GRANT
WILLIAMS

GRANT WILLIAMS

by

Giancarlo Stampalia

BearManor Media

2018

Grant Williams

© 2018 Giancarlo Stampalia

All rights reserved.

Front cover illustration: an elegant Universal Pictures portrait of Grant Williams, © 1957, Universal Pictures Company, Inc.

Published in the United States of America by:

BearManor Media
P. O. Box 71426
Albany, GA 31708
BearManorMedia.com

Printed in the United States.

Typesetting and layout by John Teehan

ISBN—978-1-62933-233-8

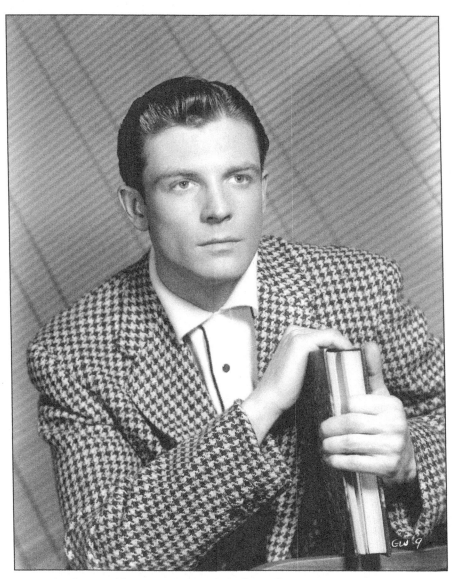

An elegant publicity portrait of Grant Williams from Universal-International.
© 1957, Universal Pictures Company, Inc.

Table of Contents

Preface

IT WAS ITALIAN PLAYWRIGHT and Nobel-prize winner Luigi Pirandello who said,[1] and I am paraphrasing from his novels and plays,[2] that the ultimate truth about people cannot be established definitively. What a person is, what we are, is refracted through hundreds, thousands, millions of subjective, imperfect views; people view people through an inextricable tangle of perception, opinion and prejudice that yields at best an unreliable composite picture. This unreliable picture, whether written or remembered, is then subjected to the ravages of time and has a way of becoming warped or dissolving altogether.

Over the years, the few facts that were known about Grant Williams have been synthetized and misconstrued beyond recognition, or forgotten; other facts were never known in the first place, or have vanished. Williams was a guarded person, very private about his life, and was a willing accomplice to the tales the Hollywood publicity machine spun about him in the press, with their brazen mix of truth and fabrication. Sixty years later, separating the truth from the fabrication is no easy exercise. To add to the confusion, no biography of Williams has ever been published, with

---

1. Perhaps no other playwright like Luigi Pirandello (1867–1936) was responsible for carrying playwriting into the twentieth century. Pirandello transformed the early experiments of the "theater of ideas" (Ibsen, Strindberg, Shaw) and made them uniquely his by adding two seminal concepts: meta-theater (or theater within theater) and the modern identity crisis. Without Pirandello's "theater of doubt," there probably would have been no Beckett, no Ionesco, no Sartre, no Pinter, maybe even no Brecht.

2. Particularly from his remarkable novel *Uno, nessuno e centomila* (Bemporad, 1926), translated into English as *One None and a Hundred Thousand* and published by E.P. Dutton & Co., 1933.

the exception of synthetic blurbs on the World-Wide Web (sometimes containing significant errors). As a result, the man is something of a mystery, a blip in the global-village movie database.

A Darwinian assumption has persisted in the world's evaluations of Williams: that he was a minor player, not among the fittest in the natural selection of the Hollywood jungle, and therefore worthy of summary judgment or dismissal. Williams is often depicted as a loser, as one who "didn't quite make it." Had he been just another pretty face in a Hollywood crowd of hopefuls, this opinion might be partly justified. Yet, in terms of charm, skill, sensibility, and experience, Williams was as good as, or better than, many of his more successful peers, and an interesting—if unhappy—individual with a number of fine artistic talents. He also left behind a hefty body of work, and was the protagonist of one of the most beautiful films in the history of Hollywood, *The Incredible Shrinking Man* (1957).

Stardom brushed against Grant Williams and then passed him by; so did that special brand of idolatry that has made myths of ephemeral stars such as James Dean, Grace Kelly, Marilyn Monroe, and Natalie Wood, or of minor talents such as Rock Hudson. Williams has been, at most, the object of science-fiction cult or of whatever-became-of curiosity and gossip.

It was my intent to carry out a full-blown factual investigation of Grant Williams, man and actor. More than three decades from his death at the age of fifty-three, however, the starting point was somewhat disheartening: a thick haze enveloped his person, obscuring it from view. Objective facts about him were scarce, and most contemporary eyewitnesses were either dead or unavailable for comment.

The press of the 1950s and '60s, luckily, turned out to be a gold mine of facts, big and small, true and untrue. Gradually, as I became acquainted with the work of the famous columnists that were active during Williams' career, I learned to distinguish the cryptic Winchell-like innuendo of a Harrison Carroll from the exploratory insight of an Eve Starr, the snappy elegance of an Emily Belser from the acidic cynicism of a Lee Mortimer, the straightforward tale spinning of an Armand (Army) Archerd from the brazen fabrications of a Liza Wilson.

A dual revelation transpired from such frequentation of the press. As I became familiar with the styles of those articles, two ghostly figures began to emerge from between their lines: on the one hand, a possible

Grant Williams, on the other, the columnists themselves. Facts aside, the best statements that those columnists made about Grant Williams were not expressed through the facts but between the facts.

Facts, however, are important, and in order to reconstruct or ascertain them as accurately as possible, this book goes back to the sources, such as articles in dailies and magazines, press releases, publicity material, personal documents, archival material, government records, and the few surviving statements by the Actor. From these sources, and from people who knew Williams personally, the book quotes extensively, to preserve the original "subjective, imperfect views" of Grant Williams. The facts are laid down as originally stated or reported, and their truthfulness is carefully weighed and—where possible—verified, always making a clear distinction between the quotations and the interpretations or hypotheses. Especially in the case of the press, this preservation of the source yields an interesting side effect: it reveals, when not Williams, the *Zeitgeist* of the period, the spirit of Williams' times. Expanding the field of vision slightly to the historical periphery through the press helps us illuminate Grant Williams' world directly and Grant Williams indirectly.

Inevitably, this could not be a traditional narrative biography. Turning the incomplete (and often unreliable) information gleaned from those sources into a romantic novelization of Williams' life would have meant creating more lies, and more uncorroborated hearsay. Hence the tendency of this book to become archaeological dig or philological examination; hence its tendency to treasure the fragment, the source, in order not to spoil even the smallest of finds by judging or interpreting; hence its insistence on making prudent conjectures about the meaning of such finds. The result is not so much a biography as an archaeological reconstruction of Grant Williams' life based on the principles of "abductive" reasoning: the most likely hypotheses or theories are inferred from the available data.

This book is, above all, an attempt to re-examine Grant Williams, thoroughly and lovingly. It may appear to be a belated gesture, but historical fairness is never hindered by coming late—one might, in fact, say that it profits from putting some distance between itself and its subjects. If nothing else, the grafting together of all those partial, imperfect views of the person is a step towards the unknowable truth about him. Short of summoning Grant Williams from the dead, this is as far as one could go.

Note: Grant Williams' career in theater, film, television, and radio is examined in considerable detail in this book. Some of Williams' work on television and in film, however, is either lost to the world forever or nearly impossible to track down; where I was not able to view a television show or film, I limited my comments to plot outlines and/or reviews. Some rarities I was able to watch in kinescopes or transfers of varyingly mediocre quality, which explains the fuzzy frame captures I occasionally felt obliged to include in the book.

Grant Williams in his Los Angeles apartment with best friend, circa 1956.

1

Roots, Education and the Air Force

CAMBRIA HEIGHTS DAYS

John Joseph Williams—social security number 056-24-6621—was born in New York City on August 18, 1931. Williams' real name was only ever mentioned by one Hollywood Columnist, Emily Belser of the International News Service (INS), during her interview with Williams in July 1956.[3] Some sources have listed Williams' birth year as 1930,[4] and Williams himself may have been responsible for not correcting some erroneous contemporary reports, but his tombstone at the Los Angeles National Cemetery confirms the former version.[5] The April 1940 Census of the United States cites his birth date as "abt. 1932."

Said Census lists the Williams family as living in their own house at number 219-17, 114th Avenue in St. Albans (Queens), New York.[6] It

---

3. Emily Belser (INS), "Actor Finds Movie Life Has Headaches" *Kingsport (TN) News*, July 5, 1956. Further references to Belser's interview are cited in the text using the abbreviation EB.

4. Such as, for example, the BFI, the NNDB database, the website Rotten Tomatoes, the *International Motion Picture Almanac* (1961 and 1963) and several articles in the 1950s press.

5. Los Angeles National Cemetery, 950 South Sepulveda Boulevard (at Constitution Avenue): Section 218, Row C, Space 83 (Souce: National Cemetery Administration, *U.S. Veterans Gravesite Locator*).

6. This particular suburban neighborhood of Queens, NY, is known as Cambria Heights, and is today prevalently African-American.

also lists the members of the household and their respective ages at the time of the Census as follows: Thomas (Grant's father), 42; Helen (Grant's mother), 40; John J., 8; Robert (Grant's brother), 2; and Sarah (Grant's maternal grandmother), 68.[7]

Thomas Williams (born in Scotland, like his parents) worked as a "Foreman" in the insurance field and was in possession of "first papers" towards his US citizenship. Both he and his wife Helen Tewes Williams (born in New York) had completed the fourth year of high school; Thomas and Helen had married in Manhattan on August 8, 1929.

Sarah Tewes was Helen's widowed mother, i.e. Grant's maternal grandmother, born "abt. 1872." She had been born in Ireland, as had her parents. Her husband had been born in Germany. Sarah's US naturalization certificate was issued on February 18, 1944.

The house, a two-story, 2,141 square-foot property built in 1925, sat on a 3,000 square-foot lot zoned R3A; the building still exists.[8] The Williams' telephone number was HO8-4147.[9]

The 1930 Federal Census, on the other hand, lists the same family unit (minus children) as living in a rental apartment in Manhattan, at 99 W. 20th Street. The family owned a radio set. Thomas's occupation was recorded as "labor." Thus, it is evident that between 1930 and 1940 Thomas had advanced to middle management. Curiously, under the item "language spoken," Thomas Williams is listed as speaking "Scotch." The word "Scotch" is written over the word "English," replacing it.[10]

Grant's brother, Robert Francis Williams, was born on January 25, 1938; he died on August 25, 2007. He was a Corporal in the U.S. Marine Corps, and is buried at Sandhills State Veterans Cemetery, Spring Lake, Cumberland, North Carolina.[11]

---

7. Source data: United States of America, Bureau of the Census. *Sixteenth Census of the United States, 1940*. Washington, D.C.: National Archives and Records Administration, 1940. T 627, 4,643 rolls.

8. Source: www.realdirect.com real estate.

9. Grant Williams' Blackfriars Theatre registration form, September 17, 1953.

10. Source data: United States of America, Bureau of the Census. *Fifteenth Census of the United States, 1930*. Washington, D.C.: National Archives and Records Administration, 1930. T626, 2,667 rolls.

11. Source: Ancestry.com, *Find A Grave Index, 1600s-Current*; also, *Social Security Death Index, 1935–2014*.

A recent photograph of the former Williams home at 219-17, 114th Avenue, Queens, NY. Photo: Benjamin Hoyer, New York.

The above facts, at least, are corroborated by hard evidence, and constitute incontrovertible proof. Everything else, including what one finds printed in contemporary newspapers and magazines, must be taken with a grain of salt.

In March 1957, *Dallas Morning News* Arts Columnist Rual Askew[12] conducted a lengthy interview with Williams, one that left Williams enthusiastic, as proven by his note to Askew thanking him for both the interview and the article that appeared in the newspaper on March 5, 1957. The text of Williams' thank-you letter was as follows:

12. Journalist, Art Expert, Poet, and amateur Pianist Rual Askew (1920–1979) worked for the *Dallas Morning News* from 1947 to 1964, first as Arts Critic and later as Assistant Editor under John Rosenfield (1900–1966). (Source: Dallas History and Archives, Rual Askew Collection, Dallas Public Library, Dallas, Texas).

Dear Rual,

My sincerest thanks for your kindness in listening to an actor expound. I know how busy you guys are. May I say that your writeup was one of the tastiest pieces of publicity I have ever had. Best of luck and continued good fortune in your work.

Gratefully,

Grant Williams[13]

The letter was written on Williams' Universal-International stationery rather than on his personal letterhead, but there is no reason to suppose it was not written by Williams personally. Though undoubtedly a product of convention and etiquette, it provides us with preliminary evidence of a genuine character trait of Williams': his old-fashioned politeness. Williams liked talking about his craft and career (but not about his private life) and could "expound" when the occasion required it, but tended to do so in a jocose, self-effacing manner; by all accounts—and there are many, from witnesses both living and dead—Williams was a gracious, polite person. The letter also proves that Williams was not averse to "tasty" pieces of publicity when they could help his advancement.

The story that Rual Askew wrote as a result of that interview, together with a handful of pieces by other celebrated columnists of Williams' times (such as Emily Belser, Mel Heimer, Armand Archerd, Bob Thomas, Eve Starr, and Don Alpert), forms an important basis for most of what we know about the Actor. Bits and pieces of these articles are used as corroborative exhibits throughout the book.

In-print evidence about Grant Williams can be grouped into two main blocks, corresponding to the two main phases of his Hollywood career: the 1955–1957 block, connected to Williams' arrival in Hollywood and to his contract with Universal-International (U-I), and the 1960–1962 block, linked with Williams' Warner Bros. contract. Each of the two studios was heavily involved in promoting Williams, each with a personal style that colored the information differently. Directly or indirectly, each studio guided the flow of information, putting the accent on different aspects of their contract player and his career. Columnists too had preferences, and styles; they shaped the information, somehow

---

13. Grant Williams, personal letter to Rual Askew. Undated (circa 1957).

expressing themselves through what they wrote about Williams. The studios, however, commanded the lion's share.

In Williams' case, U-I chose a rather straightforward approach that emphasized certain aspects of Williams' life and avoided others. In the 1955–1957 block, the bulk of the information about Williams tends to concentrate on his family, his past work experience, his Air Force service in Korea, and his Hollywood ambition. The studio seems to have paid little or no attention to romance and dating, which might suggest either that there were no big secrets to hide or that Williams (or the studio) objected to that line of questioning. As we will see, Williams was something of a melancholy loner, and his private life (in his own view) was unexciting.

Warner Bros., on the other hand, spent much of its promotional energy engaging Williams in a number of (probably fabricated) affairs with young women, many of whom were connected in some way to the studio. Romance aside, Warner's concentration was on Williams' craft—with special attention to his Method technique—as it related to Williams' psyche, and on his career in television. Warner Bros. also rehashed much of the information previously used by U-I.

In hindsight, it is especially because of Warner's tendency to fabricate romances that the 1960–1962 block appears less reliable in the truth department. Both studios produced exaggerations, contradictions and probably lies, but somehow U-I's support of Williams seemed more discreet and less calculated. On the surface, the Warner Bros. information appeared more enthusiastic, but such enthusiasm was buoyed by heavy (and suspicious) doses of hyperbole and invention.

There is also a question of style. The articles by Rual Askew, Emily Belser, or Bob Thomas—to name but a few journalists from the first block—had a simple elegance to them that was often missing from the later efforts by Don Alpert, Armand Archerd, and the many anonymous press-release writers of the 1960s. The less famous Eve Starr was an exception: her 1961 profile of Williams was constellated by subtle insights.

Here, then, is Rual Askew discussing Williams' family in March 1957:

> Grant Williams, a distant relative of opera singer Mary Garden and writer Stark Young, has been in Dallas over the weekend calling attention to Universal-International's "The Incredible Shrinking Man" due late in March at the

Majestic. The young actor [...] has been making radio and TV appearances since his arrival here Friday from Charlotte, N.C.

From his first personal appearance tour around the country he is currently testing reaction to his film career (eight to date). [...]

Of Scottish-German parentage, the young actor is of the clan of Grant on his father's side of the family, which also brought his relationship to Miss Garden and Mr. Young. His parents are Thomas Ian and Helen Tewes Williams. Williams Senior, Glasgow-born, is now a construction supervisor for Metropolitan Insurance Company and former member of the Gordon Highlanders and the British Navy. Father's career allowed young Grant to make his stage debut at age 12 in a Glasgow production of "Richard III."[14]

Mary Garden (1874–1967) was Williams' Scottish aunt (so Williams describes her in a personal letter dated July 1957,[15] probably meaning great-aunt; other biographical sources refer to her as his cousin or as a distant relative). Garden was a world-famous soprano who, among other things, premiered the role of Mélisande in Claude Debussy's opera *Pelléas et Mélisande* (1902) and the title role in Jules Massenet's opera *Chérubin* (1905), which was written especially for her. Garden also sang in the United States for many years, and was briefly connected to the film industry: she starred in two silent films for Samuel Goldwyn (*Thais* in 1917 and *The Splendid Sinner* in 1918) and worked as a talent scout for Metro-Goldwyn Mayer (MGM) in the 1930s. In her capacity as talent discoverer, Garden helped launch the career of a young actor-singer who went on to a successful career with Warner Bros.: Dennis Morgan. This last fact about Garden's life was stated *ad nauseam* by many press releases aimed at showcasing Grant

---

14. Rual Askew (signing himself R.A.) "Top Star Contender Ready for Whatever is Demanded," *Dallas Morning News*, March 5, 1957. (Further references to Askew's article are cited in the text using the following abbreviation: RA.)

15. Grant Williams, personal letter to L. Allan Smith, dated July 31, 1957, 1. The return address on letter and envelope is 1314 N. Hayworth Avenue, Hollywood, California. Further references to this letter are cited in the text using the abbreviation GW2.

Newspaperman Rual Askew of the *Dallas Morning News* checks what the
competition has to say in this undated press photo. From the collections of the
Dallas History and Archives Division, Dallas Public Library, Dallas, Texas.

Williams' contract with the latter studio.[16] It is unclear whether Williams
had any actual contact with Garden.

Stark Young (1881–1963) was an American playwright, novelist,
painter, literary critic, drama critic, and translator. He also served on the

16. For example, "Grant Williams Kin of Mary Garden," *Camden (NJ) Courier-Post*,
    December 10, 1960. Garden's role in promoting Dennis Morgan (or Stanley
    Morner as he was billed in the thirties) was confirmed by the press devoted to
    the actor in the thirties. For example, see: Edwin Schallert, "General Shifting of
    Actor's Films Noted," *Los Angeles Times*, January 11, 1936; John R. Woolfenden,
    "Flock of Handsome Brutes Spring up as Leading Men," *Los Angeles Times*, May
    17, 1936. For information about Garden's opera roles, see her autobiography:
    Mary Garden and Louis Biancolli, *Mary Garden's Story*, Simon and Schuster,
    1951, 60–89, 137–138.

Board of Trustees of New York University. Young's relation to Williams was only mentioned once, by Askew.

An article by Associated Press (AP) Columnist Bob Thomas, published on February 8, 1957, provided a physical description of Williams: "Grant is tall, 26, with handsome blond Germanic looks (he's half-German)."[17] A June 1960 United Press International (UPI) release placed considerable weight on Williams' shoulders because of his famous relatives, and reiterated Williams' connection to Germany:

> Grant Williams, one of Hollywood's busiest young actors, [...] had to make good in movies to uphold his family's reputation.
>
> Mary Garden, one of the greatest opera singers of all time, is his great-aunt, while his grandfather was court chef to Kaiser Wilhelm, of Germany.[18]

More information about Williams' family and heritage appeared in a Hollywood-written syndicated article on August 13, 1961:

> New York-born Grant Williams might today be striding the quarterdeck of one of Her Majesty's warships, if the urge to become an actor had not been just a bit stronger than his love for the sea. Williams [...] was entitled to a scholarship at the Royal Naval College as the oldest son of a Victoria Cross holder.
>
> Williams' father had been given Great Britain's highest decoration for valor during World War I. Though Grant was born and educated in New York, his boyhood dream was to become a British naval officer.
>
> The Senior Williams had been a Merchant Marine captain and for generations the Williams males had been seafaring men. The naval ambitions were sharpened when as a little

---

17. Bob Thomas, "Inside Hollywood," *Newport (RI) News*, Friday, February 8, 1957. Williams was 25 at the time, and technically only one-fourth German.

18. Phil Newsom, UPI Foreign News Editor, "Foreign News Commentary," *Shamokin (PA) News-Dispatch*, June 22, 1960.

boy Grant was presented to King George VI during the latter's visit to the United States.[19] On weekends Grant went sailing with his father on Long Island and was taught navigation and seamanship.[20]

The British National Archives contain no mention of a Thomas Williams being awarded a medal during or after the First World War, so the heroic claim is dubious. There was, however, a recipient named Thomas William, Private of the 4th Battalion, Canadian Mounted Rifles, who received a Victoria Cross for an act of bravery on October 26, 1917.[21]

As for Williams' seafaring proclivities, they might well have been true. The dubiousness of the above report on Thomas Williams' Victoria Cross investiture, however, also casts doubt on the remainder of the statement, as the two parts are interlocked. Thomas Williams' being a medal holder is connected to Grant's entitlement to a scholarship at the Royal Naval College, which in turn is connected to his love for the sea and his sailing on Long Island, etc.

The search for a heroic past in Williams' family, at any rate, makes for poor portrait painting on the part of the anonymous writer of the above quotation. If such writer had left wartime heroism alone and deigned to report something truthful about the actor's early family life (for example Williams' feelings about his parents and sibling), we might be in possession of enough known points to triangulate the facts of Williams' inner life as a child. As it is, the few mentions of family problems have come to us through later second- and third-hand reports,[22] and cannot be sufficiently corroborated. All the members of the Williams family are now dead, so there are no surviving witnesses to this phase of Williams' life.

---

19. George VI and Queen Elizabeth visited New York (and the New York World Fair at Flushing Meadows Park) on June 10–11, 1939. Williams was seven years old.

20. "Williams' Urge to Act Stronger than Sea Life," *Arizona Republic* (Phoenix, AZ), August 13, 1961.

21. The [British] National Archives—War Office, Armed Forces, Judge Advocate General, and related bodies: Reference: WO98/8/483

22. See Chapter 14.

Teacher's Pet

According to the promotion launched by Warner Bros. in 1960, Williams attended two years of high school in Glasgow, Scotland, but graduated from Andrew Jackson High School in Queens, NY.[23]

Andrew Jackson High School yearbook, thumbnail portrait of graduating senior "John Williams," 1948.

The Andrew Jackson High School yearbook of June 1948 lists graduating senior John Williams as an honor-roll student whose dream is to become a professional photographer; after graduation, he sees himself working for the Associated Press. Williams' yearbook bio lists his extracurricular activities (Spanish Tutor, Squad, Lunch Patrol, and Library Clerical Aid to Teacher) and ends with the ditty: "*To be a photographer is John's aim; In this field he will surely reach fame.*"

No mention is made of Williams' interest in music, or of his involvement in musical activities. We know from both the press and numerous eyewitnesses, however, that Williams was a music lover and an accomplished pianist all his life. It is therefore reasonable to assume that his piano studies started early in life and continued at least through his high school period. Williams probably studied piano at home. In his cited July 1957 letter, Williams writes that he is "back studying the piano very seriously," implying an interruption in his musical studies; this interruption presumably started either when he left New York to pursue his film and television career in 1955 or when he began his military service in 1948.

Williams graduated from high school at the age of sixteen, and this fact, together with his status as an honor-roll student, allows us to infer

---

23. "New 'Hawaiian Eye' Actor Had Many Other Roles," *Dover (OH) Daily Reporter,* December 17, 1960. Williams' attendance of the New York high school is confirmed by the school's online list of alumni and by the 1948 yearbook. Andrew Jackson High School (opened in 1937 and closed in 1994) was located at 207-11 116th Avenue in the Cambria Heights neighborhood, Queens, NY (walking distance from the Williams' home).

Andrew Jackson High School Lunch Patrol, yearbook picture, 1948
(Grant Williams standing, far right).

that he was an intelligent, studious person. In the absence of corroborative anecdotes, we can only guess about his feelings. As we will learn in
the following chapters, Williams' disposition was a melancholy one, and
candid photos invariably show how tentative his smiles were. One can
safely assume that his high school years were no exception to that rule.

Service before Self

After finishing high school in 1948, Williams enrolled in Queens
College, Flushing, NY, but cut his attendance short when he enlisted in
the United States Air Force.[24] He served from September 2, 1948 until 1952,[25] and was discharged as a Staff Sergeant. Williams' tombstone
makes no mention of his artistic career, but only of his status as "SSGT US
AIR FORCE" in Korea. One tidbit about his military service appeared in
the Warner Bros. pressbook for *The Couch* (1962):

24. *Dover (OH) Daily Reporter* (1960), op. cit.

25. The start date of Williams' service is also confirmed by the National Cemetery
Administration data. *Dallas Morning News* critic Rual Askew, on the other hand
(RA), cited Williams' "war service" as taking place from 1949 to 1952.

Grant Williams, who did a lot of boxing when he was in the
Air Force, had to forget what he'd learned and take lessons in
fighting "dirty" for his role in the Warner Bros. thriller 'The
Couch' […]."

Coached by "Battling" Burrows, an erstwhile pug who
boasts he is an expert in fistic skullduggery, Williams slugs vi-
ciously as the psychotic killer in the suspense drama.[26]

Which seems like pure invention, especially since Williams engages in
no physical fighting whatsoever in *The Couch*. In his 1957 profile of Williams, Columnist Bob Thomas added some puzzling information about
both Williams' military service and his personal life:

Grant enlisted in the Air Force in 1948, more or less to get
away from home. During his Stateside training, he met a girl
who was training to be a nurse. They fell in love.

Grant would have gotten out of the Air Force except for
the Korean War. He was sent to the Far East and flew on recon-
naissance missions. The nurse was also shipped to the war zone
and they were married in Tokyo. She was killed in Korea.[27]

This sudden appearance of a dead wife in the national press is particularly
startling. The US National Archives reveal that, actually, there were no
nurse casualties during the Korean War, at least not as a result of hostilities, and only one as a result of an airplane accident which occurred
over the Ocean about ninety miles south of Tokyo on July 27, 1950. The
nurse in question was Major Genevieve Smith, Army Nurse Corps, class
of 1904, who had never married. She had also never served in Korea: she
was on her way there from the Philippines when her plane crashed. Arguably, Nurse Smith would have been too old to be Williams' wife: at the
time of her death, she was 46 and Williams 18.[28]

26. Warner Bros. pressbook, *Malaga* and *The Couch*, 1962, p. 17. Further references
to this pressbook are cited in the text using the abbreviation WBC.

27. Thomas (1957), op. cit.

28. Sources: National Archives (www.archives.gov); Ancestry.com, *Find A Grave
Index, 1600s-Current*; also, obituary in the *Cascade Pioneer*, August 3, 1950.

Speaking of marriage, the 1958 edition of the magazine *Who's Who in Hollywood* ended its capsule biography of Williams thus: "A handsome blond, Grant is happily married [...]." No further specification. The same news was repeated in the 1961 edition, while it had not appeared in 1957.[29] Again in 1958, other items in the American press reported the opposite: for example, the press information for Williams' television appearance on *Shirley Temple's Storybook* (September 1958) stated, "He is 28 and a bachelor."[30] Williams himself confirmed his bachelorhood in a personal letter dated April 16, 1957.[31]

Nina Ingris (born 1931), his Secretary between 1958 and 1965, is positive that during the period she knew him Williams was not married, and is confident that the story of his Tokyo marriage was a fabrication. She adds: "Maybe he was married... to his career? More than likely."[32]

These publicity fabrications about actors' lives were customary enough in the golden age of Hollywood, and can be viewed today with benevolent humor; the difficulty for the researcher is that the persistence of such fabrications pushes the truth deeper under the surface.

The Warner Bros. publicity machine of 1960 added some detail about Williams' Air Force stint in the Far East:

> [Williams served] at B-29 bases in Okinawa, Japan and Korea [...]. During his service with the Air Force, he produced, directed and acted in shows at Chanute Field in Illinois, Tokyo, and acted in 127 USO plays in Okinawa and Japan.[33]

Still more news relating to Williams' Air Force years—but indirectly providing information about the man himself—can be found in Emily

---

29. *Who's Who in Hollywood*, Dell Publishing Company, 1957, 1958, 1961.

30. *Des Moines Sunday Register*, September 7, 1958.

31. Grant Williams, personal letter to L. Allan Smith dated April 16, 1957, 1. Further references to this letter are cited in the text using the abbreviation GW1.

32. Nina Ingris, personal correspondence and interviews with the author, 2016. Further quotations from Ingris are cited in the text using the following abbreviation: NI.

33. *Dover (OH) Daily Reporter* (1960), op. cit.

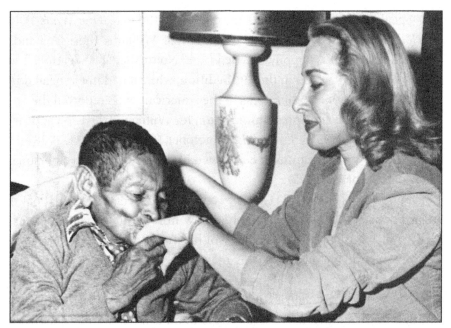

New York, September 28, 1956: popular 1950s INS Reporter Emily Belser (right) receives chivalrous homage from Javier Pereira of Colombia, thought to be born circa 1789 and therefore the "oldest man in the world." Photo: INP Soundphoto/Jack Balletti.

Belser's interview,[34] which was conducted during the shooting of *The Incredible Shrinking Man* (1957). The discussion about the film, and about the shrinkage of its protagonist, led to other considerations:

> "This [premise] is not really as crazy as it seems," Williams insisted, "in fact, I'd say this is just about the most possible—or probable—of the science fiction movies made so far.
>
> "I was an aerial photographer during the war and also happened to be present when the A-bombs were dropped on Bikini Atoll. It's quite possible for an atomic fallout to travel 1,000 miles before dispersing.
>
> "Evidence of shrinkage on the human body were [sic] discovered in Japan after Hiroshima," he went on, "when several of the bodies had shrunken as much as three inches. Of course

34. Aside from being a reporter for INS, Belser also made a few cameo appearances in films, for example in *The Best Things in Life Are Free* and in *The Harder They Fall* (both 1956); as actress and columnist, she also used the name Lee Belser.

there's no reason to think a body would shrink any more than that, but who knows?" (EB)

Many of the stories that were spun about Grant Williams during his early years in Hollywood dealt with his service in the Korean War. This is natural enough: the "mythology" of the time demanded Korean-War heroes, just as the "mythology" of the 1940s had demanded World War II heroes. What is curious in Williams' case is the insistence on such mythology (all the way down to his National Cemetery tombstone, which only mentions his status as a veteran). The character that was being built around Williams' slender frame was that of the war veteran. Whether this was merely the product of publicity convenience or whether it was Williams' own preference, it is difficult to determine. In all likelihood, it was a combination of the two.

Campus Mysteries and Tales of Employment
Askew's *Dallas Morning News* article contained an impressive list of jobs held by Williams before arriving in Hollywood:

> The young actor, whose career almost embraces the book in versatility, has […] taken his turns as concert pianist, publicist (M.C.A.), singer, lyricist, set designer, TV scripter, director, producer and much acting, legit, films and airwaves. […] Williams is serious about making his mark as an actor in all mediums. […] From the list of credits to date he's prepared for whatever his future career dictates. (RA)

According to the U-I pressbook for *The Incredible Shrinking Man*, Williams had also devoted time "to producing, to directing, to public relations, to accounting, to photography, and to journalism."[35] Exactly what this list entailed is unclear, as there appears to be no objective trace of most of the endeavors mentioned. Only his "public relations" job is attached to a specific name in most reports: the Music Corporation of America (MCA).

---

35. *Showman's Manual*, Universal-International pressbook for *The Incredible Shrinking Man*, 1957, 3. Further references to this pressbook are cited in the text using the abbreviation ISM.

Nevertheless, for a man of twenty-five, both lists are indeed impressive. Which points to a singularly annoying trait of the gossip, or publicity, writing of the era: it was simultaneously coy and boastful, exaggerated and reticent, withholding and giving information in the same breath.

The same spectacular eclecticism was indicated by a list of previous occupations in Emily Belser's interview in July 1956:

> Williams, a former New York photographer, publicity man, stock company Barrymore, and TV performer, has been in movietown long enough to snag featured roles in five major films [...] (EB).

Society Columnist Mel Heimer (in his syndicated column, "My New York") added one more detail to the above whirlpool of jobs:

> Grant Williams, a big blond actor who has matinee-idol prospects, was salvaged by a Hollywood Studio from a fate worse than death. He was a press agent with a show-business talent agency. He also was once an accountant for an auto tire manufacturer, or how prosaic can you get? A New Yorker, he's the son of a Scot who in World War I won the Victoria Cross with the Gordon Highlanders....[36]

According to some Internet sources,[37] upon his return from Korea Williams studied at the University of Illinois and finally at the City College of New York in New York City. According to Askew, on the other hand, Williams enrolled at New York University and received an A.B. in Journalism (RA). Brian's Drive-In Theater website only mentions that Williams "enrolled in college courses" and was "initially interested in singing."[38] The Warner Bros. 1960 press stated that Williams had com-

---

36. Mel Heimer, "My New York," *Kane (PA) Republican*, October 10, 1956. Biographer, historian, novelist, and scandal recorder Mel Heimer (1916–1971) penned his popular syndicated column, "My New York," circa 1947–1971.

37. For example, Wikipedia.

38. This particular musical detail was probably a fabrication meant to set up Williams' alleged career as an operatic tenor. See Chapter 13.

Columnist and Author Mel Heimer in a Central Press Association
press photograph, 1947.

pleted his higher education at Columbia University and had received a
Bachelor of Arts degree.[39]

Here the sources are deeply discordant, and, if one considers all the
information provided, somewhat improbable, if not unbelievable: it is
unlikely that any one person would have been able to attend all those
universities in such a short time span (a span that included a four-year
Korean hiatus).

That is not all. The *Daily Herald* of Provo, Utah, in an article intended to plug Williams' 1959 television role as composer Pyotr Ilyich

---

39. *Dover (OH) Daily Reporter* (1960), op. cit.

Tchaikovsky,[40] provided yet more information about both study and employment:

> And somehow along the way [Williams] managed to vary the routine by earning a degree in journalism from a correspondence school, studying at New York University, working as an accountant,[41] press agent, stage and TV producer and director, secretary and salesman and serving a hitch in the Air Force as a photographer and lab technician.
>
> Grant's appropriately intellectual mien in his Tchaikovsky role is not without bias. He was somewhat the Quiz Kid type, having entered high school at 12 and graduated at 16 [...].[42]

The information about Williams being "a photographer and lab technician" during and after his military service, at least, is consistent both with Williams' statements (reported earlier) and with the ambition cited in his high school yearbook. His body of work as a photographer, if ever there was one, appears to have vanished without a trace.

In his years of self-promotion under U-I, Williams was willing to expound about his accomplishments, spinning tales simultaneously laced with boastfulness and self-deprecation. Here he is in 1955, talking about his eclectic curriculum:

> There have been frequent breathing spells in my acting career. Frankly, I can't readily remember all of them, but I guess I've tried producing, directing, accounting, journalism-publicity and professional photography. [I was] a flack—publicist, that is—for the Music Corporation of America for six months and also helped found an investment group for Broadway shows and TV packages.
>
> This may show a little range of jobs, but it didn't seem to matter much what I did. I returned to the stage as an actor.

---

40. See Chapter 9.

41. "He's a CPA," announced the 1957 magazine *Who's Who in Hollywood*.

42. "TV Star Rises From Stinker To Thinker Actor," *Provo (UT) Daily Herald*, February 2, 1959 (probably UPI).

Maybe I'd better stop being a job-jumper. [...] I guess I'll stick with it for a while. It's not only handy for credit purposes, but I happen to like it.[43]

---

43. "Williams Infected By Acting Bug" (UP), *Arizona Republic* (Phoenix, AZ), November 27, 1955.

Grant Williams and Sheila Fallon in Charles Oxton's play *Late Arrival* (New York, October–November 1953). Courtesy of the Blackfriars Guild Collection, Providence College, Phillips Memorial Library, Special and Archival Collections.

2 Treading the Boards

MELPOMENE'S BOY[44]

Most sources agree that Williams' interest in acting predated his teenage years, and mention his working in summer-stock productions while still a boy. The pressbook for *The Incredible Shrinking Man* (1957), in presenting Universal-International's new leading man, stated: "Although he has been a professional thespian since he was 12, the burning question in the mind of Grant Williams has been until very recently 'to act or not to act.'" (ISM, 3) An account of Williams' early encounters with the theater appeared in a 1961 syndicated article:

> Grant's acting career began accidentally when at 12 he was sent to a summer camp near Garrison, New York.[45] There was a strawhat theatre in town and he was asked to appear in a production of "Ah, Wilderness."
>
> In subsequent school vacations he continued to act in summer theatres. This experience convinced Grant that his future lay in "treading the boards" [...].[46]

---

44. In Greek mythology, Melpomene was the Muse of Tragedy.

45. This contradicts the facts reported by Rual Askew in his 1957 *Dallas Morning News* article, which placed Williams' theatrical debut at age twelve in Glasgow, Scotland.

46. *Arizona Republic* (1961), op. cit.

After his Korean parenthesis, Williams took lessons at Lee Strasberg's Actors Studio,[47] lessons that left a deep impression on him. Williams was deeply committed to the Stanislavsky Method, and to the truthfulness it required. This commitment he clearly demonstrated in his film and television performances, as well as in his statements and in his teaching.

The combination of Strasberg's teachings and Williams' personality made the actor more adept at somber, melancholy drama than at comedy. This is logical: since the Method entailed searching for points of contact between the characters he was portraying and his own disposition, in most characters Williams found something sad or despondent, he found an aspect of his own personality. In any case, the kind of personal soul searching dictated by Stanislavsky/Strasberg made Williams a perfect candidate for the exploratory rehearsal work traditionally associated with the theater. The theater stage was Williams' natural element, and a model to which he would refer repeatedly even when preparing his film and television characters.

It is clear from his own statements and from most printed reports about him that Williams had not always been sure whether he wanted to act for a living or not. What is less clear is when he made that decision, and what exactly sparked it. Most stories that were written about Williams placed this decision somewhere between his Actors Studio lessons and his stage debut, or between his work on the New York stage and his first appearances in television dramas. Either way, the transition in those stories is usually a smooth one (from acting to acting). Only one source is discordant. In a brief 1961 article, Columnist Harold Heffernan of the North American Newspaper Alliance (NANA) gave a brazenly divergent version of Williams' vocational call. The information presented by Heffernan appears unlikely, but the events described are so karmically eccentric and so down-to-earth that they might just be true.

Acting careers are inspired by devious circumstances. For instance, Grant Williams is one who wasn't consumed with

---

47. This is also confirmed by direct testimony from Williams' acting students, and by Richard Lamparski's 1982 interview with Williams (Richard Lamparski, *Whatever Became of...?* Crown Publishers, Inc., 1982, 292. Further quotations from Lamparski's book are cited in the text using the abbreviation RL). According to the cited 1961 *Arizona Republic* syndicated article, this training occurred after Williams' 1953 summer stint at the Barter Theatre. The Actors Studio itself could not find any record of Grant Williams' attendance.

such desires until an incident in his early 20's. At the time, he couldn't decide whether to become a photographer, a publicist, or a journalist.

"You've heard the old adage 'I complained my legs hurt until I saw a man with no feet'!" says Grant. "Well, I was plugging along, constantly changing jobs, until I met a man named Hank Viscardi, founder of Abilities, Inc., an electronics plant on Long Island employing 600 people—all handicapped.[48]

"I first met Hank when he walked into a restaurant in New York and a mutual friend introduced us, mentioning that I was a 'spare time' actor."

A TV play later was written about Viscardi and the manufacturer suggested that Williams was just the fellow to star in its off-Broadway stage production. Grant agreed and has been an actor ever since.

"No," he smiled, "it wasn't that the play got good notices, but it was the fact that Viscardi's accomplishments showed me that a man's life should have a purpose. You see, he was born with two shriveled stumps in place of legs, yet he never wasted time sitting around 'wishing' his body were normal. Instead, he went out and did something—not only for himself but for others."[49]

Whether the inspirational story was true or not, Williams told it to Heffernan. If not for the facts it describes, that story is interesting for what it reveals about Williams, for the personality traits that quiver between Williams' words: his restlessness and dissatisfaction, his undecidedness, his aspiration towards altruism, and his thwarted desire to find a "purpose." As we will see, these personality traits would grow over the years and ultimately be his undoing.

48. Henry Viscardi Jr. (1912–2004) was a celebrated Businessman and Philanthropist. In the words of *The New York Times* obituary (April 16, 2004), he "became a leader in integrating disabled people—like himself—into America's work force […]." Founder of Abilities Inc. and of the National Center for Disability Services, Viscardi advised "every president from Franklin D. Roosevelt to Jimmy Carter," and wrote eight books and many articles on the subject of disability.

49. Harold Heffernan, "'Babes in Toyland' Nostalgic Setting," *Pittsburgh (PA) Press*, July 16, 1961.

Oddly enough, of his stage experience Williams spoke only fleetingly and in general terms. Here is one statement he made in the Warner Bros. pressbook for *The Couch* (1962):

> I did two plays on Broadway.[50] Both of them were flops. Someday I'd like to play Broadway in a hit. I guess that's the dream of every ambitious actor. This is what many of us work towards. It is much more rewarding than the immediate paycheck. It signifies accomplishment and a job well done (WBC, 18).

Williams was much more talkative about the actor's craft and about the discipline that came with it. In a 1961 interview with Central Press Association Columnist Armand Archerd, Williams expounded about his views on acting and about the theater as training ground:

> In the 'old days,' young actor Grant Williams recalls, a young actor (like Grant Williams) would receive his training via the tried-and-true stock company. It meant playing a juvenile in one show, a character role the next. Stock companies were rough going—but fun for a young actor with only one place to go, anyway: the theater.
>
> "That's all gone now," Williams sighs. "There are the 'little theaters,' but too many of them use directors who are just as inexperienced as the inexperienced actors who are trying to learn there! It boils down to the amateur leading the amateur.
>
> "The results of this kind of training can breed mannerisms in an actor that take a lot of overcoming. It goes beyond the obvious needs of an actor and includes such things as poor posture, sloppy diction and a host of other things a young actor must have corrected by a seasoned expert."[51]

---

50. Williams did one play off-Broadway; as we will see later in this chapter, there is no evidence supporting his claim of a second New York play, but only unconfirmed rumors (including his own statements).

51. Armand Archerd, "'Good Old Days' Vanish for Juvenile Hopefuls," *Pottstown (PA) Mercury*, August 26, 1961.

An elegant headshot of a youthful Grant Williams, one of two that Williams
used for his Barter Theatre auditions. Circa 1953. Courtesy of the Barter Theatre,
Abingdon, Virginia.

Williams then described how the film and television studios were the
closest approximation of such stock-company experience. Many of the
above statements, though derived almost verbatim from the Warner Bros.
pressbook for *The Couch*, undoubtedly came from Williams in some
form. If one reads between the lines, one can see that Williams was ultimately more concerned with versatility, and with stretching the acting
muscle, than with stardom per se. This preference would simultaneously
be a blessing and a curse in his career.

Rosalind Russell and the Virginia Ham

In May 1953, at the age of twenty-one, Williams, armed with his
limited training and experience and with the golden calling card of his

considerable talent, took a giant step in his theatrical career: he won the Barter Theatre auditions and was chosen by Barter Theatre Award winner Rosalind Russell for a salaried summer season at the Abingdon, Virginia, theater.[52]

The Barter Theatre was inaugurated in June 1933 by actor Robert Porterfield[53] and is still active today. Many actors have performed there over the years, before, or while, achieving bigger fame on Broadway or in Hollywood. To name a few: Ned Beatty, Ernest Borgnine, Hume Cronyn, Patricia Neal, Gregory Peck, Kevin Spacey, and Fritz Weaver. The venue was named Barter because in its early days during the Great Depression and at least until World War II, its policy allowed patrons to pay for theater tickets with goods and produce.

The Barter Theatre was a daring, enlightened experiment. Decades before Joseph Papp's Public Theater in New York,[54] it was the first example of a true public theater: a publicly funded non-profit venue with a stable company of players. In this respect, it was akin to the *teatri stabili* of Italy, state-supported non-profit theaters devoted to the classics and to modern works. (The seminal example in Italy was the Piccolo Teatro di Milano, founded in Milan in 1947 by legendary Stage Director Giorgio Strehler and Managing Director Paolo Grassi.) The Barter Theatre found staunch supporters in the local and Federal Governments in its formative years, and was promoted by illustrious spokespersons such as Eleanor Roosevelt.[55] As Robert Porterfield wrote in 1940: "My dream is to have the first state theater in the Commonwealth of Virginia. Wouldn't it be grand if we had 48 state theaters? Then we would have a national theater."[56]

---

52. Rosalind Russell (1907–1976) was an American Actress of stage and screen. She is probably best known for her roles in the films *The Women* (1939), *His Girl Friday* (1940), *Auntie Mame* (1958) and *Gypsy* (1962).

53. Stage Actor and Director Robert Porterfield (1905–1971) worked in film only sporadically; his most famous screen role was Zeb Andrews in Howard Hawks' *Sergeant York*, 1941.

54. Founded as the Shakespeare Workshop in 1954 before settling into its permanent home in 1967.

55. Mark Dawidziak, *The Barter Theatre Story*, Appalachian Consortium, Inc., 1982, 10–15, 29–31.

56. Ibid., 34.

A bespectacled Grant Williams helps put on a show by painting a set at the Barter Theatre, 1953. Courtesy of the Barter Theatre, Abingdon, Virginia.

While the prewar Barter Theatre was a community affair, based on voluntary work and cooperative effort, the postwar Barter abandoned its "barter" policy and put its actors on salary, establishing season tickets and a cash box office. The most distinctive element of the theater's character, and its main contribution as an actor's training ground, was its repertory-company cooperation. During the theater's annual summer festival (the Virginia Highlands Festival), actors learned to study quickly, and study a lot, performing leading and supporting roles in several plays in a short period of time and memorizing hundreds of pages of dialogue in mere weeks; they also contributed to the running of the festival by building sets and performing other menial tasks. The Barter Theatre, in other words, was like an intensive actor's boot camp, but in front of a public.[57]

57. Ibid., 39–40, 63.

A large number of actors applied to the Barter Theatre and attended its auditions annually. Some of those who were not chosen for the prize might receive other offers that did not include a salary, as Robert Porterfield explains in a letter to a candidate for the 1953 season:

> I want to thank you for your audition [...]. After consideration, we find that the only place we could offer you this summer at the Barter Theatre would be apprenticeship. Apprentices receive no salary and take care of their room and board which amounts to $25.00 weekly. However, they are members of the resident company in that they have an opportunity to work into any position (acting or otherwise) for which they show ability. Also there is the strong possibility of being accepted into the winter touring company on salary. The summer season will open on June 15 and will run through September 5. We would like to have you here a week previous to opening if possible.[58]

In May 1953, stage and screen Star Rosalind Russell won the fifteenth annual Barter Theatre Award for "the most outstanding performance given by an American-born actor during the current New York season." Robert Porterfield made the announcement on May 6; newspaper reports appeared between May 6 and May 18.[59] On May 22 and 25, Barter Theatre auditions were held at the Winter Garden Theater in New York City (where Russell was performing in the successful musical *Wonderful Town*),[60] with Russell in attendance as judge.[61] On Tuesday, May 26, Ms. Russell and the audition winners were feted at a luncheon held at

---

58. Robert Porterfield, typed letter dated March 24, 1953.

59. The earliest: "Rosalind Russell Is Named Winner Of Barter Award," *Kingsport (TN) Times*, May 6, 1953.

60. The 1953 musical *Wonderful Town*, with book by Joseph A. Fields and Jerome Chodorov, lyrics by Betty Comden and Adolph Green, and music by Leonard Bernstein, was based on Fields and Chodorov's 1940 play *My Sister Eileen*, which in turn was based on a series of short stories by Ruth McKenney first published in *The New Yorker* in the late 1930s. The musical ran for 559 performances.

61. "Plum for Miss Russell," *New York Times*, May 6, 1953.

the New York Town Hall Club.[62] The following day, *The New York Times* wrote:

> Rosalind Russell, star of "Wonderful Town," received the fifteenth annual Barter Theatre Award yesterday for "the best performance given by an American-born actor during the current New York season."
>
> Cornelia Otis Skinner, last year's winner, made the presentation before several hundred members of the Town Hall Club after a luncheon.[63] The award consists of an acre of land on the side of a mountain near the Barter Theatre in Abingdon, Va., a Virginia ham and platter and the honor of choosing two young actors for stage grooming.[64]
>
> In presenting the ham and platter to Miss Russell, Miss Skinner remarked that it was "a great joy to welcome this lovely new hamster." Robert Porterfield, who served as master of ceremonies, presented the title to the land, observing that other distinguished holders of real estate on the Virginian mountainside were Helen Hayes, Henry Fonda, Tallulah Bankhead, Dorothy Stickney, Louis Calhern, Frederic March, Shirley Booth, Ethel Barrymore and Mildred Natwick.
>
> Tributes to the actress were paid by Dennis King, Miss Stickney and Hedda Hopper. Bob Pastene, one of the young actors selected to study at the Barter Theatre several years ago, […] read the deed to the acre of land.
>
> […] Selected by Miss Russell to receive further stage experience and training at the Barter Theatre, which opens its

62. Town Hall, a performance and meeting space in New York, located at 123 W. 43rd Street and designed by the renowned architectural firm McKim, Mead, and White, was known for its outstanding acoustics. It was inaugurated in 1921 and was designated a National Historic Landmark in 2012.

63. Cornelia Otis Skinner (1899–1979) was an American Author, Actress, and Comedienne.

64. In his May 6 press conference to announce Russell's Award, Porterfield described the land as "an acre of some of the most perpendicular land in the Virginia Highlands." A special piece of land nonetheless: a hunk right off the Porterfield Farm at Glade Spring. (See: "Barter Award Winner Named," *Kingsport (TN) News,* May 7, 1953.)

In this photo, probably taken at the Town Hall Club luncheon on May 26, 1953, Rosalind Russell poses graciously to commemorate her own Barter Theatre Award and the victory of the three young actors she has selected. Left to right: Robert Porterfield (holding Russell's ham), June Moncur, Charles McCawley, Rosalind Russell (with platter), and Grant Williams. Courtesy of the Barter Theatre, Abingdon, Virginia.

season June 15, were June Monceur[65] of Salt Lake City, Charles McCawley[66] of Louisville and Grant Williams of New York. Since Russell could not decide which of the two young male actors should be the winner, it was decided to honor both. She recently had held auditions for various candidates.[67]

---

65. The Barter Theatre programs referred to her by her correct name, "June Moncur." The press, on the other hand, oscillated between two spellings: "Monceur" and "Moncure."

66. Later known as Charles Macauley. Macauley (1927–1999) had studied at London's Royal Academy of Dramatic Arts (RADA) and made his American stage debut in New York in 1952. He went on to a long television career, guest-starring in some 200 television shows. He became a close friend of Raymond Burr (and partner in his Sonoma County vineyards) and played District Attorney Hamilton Burger in the 1980s *Perry Mason* TV movies. From 1986 to 1992, he taught at the University of Southern California School of Theater.

67. "Miss Russell Wins a Ham for Effort," *New York Times*, May 27, 1953.

1953 was an important year for Rosalind Russell. For her overwhelming success in the Broadway musical *Wonderful Town*, she was on the cover of *Life* magazine and of several other national periodicals, and was the recipient of many prestigious awards, such as the Tony Award, the New York Drama Critics Circle Award and the *Los Angeles Times* Woman of the Year Award. In her autobiography, Ms. Russell shares no details about the Barter Theatre Award or about Williams; she only mentions the accolade along with a dozen other recognitions for her performance in the Broadway musical.[68]

Williams' co-winner June Moncur (now Sister June Moncur Waite of Orem, Utah) shares some memories of her May auditions:

> A friend of mine had done an apprenticeship at the Barter Theatre in 1952, and had told me all about it with enthusiasm. That summer, after graduating from the University of Utah in Theater and Communication, I spent time at the Highfield Theatre in Cape Cod, where one of my drama professors was spending his sabbatical year to direct. After the summer, I stayed in New York City and did odd jobs (I worked at *The New York Times*, and as a guide at NBC for a while).
>
> One day, my friend called and said the Barter was holding an open audition. (There were very few places that had open auditions in New York City.) She had signed up for the audition but had decided not to go, so she told me I could go and take her number. I stopped at a library and read through a script that I was familiar with, to memorize the lines, and with that little monologue I did my first audition for the Barter Theatre. We were only given one minute for the first audition.[69]
>
> My audition must have gone well, because the Barter people called my friend, asking who that person was that had auditioned in her place. My friend gave the Barter people my telephone number. They contacted me and asked me to come back for another audition.

---

68. Rosalind Russell and Chris Chase, *Life Is A Banquet*, Random House, 1977, 160.

69. This one-minute time limit originated with 1941 Barter Theatre Award winner Ethel Barrymore. Her explanation for the time limit was, "If they have talent, you'll know it. If they don't, you'll think your watch has stopped." In Dawidziak (1982), op. cit., 31.

We did not have the same strict time limit for the second audition, we could pretty much do what we wanted. That went well too.

To be chosen as a winner was an exciting experience. We were introduced to Rosalind Russell, who had judged us; she was very gracious to us, but we had little contact with her. I had little contact with Grant, too, until we went down to the Barter Theatre. I met him briefly at the Award banquet, but did not see his auditions.[70]

A mention of Williams' Barter tenure appeared in Rual Askew's article for the *Dallas Morning News*, along with a list of other theatrical engagements:

[Williams] toured with Judith Anderson in "Family Portrait," performed Shakespeare at the Antioch Festival in Ohio, acted for Virginia's Barter Theater, has both directed and acted for Hollywood's Stage Society and many more. (RA)

Askew's mention of the *Family Portrait* tour with Judith Anderson[71] did not refer to the original 1939 Broadway production of the Lenore Coffee–William Joyce Cowen play (a telling of the life of Jesus Christ as seen through the eyes of his family). Rather, it referred to the revival produced and directed by Robert Porterfield at the Barter Theatre in 1953.

According to June Moncur, the three co-winners chose to limit their participation to the 1953 summer festival (June–September):

We were at the Barter Theatre for the 1953 season of spring, summer, and early fall. Grant, Charles and I chose not to stay for the winter touring. The winter company actors did

---

70. June Moncur Waite, correspondence with the author, June 2016, and interview with the author, October 2016. (Further quotations from correspondence or interview are cited in the text using the abbreviation JMW.)

71. Classical stage, screen, television, and radio Actress Judith Anderson (1897–1992) had a long and successful career in all four media; she may be best known to filmgoers as the sinister Mrs. Danvers in Alfred Hitchcock's *Rebecca* (1940).

the winter touring, and also served as a company during the summer, playing parts in the plays we did during the Festival. (JMW)

Because the Barter Players were fundamentally a repertory company, the audition winners alternated between leading and supporting roles. The Barter Prize was, in effect, a glorified scholarship to a prestigious theatrical university. Much like the Universal-International School for Actors would be two years later, the Virginia theater was an occasion for Williams to hone his craft while performing a variety of tasks in a professional context—and receiving a salary.

Moncur has fond memories of her Barter experience with Williams:

Grant was a good actor, but he was somewhat at a disadvantage at Barter because he had to share leading roles with co-winner Charles McCawley *and* with Jerry Oddo, a talented Marlon-Brando type who was a Barter regular.

We did not have much time at Barter to develop deep friendships. We were all living together at this great big inn, but, because we were so involved in rehearsing and performing, there was virtually no time to socialize. We did a new play each week; we would rehearse the next week's play all day and perform the current play each night. Sunday evening we had a dress rehearsal for Monday's opening. At the end of the summer, we performed all the plays again two or three times each, and we did not even have time for a run-through before these performances, so we just went on stage and hoped that we would remember our lines!

Between the studying, the rehearsing, and the performing, by the end of the summer I felt I could not tell when I was acting and when I wasn't: as if I didn't know who the real me was.

Mr. Porterfield was very supportive after the summer season, and gave me nice letters of introduction for some of the directors he knew in New York. But I quickly tired of having to promote myself and "push" myself all the time in the interest of a career: I soon abandoned theater, at least professionally. (JMW)

The list of the productions in which Williams was involved between June 15 and September 5, 1953 is impressive indeed.

As a warm-up for the *tour de force*, Williams played a mere Young Collector in Tennessee Williams' *A Streetcar Named Desire* (June 15 and June 25–27; August 3–4); June Moncur played Blanche DuBois and Jerry Oddo played Stanley Kowalski; Charles McCawley played the secondary role of Steve Hubbell. Alex North provided the music; the production was directed by veteran Barter Player Owen Phillips.

Williams then played the unsympathetic but important role of Anthony Marston in Agatha Christie's *Ten Little Indians* (June 29–July 1; July 9–11; August 24–25).

Williams' first large role was Joseph, opposite Judith Anderson's Mary (yes, *that* Mary), in *Family Portrait* (August 10–15, 1953); the role, that of Mary's third son, entailed learning about 190 lines spread over three acts. Ms. Moncur was not cast in the play. Kalita Humphreys played Mary Cleophas, Kay Kendall Mary of Magdala. Robert Porterfield directed.

On August 17–19 (and again on August 28 and 29), Williams went back to minor roles, by playing the part of Tosspot in Frank Lowe and Robert Gallico's adaptation of James Thurber's *The 13 Clocks*.[72] Other members of the cast included Eric Blore,[73] Charles McCawley, and familiar Barter names Jerry Oddo and Kay Kendall. The production was directed by Owen Phillips.

An inspired casting choice occurred in Garson Kanin's *Born Yesterday* (July 13–14; July 25; August 7–8; August 13; August 26 and 27), where Williams, third-billed, took on the role of Paul Verrall (which William Holden had played in the 1950 film version and Paul Douglas had played in the 1946 Broadway run), acting against Ms. Moncur and Mr. Oddo.

Another play in which Grant Williams was ideally cast as a leading man was William Shakespeare's early comedy *The Two Gentlemen of Verona*, which ran from August 31 to September 5, 1953.[74] Williams played

---

72. James Thurber, *The 13 Clocks*, Simon & Schuster, 1950.

73. Eric Blore (1887–1959) from Great Britain had an extensive career in Hollywood as character (especially comic) actor. Among his many films, let us mention at least two directed by Preston Sturges: *The Lady Eve* and *Sullivan's Travels* (both 1941).

74. Reportedly, this was "the first professional production of the play to be given

Proteus, one of the eponymous gentlemen (the conflicted one); the co-protagonist was Charles McCawley, who portrayed Valentine. Ms. Moncur was cast as Silvia. The production was designed and directed by John Edward Friend.[75]

(Shakespeare and Kanin leading roles weeks apart! Williams' part in *The Two Gentlemen of Verona* alone amounted to some 460 lines, and Paul Verrall is a sizeable leading role, occupying sixty-eight pages in the published play.)[76]

Williams' participation in Elmer Rice's *Street Scene* (July 6–8, 1953; August 5, 6 and 20–22, 1953) is uncertain.

Also uncertain is the touring of any or all of these plays in subsequent months. We know from June Moncur that the three Barter co-winners did not participate in the tours. *The Two Gentlemen of Verona*, the local press tells us, enjoyed a college tour in 1954, but with a different cast: Lauren Farr and Jerry Oddo played the two gentlemen, Kay Kendall and Peggy Collins Julie and Silvia, respectively.

June Moncur sums up her Barter Theatre experience:

> We worked hard, and we worked fast; we learned, rehearsed, and performed in a large number of plays in a short period. There wasn't time for any in-depth exploration of anything, but the Barter Theatre had some talented people working for it, who did an excellent job with the plays.[77] The shows all turned out well.
>
> In the fall of 1953 the three of us returned to New York City. I don't remember ever seeing Grant again. (JMW)

Williams' stint at the Barter Theatre was a key moment in his acting career, and, one can imagine, an emotional one. He was getting a name for himself, receiving invaluable repertory experience, and rubbing elbows with famous players such as Judith Anderson, Eric Blore, Robert Porter-

in the United States in the Twentieth Century." *Kingsport (TN) Times-News*, August 30, 1953.

75. "Current Theater Notes," *Shakespeare Quarterly*, vol 5, no. 1 (January 1954), Folger Shakespeare Library in association with George Washington University; also, Barter Theatre playbill, *The Two Gentlemen of Verona*, 1953.

76. Garson Kanin, *Born Yesterday*, The Viking Press, 1946.

77. For example Barter's set designer, Mack Statham.

field, and Rosalind Russell. If ever there was a pivotal transition in Williams' artistic progress, this was it. Simultaneously, and paradoxically, that moment turned into a missed opportunity. Williams was obviously harboring an important ambition; whether this ambition was already oriented towards Hollywood or whether the idea came to him after the 1953–54 theater season, we do not know,[78] but one thing is certain: acting was becoming a central factor in Williams' life, and his other career paths were forgotten. Judging from his statements on the craft and from his film and television performances, Williams remained at heart a stage actor, or at least an actor who needed to test himself in a variety of different roles: an actor who valued acting and character exploration. Yet, he was also impatient to move on to a more remunerative career in the film industry: this impatience created something of a contradiction for him.

Coincidentally, and probably not referring to Williams at all, Robert Porterfield himself commented on this impatience during a panel discussion that took place at that same summer festival on August 11, 1953. This is what he said about actors: "Some actors want to get ahead too quickly. It takes at least ten years of wearing out your soul as well as the soles of your shoes."[79]

Had he allowed his stage career to develop slowly, Williams might have expanded his skill and repertoire and acquired a name as a serious thespian, for example by graduating to Broadway. Williams eventually fared well enough in film and television, and in a couple of instances was able to be involved in minor masterpieces; in his westward thrust, however, he also lost something vital for the organic growth of himself and his career. Williams' entire Hollywood career (not counting those pitiful late entries between 1967 and 1977) lasted ten years, which, according to Porterfield, was just the groundwork.

The contradiction between serious acting and "business" success, between art and commerce, would be painfully evident in Williams'

---

78. The exact event that triggered Williams' definitive move to the West Coast is not documented, but it must have coincided with his trip to Los Angeles to film his television appearance in the television series *Soldiers of Fortune* (February 1955, see next chapter). According to columnist Hedda Hopper, by March 1955 Williams had signed his contract with U-I.

79. Robert Porterfield, quoted in Frances Roberts, "Actors Lead Discussions During Festival Panels," *Kingsport (TN) Times*, August 12, 1953.

Hollywood tenure. Talent, truthfulness, and versatility were not prime commodities in Tinseltown, at least not the way they were on the theater boards; yet somehow Williams kept playing by the rules of the theater, concentrating on his craft and changing agents and jobs as if jumping from audition to audition or from theater to theater. Even when talking about his career, Williams tended to dismiss his accomplishments and focus on the technical lessons he had learned. Acting itself—rather than its results—was his primary concern. Consciously or not, Williams'

The second headshot Williams provided for his Barter Theatre auditions. Undated, circa 1953. Courtesy of the Barter Theatre, Abingdon, Virginia.

restlessness in Hollywood was the expression of that conflict, as was his entire Hollywood output, which (with one notable exception) was—and is—more interesting from a theatrical or thespian point of view than from the point of view of stardom or financial success.

This contradiction was implied rather forcefully (though perhaps unintentionally) by the witty introduction to a syndicated article about Williams that appeared in newspapers nationwide in November 1955:

> Grant Williams has a deep-seated infection caused by a mean bite from the acting bug. And no medicine, even an antibiotic called success, seems able to effect a permanent cure.
>
> Williams figures that he has given up acting about as often as a chronic liar casts aside his New Year's resolutions. Apparently the guy just likes the work.[80]

The Blackfriars Guild

After his summer season at the Barter Theatre, Williams was cast in the play *Late Arrival* (October 19–November 24, 1953) by Charles Oxton, staged at the Blackfriars Theatre (off-Broadway) in New York City. In his book about the venue, Matthew Powell, O.P., describes the theater's genesis:

> In 1940 two Catholic priests of the Dominican Order rented a small auditorium on West Fifty-seventh Street in New York. Thus began the Blackfriars Theatre, also known as the Blackfriars Guild of New York, a part of a larger national Blackfriars Guild movement. This experiment in Catholic theatre would last for thirty-two years.
>
> Blackfriars was one of the very few attempts by a religious group to conduct a professional-level theatre, the only professional-level theatre ever conducted by a Catholic organization in the United States and the first religious theatre ever tried in New York City.[81]

---

80. *Arizona Republic* (1955), op. cit.

81. Matthew Powell, O.P., *God Off-Broadway: The Blackfriars Theatre of New York*, The Scarecrow Press, 1998, 1. Williams' association with, or interest in, religion would form a constant thread in his life, for better or worse, as we will see later.

A scene from the play *Late Arrival*, October 1953. Left to right: Sheila Fallon, Tom Gorman, Marion Fay, Al Mifelow, Marilyn Fay, Grant Williams, Ilse Bernnard, and Mary Berkeley. Photo: Adrien Boutrelle, New York. Courtesy of the Blackfriars Guild Collection, Providence College, Phillips Memorial Library, Special and Archival Collections.

The Blackfriars Theatre was a small but important venue, where many celebrated actors showcased their talents early in their careers. Among them, Eileen Heckart, Darren McGavin, Patricia Neal, and Geraldine Page.

Powell also provides a brief synopsis of *Late Arrival*:

> The central character of the play is a nineteen year old college girl, campaigning for the need for women to elevate themselves above their routine functions of housewife and mother. Her campaign is upset when her mother becomes pregnant and eventually gives birth to a son. By the end of the play the girl is engaged to be married and is planning a family of her own. The cast included John G. Williams as the girl's boyfriend.[82]

The play received praise from both critics and audiences. As Williams would later put it in his July 1957 personal letter, the play "was very successful and […] gave me a healthy shove in the business" (GW2, 1). This

---

82. Ibid., 83.

Another scene from *Late Arrival*, 1953. Left to right: Marilyn Fay, Al Mifelow, Marion Fay, Grant Williams, Ilse Bernnard. Photo: Adrien Boutrelle, New York. Courtesy of the Blackfriars Guild Collection, Providence College, Phillips Memorial Library, Special and Archival Collections.

appraisal of Williams' contrasts with the antithetical one he made in later years, where the key word he used was "flop" (see Williams' 1962 quotation from the beginning of this chapter); yet the play's success was, in fact, above average for an off-Broadway production, in terms of both audience reaction and critical reception.[83] It seems that by 1962 Williams felt obliged to categorize things in terms of fame and success rather than in terms of quality and experience—that old contradiction between art and commerce again.

About Williams' performance, the *New York Journal-American* wrote, "John G. Williams is an engaging and competent leading man." The same daily was backhandedly positive about the play itself: "There is a certain freshness and enthusiasm that transmits itself to the audience [...]," it commented, defining the play "a gentle and innocuous little comedy."[84]

---

83. The 1957 quote comes from a personal letter, and I would be inclined to consider it more credible than the negative statement he made in 1962 for a studio pressbook.

84. Powell (1998), op. cit., 83.

The New York Times was pleased with the play ("*Late Arrival* has good taste and humor and should provide rich enjoyment for many patrons.") [85] and with its creative team, but was synthetic about Williams (billed as John J. Williams):

> Father Thomas F. Carey and Father Robert A. Morris, who control the destinies of the Blackfriars Guild, have reason to offer a special prayer of thanksgiving this morning. [...] The play [...] found quick favor with the audience at last night's premiere at the Blackfriars' Theatre. [...] John J. Williams and Al Mifelow, as young men who come a-calling, complete the capable cast. [86]

The *Brooklyn Eagle* was slightly more positive about Williams:

> Among the more effective performances are those by Marion Fay as the gossip, John J. Williams as the level-headed boy friend, Ilse Bernnard as the housemaid, and Marilyn Fay as the younger daughter.[87]

The success of *Late Arrival* may have been limited, but Williams kept in touch with the Blackfriars Theatre management loyally in later years. In his cited July 1957 letter, Williams writes about this affection when mentioning some guests who had visited him in Los Angeles from the East Coast:

> Among those from the East were Fr. Robert A. Morris who with a Fr. Carey, runs a theatre known as the Blackfriars Guild in New York on 57th St.[88] I did a play there in 1953 which was very successful and which gave me a healthy shove in the busi-

---

85. J.P.S., "The Theatre: Blackfriars' 13th Season," *New York Times*, October 20, 1953.

86. Ibid.

87. Louis Sheaffer, "'Late Arrival' Opens New Season at the Blackfriars," *Brooklyn (NY) Eagle*, October 20, 1953.

88. Father Thomas Carey, O.P. co-founded Blackfriars with Father Urban Nagle, O.P.; Nagle was subsequently removed as co-Director of the theater in September of 1951 and replaced by Father Alan Morris, O.P. in 1952. See Powell (1998), op. cit., 73–82.

Thomas Carey, O.P., standing backstage at the Blackfriars Theatre; undated.
Courtesy of the Blackfriars Guild Collection, Providence College, Phillips
Memorial Library, Special and Archival Collections.

Robert Alan Morris, O.P., of the Blackfriars Guild; undated. Courtesy of the
Blackfriars Guild Collection, Providence College, Phillips Memorial Library,
Special and Archival Collections.

REGISTRATION FORM

KINDLY FILL IN AND RETURN TO

BLACKFRIARS' GUILD
316 West 57th St.
New York 19, N. Y.

(DO NOT WRITE IN THIS SPACE)

Have you registered
before? _*NO*_

Are you male? _YES_ or female? _____

NAME _GRANT WILLIAMS_

ADDRESS _219-17 114 AVE CAMBRIA HTS 11 LI NY_

TELEPHONE _HO 8-4147_

Are you a member of Equity or any theatrical union? _Equity_
Have you played with Blackfriars? _NO_
Name Production _____

Experience (If professional, please cite plays and roles; if school
and amateur, please state number of years and names of organizations)

"FAMILY PORTRAIT" WITH JUDITH ANDERSON (JOSEPH)
"TEN LITTLE INDIANS" (MARSTON)
"BORN YESTERDAY" (VERRALL)
ETC.
BARTER THEATRE, ABINGDON, VA.
YELLOW SPRINGS PLAYHOUSE, OHIO
TENTHOUSE THEATRE, ILL.
T.V. + RADIO NBC, CBS, WOR

References:

MUSIC CORPORATION OF AMERICA
ROSALIND RUSSELL
JUDITH ANDERSON

Are you interested in any other department than acting; such as
directing or technical work? _NO_

Height _6'_ Weight _170_

Age _23_ Color of Eyes _BL_

Color of Hair _BLONDE_ Today's Date _9/17/53_ Form AA

Grant Williams' registration form for the Blackfriars Theatre, dated September 17, 1953.
Courtesy of the Blackfriars Guild Collection, Providence College, Phillips Memorial
Library, Special and Archival Collections.

ness. Then Ellie Evers (my galfriend in New York) was here
for three weeks.[89] I'm sure you know what it is to entertain 24
hours a day for weeks on end. I'd rather do a heavy day's work.
But I love these people. (GW2, 1)

The Blackfriars Theatre archival material[90] for *Late Arrival* contains,
among other things, Williams' handwritten registration form, which provides interesting information. Williams was already a member of Equity,
which means that his experience at the Barter Theatre had served yet another valuable purpose.[91] Probably for lack of space on the form, Williams
does not mention *The Two Gentlemen of Verona* as one of his Barter plays,
while he does mention *Family Portrait, Ten Little Indians,* and *Born Yesterday.* He also mentions his having worked in television and radio, listing
NBC, CBS, and WOR. As references, Williams lists the Music Corporation of America, Rosalind Russell, and Judith Anderson. He also lists his
height as six feet; this last statement puts an end to the doubts created
by the oscillating measurements reported by the American press of the
time. Though Williams was billed as "John G. Williams" in the play's cast
and *The New York Times* and the *Brooklyn Eagle* referred to him as "John
J. Williams," it would appear from his registration form—and from his
Barter Theatre season—that by 1953 he was already introducing himself
by his definitive stage name, Grant Williams.

Lies and *The Cretan Woman*

The second play Williams allegedly (RL, 292) did in New York was
The Cretan Woman (1954) by Robinson Jeffers (1887–1962), a poet with
a reputation for well-crafted translations or adaptations of classical trag-

---

89. Ellie Evers was described thus in a 1959 newspaper: "Ellie Evers left college
when she was elected "Miss German-American." She started modeling and
now appears in "The Big Payoff" daytime [game show]." *Cincinnati Enquirer,*
February 16, 1959.

90. The Blackfriars Guild Collection, Providence College, Phillips Memorial
Library, Special and Archival Collections.

91. The origin of Williams' Equity status may have lain elsewhere. In a 1955 UP
interview, Williams stated: "I've actually been a professional actor since the age
of 12." *Arizona Republic* (1955), op. cit.

edies; Jeffers' biggest theatrical success had been his 1946 poetic translation of Euripides' *Medea*, performed on Broadway by Judith Anderson. Facts about *The Cretan Woman* are contradictory.

The New York Times reviewed an off-Broadway production of the Jeffers play that ran at the 182-seat Provincetown Playhouse in New York from July 7, 1954 to September 26, 1954.[92] The play had previewed at New York's President Theatre in March[93] and in Washington, D.C. in May.[94] The success of the Provincetown Playhouse engagement prompted the producers to extend its run and try to arrange a move to Broadway; an opening at the Bijou Theatre was announced by *The New York Times* in two short articles.[95] However, no further mention was made of the production after September 1954.

Grant Williams' name appeared neither in the off-Broadway cast listed by the New York newspapers nor in the annual review of the New York theater season, *Theatre World*.[96] As late as January 1955, in an interview he gave to the *Los Angeles Times*' Cecil Smith, Robinson Jeffers lamented that no Broadway production had materialized.[97]

If one were to look for abstruse reasons why the legend of Williams' participation in this second New York play was created (by Williams himself, no less), one could cite, for example, an early mention of the Provincetown Playhouse cast made by the *Brooklyn Eagle* in June 1954, about two weeks before the play's premiere.[98] In this announcement of the "completed" cast, the article listed the name of Charles McCawley—Williams' Barter Prize co-winner and Barter Theatre colleague during the previous summer season. McCawley, however, was not in the final cast when

92. *New York Times*, July 8, 1954; according to the same newspaper, plans were made to extend the run to September 28, 1954; the play closed on September 26 instead.

93. "Cast Rex Ingram in Greek Drama," *New York Age Defender*, March 13, 1954.

94. Walter Winchell, "Theatrical Arithmetic," *Shreveport (LA) Times*, June 2, 1954.

95. *New York Times*, August 14, 1954 and September 5, 1954.

96. *Theatre World, Season 1953-54* and *Theatre World, Season 1954-55*, Daniel Blum, ed., Greenberg: Publisher, 1954 and 1955.

97. Cecil Smith, "Jeffers' Poetry Gives Stage a New Language," *Los Angeles Times*, January 9, 1955.

98. "The Cretan Woman," *Brooklyn (NY) Eagle*, June 24, 1954.

The Cretan Woman premiered in July. Perhaps McCawley was mistaken for Williams in later reports; perhaps Williams himself was considered for the play, and then discarded; or perhaps Williams thought that if he claimed he had appeared in the play no one would bother to check.

Or perhaps, during his last interview with Richard Lamparski in 1982, Williams found himself having to explain the promotional statements made by the press in the fifties and sixties, statements that had mentioned his having done "two plays on Broadway." Those original statements had been lies, or at least exaggerations, designed to allow U-I and Warner Bros. (and hence the press) to label Williams as a "Broadway actor"; and lies have consequences.

As for the Antioch Shakespeare Festival mentioned by Askew in his 1957 article and by Williams himself in his Blackfriars Theatre registration form, it was also known as "Shakespeare Under the Stars" and was founded in 1952 by Arthur Lithgow (1915–2004, Associate English Professor at Antioch College and father of Actor John Lithgow) in Yellow Springs, Ohio. The festival set out to perform the entire Shakespeare canon in its six years of existence, which it did. Consultation of the "Antiochiana Collection" archive at Antioch College, however, has revealed that no Grant, or John, Williams seems to have performed at that festival.

Limited archival material exists about the interesting Tenthouse Theater in Highland Park, Illinois (also mentioned by Williams in his registration form). The venue, established in 1948 by Producer Herb Rogers (though its opening season only took place in 1950), was an "all-Equity" repertory-company theater "in the round" with a yearly summer season (typically from June to September). I could find no mention of Williams appearing at the defunct venue in the contemporary Illinois press of the period, nor in the few surviving playbills for 1952 and 1953. The theater closed in 1965.[99]

Oregon Cowboy

On September 8, 1958, a curious article appeared in the *Medford Mail Tribune* of Medford, Oregon, announcing the play that was to close the summer season of a stock-theater company, Bridge Bay Summer Theater. The article stated the following:

---

99. Chicago History Museum; Highland Park Public Library.

> Redding – Bridge Bay Summer Theater will bring the season
> to a close with the Broadway hit "Bus Stop." With Grant Wil-
> liams and Sonia Torgenson in the leading roles,[100] "Bus Stop"
> will open September 9 and run through September 14, closing
> the summer stock theater's 14-week season.[101]

My first thought when I read the above was that the announcement might
be referring to some other Grant Williams (Redding seemed an improb-
ably remote location), until I read the paragraph that followed:

> Williams, currently doing a television series, has appeared in
> nine motion pictures, including "The Incredible Shrinking
> Man." He toured with the famous Judith Anderson and his
> roles in several western films and on the stage gives [sic] him
> background for the impetuous cowboy role in "Bus Stop."[102]

The theater was located twelve miles north of the town of Redding, Oregon, on the shore of Lake Shasta. No reviews of the play appeared in the
local newspapers.

In September 1958, Williams had already been dismissed by Universal-International and was mainly busy with guest-starring appearances
on television. Since his contract with Warner Bros. was still two years
away, Williams must have been worried. Even so, from the point of view
of his career, and with all due respect to summer-stock theater companies, playing Bo Decker in William Inge's *Bus Stop* in Redding, Oregon,
seems like an over-reaction on his part.

Stage Society, Inc.

Puzzlingly, the 1960 biographical article about Williams in the
Daily Reporter of Dover, Ohio, claimed that he had appeared in for-

---

100. Sonia Torgeson had been a Barter Player during the 1953 summer season,
playing small parts, including Ursula in *The Two Gentlemen of Verona*, where
Williams was a leading man.

101. "Stock Company To Close Season With 'Bus Stop,'" *Medford (OR) Mail Tribune*,
September 8, 1958.

102. Ibid.

ty-nine stage plays (not counting, I suppose, the 127 USO plays cited by the same article).[103] There is, alas, no hard evidence corroborating such claim. The only *direct* account by Williams of his stage work after his arrival in Hollywood is a sentence in his July 1957 letter, where he announces: "Will open in the play 'Rope' approx. first week of Sept. Stage Society Theatre—Hollywood." (GW2, 3)Williams' acting students claim Williams knew Frederick Knott's play *Rope* (1929) quite well and used it as acting material in his master classes. A surviving Stage Society production list, however, indicates that no production of the play was mounted between 1954 and 1962. In fact, Rual Askew's claim that by March 1957 Williams had "both directed and acted for Hollywood's Stage Society" (RA) finds no confirmation in the California or Los Angeles press between 1954 and 1959. Still, since Williams' cited three-page letter contains no other lies or exaggerations, there is no reason to doubt that he was at least *supposed* to appear in *Rope*. In all likelihood, the production was simply canceled. Judging from the local press and from the surviving partial documentary evidence about the theater,[104] September 1957 was a "dark" month between two productions: Langston Hughes' *A Part of the Blues* (which opened on July 19) and the Shavian double feature *How He Lied to Her Husband/The Man of Destiny* (which opened on October 11).

Conversely, the press confirms that Grant Williams did appear in one of the theater's productions: *Legend of Lovers*, a telling of the legend of Orpheus and Eurydice, which had its West-Coast premiere on April 29, 1960.[105] In the cast alongside Williams were Denise Alexander, John Harding, and Peter Brocco. The production was directed by Denis Sanders.[106] As proof that one cannot believe everything that newspapers—even authoritative newspapers—print, the *Los Angeles Times* advance announcement for the play stated that "the lovely, lyrical telling of the Orpheus and Eurydice story [was] by Jean Giraudoux." The play—whose original title

---

103. *Dover (OH) Daily Reporter* (1960), op. cit.

104. Robert Richardson Collection of Southern California Theater, USC Special Collections, University of Southern California, Los Angeles.

105. *Los Angeles Times*, April 10, 1960.

106. Charles Stinson, "On Stage This Week: Giraudoux and 'Vintage '60' Due," the *Los Angeles Times*, April 27, 1960.

was *Eurydice*—was, in fact, written by French Playwright Jean Anouilh in 1941.[107]

Stage Society was a well-regarded "professional but nonprofit actors' organization which offered for the most part neglected classics but also some original works."[108] During the 1950s, Actor Richard Erdman (born 1925) was "President, Director, and Producer of Stage Society, Inc., of Los Angeles" for seven years.[109] The Stage Society Theatre (where the company finally settled after its early days in a loft) was located at 9014 Melrose Avenue in Los Angeles (West Hollywood).[110]

Here is a bit of historical perspective provided by the *Los Angeles Times* in 1962, on the occasion of the theater's tenth anniversary:

> The Stage Society was founded in 1951 by actors Arthur Kennedy, John Ireland, Akim Tamiroff and playwright N. Richard Nash. [Producer Stephen] Brown, Richard Erdman, Barbara Slate and Helena Nash are the only "old timers" left from the original assemblage which performed in a playhouse on New Hampshire Ave.
>
> "We were quite snooty," Brown recalls. "For years, we only played for our own edification. We never let anybody but the members in."[111]

---

107. It is unclear where the mistake originated, whether with the *Los Angeles Times* reviewer or with the theater's press release; in any event, said reviewer corrected his mistake in his review of the play dated May 3, 1960.

108. Arnold Rampersad, *The Life of Langston Hughes: Volume II: 1941-1967, I Dream a World*, Oxford University Press, 2002, 274.

109. George Eres, "Richard Erdman Puts 'Blame' on Luck," *Long Beach (CA) Independent*, April 7, 1956. For Stage Society history, see also: "Inside LA STAGE History: Richard Erdman & LA Stage Society" at the website "@THIS STAGE magazine" (thisstage.la/category/columns/inside-la-stage-history).

110. Subsequently the Theatre Vanguard, from 1973 to 1978. Source: *Alternative Projections: Experimental Film in Los Angeles, 1945-1980*, David E. James, Adam Hyman, eds., John Libbey Publishing, 2015. Stage Society occasionally used another venue for its productions in the 1950s: the 350-seat Ivar Theatre at 1605 Ivar Avenue, Los Angeles (Hollywood), which opened in 1951.

111. Margaret Harford, "The Fragile World of Little," *Los Angeles Times*, February 25, 1962.

Sheila Fallon and Grant Williams, joint portrait for the play *Late Arrival*, 1953.
Courtesy of the Blackfriars Guild Collection, Providence College,
Phillips Memorial Library, Special and Archival Collections.

The Stage Society Theatre went dark in 1971.

In his long review of *Legend of Lovers*, *Los Angeles Times* Drama Critic Charles Stinson was quite enthusiastic about the production, but concise about his enthusiasm for Williams: "As Orpheus, Grant Williams is personable and satisfyingly intense and interior."[112]

---

112. Charles Stinson, "Anouilh's 'Legend' Witty Morality Play," *Los Angeles Times*, May 3, 1960.

A recent photograph of the apartment building at 1314 N. Hayworth Avenue, Los Angeles (West Hollywood), where Williams lived in the 1950s. Photo: David Rodgers, Los Angeles.

3

Westward, Ho! Early Television

IN HIS EARLY ADULT YEARS,[113] Williams worked as a publicity man for the Music Corporation of America for six months;[114] according to U-I, "[it] was that job which was responsible for his latest return to the thespian art. One of the agents at that giant talent agency convinced Grant that his best hope of an exceptional career lay in the acting field." (ISM, 3) That agent, in the opinion of the blog *Poseidon's Underworld* and of Richard Lamparski (RL, 292), was Maynard Morris.

Morris died in New York City in 1964, at the age of 65. On the occasion of his passing, *The New York Times* wrote:

> [Morris] was co-Director of the theatrical department of the Music Corporation of America, […] from 1937 to 1960, when he retired for reasons of health. He was thereafter personal manager for several young performers. He helped begin the careers of Gregory Peck, Charlton Heston, Paul Newman, Joanne Woodward, Robert Goulet and scores of others.[115]

---

113. Presumably in 1952–53.

114. This piece of news was also repeated in the *International Motion Picture Almanac, 1963* (Williams' bio is on page 310) and in several interviews Williams gave in 1955–1957.

115. Maynard Morris obituary, *New York Times*, January 28, 1964.

Following Morris's advice, Williams began to work with regularity in New York live television dramas; before graduating to films, and both before and after signing with Universal-International, Williams appeared in several live television shows. He would continue to work in television even after achieving leading-man status, but his first roles for the small screen were secondary—sometimes criminally so. His smallest parts were probably those for *Kraft Television Theatre* ("Alice in Wonderland," 1954, a cameo as the Knave of Hearts with two lines of dialogue), and *Studio One* ("Sail with the Tide," 1955).[116]

The Mask: "Fingers of Fear"

To date, no online resource, not even the Internet Movie Database (IMDb), has mentioned Grant Williams' participation in the episode "Fingers of Fear" (airdate March 21, 1954) of the short-lived (a total of fifteen episodes) television series *The Mask* (1954). In fact, IMDb provides almost no information about the series' episodes.

Most contemporary newspapers limited their discussion to the series' protagonists, Gary Merrill and William Prince, who played small-town brother attorneys, Guilfoyle and Guilfoyle, in the hour-long detective melodrama produced by the American Broadcasting Company (ABC). Only one or two dailies printed a fuller cast list on the day this particular episode aired.[117] That list of four included Grant Williams.

The longest plot summary, in New Jersey's *Courier-Post*, was the following: "The story of a teenage girl seeking help for her boyfriend, a murder suspect."[118] Grant Williams played the boyfriend.

James Devane, the television Reviewer of the *Cincinnati Enquirer*, was particularly unhappy with the series two days after its January 10 debut:

---

116. "Sail with the Tide" was described by the *Brooklyn Eagle* television desk with the following outline: "The American TV debut of Mai Zetterling, an arresting and extremely talented Swedish visitor, is the primary reason this sophisticated soap opera is worth seeing. About a beautiful but icy singer devoted exclusively to her art and her equally icy French officer who succumbs to her charms. Claude Dauphin is back from Paris, playing the French Officer [...]." *Brooklyn (NY) Eagle*, January 17, 1955.

117. For example the *Brooklyn (NY) Eagle*.

118. *Camden (NJ) Courier-Post*, March 20, 1954.

ABC-TV publicists have been calling "The Mask," their new series of melodramas which debuted [...] last Sunday, a "major event" of 1954.

If the publicists actually believe what they write then their idea of a "major event" is a mystery program on a par with "Rocky King"[119] or "The Plainclothesman"[120] dragged out to an hour in length for that's just about what "The Mask" was on its debut.

Gary Merrill and William Prince, two usually competent actors, are mixed up in "The Mask" as brother attorneys, Guilfoyle and Guilfoyle. Gary is the staid type who walks around sucking a pipe while deploring his brother's interest in crime. William loves a murder and solves them, according to Gary by "taking a nap, by going down into a mental underworld, by imagining himself the criminal."

Sunday, the Guilfoyle boys were involved with a burlesque troupe scared by a slasher. [...] For approximately an hour, William and the members of the burlesque troupe shivered and lurked mysteriously in backstage shadows while an organ worried and churned. Gary, however, just took things easy, sucking his pipe and talking about how his brother was soon going into that "mental underworld" of his and make everything come out all right.

[...] Nothing much of worth was evident in this first Guilfoyle case. [...] If "The Mask" keeps up like this, ABC-TV would be wise to close down the Guilfoyle and Guilfoyle office and try something else in its place.[121]

---

119. *Rocky King* (1950–1954) was a detective series produced by DuMont Television Network and Stark-Layton and starring Roscoe Karns as the titular detective (Source: Wikipedia).

120. *The Plainclothesman* (1949–1954) was a detective series, also produced by DuMont Television Network and starring Ken Lynch. The main gimmick was the following: the Lieutenant (Lynch) never appeared on camera, as the series used the subjective point-of-view camera technique (Source: Wikipedia).

121. James Devane, "Look and Listen": "'The Mask' Is No 'Major Event,'" *Cincinnati Enquirer*, January 12, 1954.

Evidently, it did not take long for ABC-TV to follow the above reviewer's advice. The series was canceled within five months of its inception.

Kraft Television Theatre I: "Deliver Me from Evil"

Presumably, Grant Williams was a lead player in the small cast of three listed by the contemporary press (and by online sources such as IMDb in recent years) for the episode "Deliver Me from Evil" (airdate June 17, 1954) of the live drama anthology *Kraft Television Theatre* (1947–1958).

Here is a plot outline from the *Brooklyn Eagle*:

> If you're not tired of the Army-McCarthy hearings you should like tonight's Magistrate's Court scene investigating the murder and attempted robbery of a gas station owner by two boys. Anthony Ross stars as the lawyer-father of a weak son who's in a real jam.[122]

Soldiers of Fortune: "The Lady of Rajmahal"

Williams' role in the episode "The Lady of Rajmahal" (airdate February 9, 1955) of the series *Soldiers of Fortune* (1955–1957) is not much to write home about, though, fifth in a drawing-room cast of five, it is virtually a co-starring role. Young, handsome and clean-cut, Williams plays Kingsley Miller, the shady cousin/lover who visits Lady Diane (Lisa Daniels, who is not very effective), the white American wife of the local Rajah (Ian Keith, who is quite charismatic as the disenchanted Rajah). Set in an Indian ambience reconstructed at Republic Studios in North Hollywood, the thirty-minute story involves titular characters Tim Kelly (John Russell) and Toubo Smith (Chick Chandler) as mercenaries hired by the Rajah to protect a valuable painting, a domesticated tiger, and his own wife as they leave his property on their way to Calcutta. Kingsley covets Lady Diane and the painting both, and gets killed trying to steal the latter at gunpoint.

Williams can certainly act, but the part is slight. The show, as was often the case with these early live-television efforts, is awkwardly blocked and directed, using a wooden style reminiscent of early sound film theat-

---

122. *Brooklyn (NY) Eagle*, June 17, 1954.

Grant Williams and Lisa Daniels in "The Lady of Rajmahal" (1955). Frame capture.

rics. Afraid to be off their camera marks, the actors stand absolutely still during entire exchanges, speaking in an inconsistent variety of English accents: everyday American (Russell and Chandler) and three variations of mid-Atlantic or theatrical American, of which Keith's is the most British (Daniels was a British actress, but she is playing an American here).

Lux Video Theatre I: "Shadow of a Doubt"

Little was written about the *Lux Video Theatre* television drama "Shadow of a Doubt" (airdate March 24, 1955). Grant Williams, though not the protagonist of the episode, played the important role of young detective Jack Graham (which Macdonald Carey had played in Hitchcock's 1943 film), a key element in the mystery plot.

Daily Variety was enthusiastic about the show:

> Adapted from the UI film of 1943, "Shadow of a Doubt" is, in its televersion [sic], a harrowing, chilling tale of suspense—a melding of the macabre with the normal. Top-flight entertain-

ment all the way, "Shadow" also casts very fine performances by Frank Lovejoy and Barbara Rush. They help make it compelling drama.[123]

Still in a positive vein, the daily gave short shrift to the secondary players: "Good support is given Lovejoy and Miss Rush by Byron Foulger, Grant Williams, Sarah Selby, and George Chandler."[124]

Allen in Movieland

The TV movie *Allen in Movieland* (airdate July 2, 1955), on the other hand, was given extensive coverage in the press, including the trades. Here is a description of the antics on display from an announcement on the day of the broadcast:

> Ever tour a movie studio? You can tonight via remote control as the cameras […] follow Steve Allen through a 90-minute visit to the Universal-International lot. […] Tour starts promptly at 6 p.m., and Steve is the guide.
>
> Along the way you'll find Tony Curtis and two stuntmen doing a fight scene from "The Rawhide Years," and they'll show how the trick fights are pulled off.
>
> Jeff Chandler will sing his "Foxfire" (he wrote the lyrics), and show some film clips from his movie of the same name. Audie Murphy will tell of some of his experiences and show clips from the movie "To Hell and Back," based on his book of that title.
>
> Steve will visit the dramatic school to find Leigh Snowden, Dani Crayne and Mara Corday hard at work. Keith Andes does a production number with a crew of dancing lovelies. Pat Crowley and dancer Dante De Paolo [sic] do a fancy turn.[125]

123. *Daily Variety*, March 28, 1955.

124. Ibid.

125. Dante DiPaolo (Dante Cesare DiPaolo, 1926–2013) was an Italian-American dancer and actor, best remembered for Stanley Donen's *Seven Brides for Seven Brothers* (1954) and for his leading role in Mario Bava's *Sei donne per l'assassino* (*Blood and Black Lace*, 1964).

Piper Laurie sings a song and the famed Benny Goodman trio shows up.[126]

Allen in Movieland was not well received by critics; it was, for example, the object of a searing review by Paul Cotton of the *Des Moines Register*:

> If you feel oppressed by the heat these evenings, turn on your set and watch summer television. See if you forget the humidity and escape the workaday world. Are you enchanted?
>
> If so, see a psychiatrist. The heat has addled your head.
>
> Steve Allen has signed with Universal-International to impersonate Benny Goodman in a movie. TV is in the midst of an all-out courtship of the movies. So the Saturday evening NBC summer spectacular was a valentine, or 90-minute nosegay, to this movie maker.
>
> It was called "Allen in Movieland." It should have been, "Universal-International, I Love You, (signed) Steve Allen and NBC." It came from Hollywood, of course, and the plot, if any, was Allen arriving and wandering around the Universal-International lot.
>
> I counted fat-sized plugs for nine upcoming Universal-International movies, including film clips from five and a live scene from still another. So-called movie stars were in and out of the show, some of them so famous that I, for one, had never heard of them.
>
> The first part of the show was passably amusing in spots as it kidded Allen for being out of place. The last half-hour turned almost maudlin with its Allen a lonely, friendless man.[127]

Mr. Cotton will forgive me if I do not share his scorn. It is true that the television special is a shameless plug for sundry Universal-International projects, and that the final effect is that of an anthology talent show—even an awkward one at that. It is also true, however, that a few of the players shine in spite of this limitation, because of their charm and talent (Muriel

126. Terry Vernon, "Tele-Vues," *Long Beach (CA) Independent*, July 2, 1955.

127. Paul Cotton, "On Television," *Des Moines (IA) Register*, July 5, 1955.

Grant Williams in the TV movie *Allen in Movieland* (1955). Frame capture.

Landers and Grant Williams are two such players), and that at least two scenes not only redeem the movie from its clumsy format but also create some authentic theatrical poetry. One of those two scenes involves Grant Williams.

As a theatrical exercise demonstrating the quality of the Universal-International School for Actors, Williams is assigned a pivotal scene from *Bright Victory* (a 1951 U-I feature film starring Arthur Kennedy) in which he plays Sergeant Larry Nevins, blinded during World War II. The scene involves a dialogue with the Army psychologist (the rather wooden Rex Reason), who is helping him with his recovery, and a phone call Nevins is supposed to make to his mother to inform her of his injury. A twenty-five-year-old Clint Eastwood is on hand as an orderly who walks Nevins in and out of the room, and reveals to him before the scene closes that the psychologist he has just accused of not understanding his plight is—unexpectedly—as blind as he is.

The six-minute scene is quite moving, and Williams is magnificent in it—and arguably more potent and vibrant than Kennedy's original. Intense and thoughtful, Williams carefully pulls out all the dramatic stops, one by one, and delivers a powerful, intelligent performance. His youthful talent is undeniable, as is his ability to delineate his character clearly and to make every emotional change visible through his face and body. Kennedy was thirty-seven when he starred in the original film, Williams twenty-three when he made *Allen in Movieland*; and youth itself becomes a positive factor in his performance, making his character's immaturity and boyish torment all the more poignant, and all the more believable. Judging from this early test, Williams was definitely a real actor, and a good one.

Especially remarkable is Williams' command of emotional transitions. Like a true Method wizard, Williams breaks down his scene into tiny dramatic beats, and deftly (and touchingly) veers the character's feelings and thoughts (and the audience's reactions, for those paying attention) through a tortuous transformative course that is both surprising and revealing.

Williams' scene aside, *Allen in Movieland* is most successful when it finally stops trying too hard and eases into its most touching, beautiful musical number. Authentic magic happens towards the end of the movie.

Grant Williams and Rex Reason in *Allen in Movieland* (1955). Frame capture.

Grant Williams in *Allen in Movieland* (1955). Frame capture.

Left alone in the cavernous sound stage, the stage lights dimmed, Steve Allen is not too enthusiastic anymore. Having been ridiculed, bullied, or ignored by the Universal-International people, he tries to phone his agent in New York but has to compete first with an uncooperative switchboard operator and then with a charwoman who has entered the sound stage to clean and is expecting a phone call. The call comes; it is from a man who tells her that he is canceling their first date: she is no beauty, and he has just seen her photograph.

Both characters, Allen and the charwoman, have been rejected. They exchange a few words, commiserate for a moment, and then, quietly, begin to sing together. The song: "Two Lost Souls" from *Damn Yankees*.[128] Allen stops being a comedian, while his co-star Muriel Landers (1921–1977) demonstrates that she was a great actress and an even better singer. The number makes up for everything. Suddenly, this is great, intimate theater, even great television.

---

128. The original Broadway production of the successful musical comedy *Damn Yankees* opened on May 5, 1955 and closed after 1,019 performances on October 12, 1957. Warner Bros. produced the 1958 film version.

Muriel Landers and Steve Allen in *Allen in Movieland* (1955). Frame capture.

The show-stopping power of the Allen-Landers scene is such that the finale that follows it (involving Allen, Benny Goodman, and his trio) cannot be but a letdown. As good as the jamming session is, it cannot compete with the charming atmosphere of the previous scene, and feels anticlimactic, even when all the artists who participated in the television special join in to listen (Universal-International is welcoming towards Allen once more). The significance of this finale is mostly historical; Grant Williams' scene and the charwoman number are great showmanship.

Three days after the airing of the special, *Daily Variety* agreed with the complaints previously made by the national newspaper reviewers, and had some snide comments of its own to make along the same lines. It did, however, notice Grant Williams' scene work, in what (for *Variety*) was a glowing endorsement:

> There were sporadic moments of solid entertainment, as well as players who showed talent and a fine dramatic sequence from studio's upcoming [sic] "Bright Victory," re-enacted alive,

with Rex Reason and Grant Williams displaying depth in their emoting.[129]

Lux Video Theatre II: "The Amazing Mrs. Holliday"

This is how a press release for the October 1955 *Lux Video Theatre* episode "The Amazing Mrs. Holliday" described both the show and its protagonist:

> "This is Grant Williams, rising young Universal-International actor, who will co-star with Barbara Rush in the LUX VIDEO THEATRE televersion [sic] of "The Amazing Mrs. Holliday," Thursday October 6, 1955 over NBC TV. In the TV version Williams plays the role created by Edmond O'Brien in the [1943] Universal-International film, that of Tom Holliday III, who sets out to prove his grandfather's widow is an imposter."

Daily Variety was tepid about the whole affair, but had a few kind words to say about Williams (and even a few kind words from the *Variety* folks could carry some weight in the industry): "Miss Rush lent little credibility to her role; Grant Williams was much better as her young romancer."[130]

Williams would star in two more *Lux Video Theatre* dramas in 1957.

Matinee Theater: "Arrowsmith"

Virtually nothing was written about another television drama, "Arrowsmith" (aired December 5, 1955, in color), filmed live for the newly-minted dramatic anthology series *Matinee Theater* (October 31, 1955– June 27, 1958). The episode was based on Sinclair Lewis's novel of the same title and featured a young idealistic doctor (Williams) as its protagonist. Here is a brief announcement of the airing from a daily: "'Arrowsmith,' Sinclair Lewis story. Young doctor's devotion to research meets opposition. Grant Williams plays title role. In color."[131] According to

129. *Daily Variety*, July 5, 1955.

130. *Daily Variety*, October 10, 1955.

131. *Philadelphia Inquirer*, daily television listings, December 5, 1955.

television expert Larry James Gianakos, "[Williams] was a wondrous Dr. Martin Arrowsmith, exceeding in emotive temperament—in under sixty minutes—the performance of his 1931 feature-film predecessor Ronald Colman."[132] Williams would star in two more *Matinee Theater* dramas in 1957 and 1958, and almost star in a fourth.

The new series was the center of attention, and the press was quite enthusiastic. The format was daring: a daily (five days a week) live drama series with ambitious stories adapted from novels and plays. Using a "cameo technique" that privileged close-ups or medium shots with only a suggestion of sets in the background, the show was filmed in color at the NBC Studio in Burbank (or, according to some sources, at NBC's studio in Hollywood). While one episode was being filmed, the sets for the next day's program were readied on the other side of the sound stage. The newspapers of 1955 filled pages and pages with enthusiastic reports of Executive Producer Albert McCleery's bold experiment.

An article published after the airing of the first episode added details about the manpower required to pull off the enterprise.

> "Matinee Theater" has taken over almost exclusive use of NBC's vast Hollywood color studio. (Some plays, but not all, will be in color.) The production staff is almost an army—Producer Albert McCleery has 3 associate producers, 16 directors, 150 technicians, and 14 editors. Recently, 17 plays were bought in a single day."[133]

Another article presented some of the show's minuses for its actors:

> McCleery's love for the "cameo" technique—a set-saving device using one close-up after another—can become a little wearing. But it has its compensations in that the actors love it. It gives people a chance to see them, and "Matinee" is already being touted as the greatest actor's showcase yet invented.
>
> It's just as well the actors are pleased with the showcase aspects of the show, for the pay just isn't there. For the first

---

132. Larry James Gianakos, personal correspondence with the author.

133. Paul Cotton, "On Television," *Des Moines (IA) Register*, November 4, 1955.

week, in an effort to launch the proceedings with a few hefty names, the top price for an actor was $1,000. Hereafter it will be $500—and that will be just for the leads. Everybody else will be doing the show for faith, love and expenses.[134]

Matinee Theater was quite a challenge for actors. The cast and crew had a total of five days to rehearse, block, tech, and perform each episode, which was rigorously performed live and without teleprompters. Casting directors who helped build the show realized that theater actors, who knew how to sustain a performance without re-takes, were their best bet. Williams—with his Barter Theatre past—was ideally suited to these efforts.[135]

The courageous series folded under great financial duress in June 1958. Television Critic Charles Mercer wrote the heartfelt eulogy:

> There's as little sense in trying to breathe life into a dying horse as there is in beating a dead horse. You can only write him a decent obituary before someone ships him off to the glue factory.
>
> The horse in question is a gallant 3-year-old named "Matinee Theater." It has won many a race in the estimation of many a weekday afternoon viewer but it has not been able to win the grand national sponsorship handicaps. On June 27 "Matinee Theater" will present its last drama on NBC-TV.
>
> [The network] should be praised for effort and tenacity. [It] has poured about 12 million dollars into "Matinee Theater." Trade sources indicate the network's net loss is over 3 million. It reached its peak of sponsorship and estimated viewing audience last summer.
>
> [...] Although facing great difficulties doing a daily hour of live drama, "Matinee Theater" nevertheless maintained a high level of production quality—as indicated by the many awards it has received. [...] In its more than 600 productions

---

134. Eve Starr, "Inside TV," *Rochester (NY) Democrat and Chronicle,* November 7, 1955.

135. For more information, see the interviews about the show on the Archive of American Television, emmytvlegends.org.

it has ranged through every conceivable type of drama. Not the least of its contributions is the fact that it has offered experience and employment to about 5,000 actors, old and new.

Now "Matinee Theater" is going and in its place it is expected that two half-hour soap operas will be seen. [...][136]

Kraft Television Theatre II: "I Am Fifteen and I Don't Want to Die"

Contemporary reviews of the 1956 *Kraft Television Theatre* episode "I Am Fifteen and I Don't Want to Die" (color, airdate October 18, 1956) were tepid, but saw Williams as a redeeming virtue. Here is J. P. Shanley of *The New York Times News Service* commenting:

[...] [T]he TV presentation [of Christine Arnothy's novel] was spiritless and uninspiring.

Mlle Arnothy based her book on a diary that she kept during the days of horror when she and some other residents of Budapest sought refuge from death in a cellar. The city was in the hands of the Nazis and under air and artillery siege by advancing Soviet forces.

In the detached and superficial television production, the characters might have been merely pausing briefly under a shed to avoid a sudden shower.

The telecast's only moments of vitality were those in which Bennye Gatteys, as Christine, and Grant Williams, as a young Hungarian Army officer, exchanged ideas and affection. Their moments together, however, were not nearly enough to compensate for the extended sequences in which nothing of real consequence seemed to be happening on the TV screen.[137]

136. Charles Mercer (UP), "Mercer Says Matinee Theater To Breathe Its Last June 27," *Hagerstown (MD) Daily Mail*, April 15, 1958.

137. J.P. Shanley, "TV Version of 'I Am 15' Lacks Spirit of Novel," (*New York Times News Service*), *Louisville (KY) Courier-Journal*, October 18, 1956.

One of Universal-International's most striking portraits of Williams (© 1957, Universal Pictures Company, Inc.). The inscription, made out a couple of years later to Williams' Secretary Nina Ingris, reads: "To Nina, Without whose help I could not manage, Gratefully, Grant."

4

Universal-International, 1955–1957

I, Universal-International, Take You, Grant Williams

In 1957, the Universal-International pressbook for *The Incredible Shrinking Man* reminisced about Williams' arrival in Hollywood:

> [Williams] was eventually called to Hollywood to test for the lead in a projected filmed television series called *The Sword*. The series never came into being, but as long as he was in the movie capital, Grant decided to give the films a whirl. His agent started to take him on a round of the studios, but they never got further than U-I, where Grant was given a screen test and signed to a long-term contract within 48 hours." (ISM, 3)

An early mention of Williams' newly-minted (March 1955) Universal-International contract appeared in April 1955, in Hedda Hopper's syndicated column:

> For "Away All Boats" Universal-International has signed a couple of interesting characters. Grant Williams, from Long Island [sic], was a combat photographer in Korea; then an agent. [He] came out here last month for a TV show and got a U-I contract... .[138]

---

138. Hedda Hopper, "Hollywood and Vine," *Shreveport (LA) Times*, April 24, 1955.

Other mentions of the signing appeared in July 1955.[139] A tardy but more substantial reference to it appeared in *The New York Times* and other dailies less than a year later:

> Grant Williams, young contract player at Universal, is going to get star build-up treatment. He was chosen today for two lead roles in two projected features, "Star Light" (formerly known as "Star Light Star Bright")[140] and "The Incredible Shrinking Man." He will portray a Hollywood playboy in the first film and in the second will be the victim of a strange disease which causes him to diminish in size.
>
> The actor, who is 6 feet tall, was born in New York in 1930 and has played roles in three other films for the studio.[141]

According to Author/Columnist Robert Hofler, Williams was managed by Agent Henry Willson at that time and "[…] benefited from Henry's plugging him into a supporting role in U-I's *Written on the Wind*, 1956, which led to his headlining the sci-fi classic *The Incredible Shrinking Man* the following year."[142]

It would appear from the *Academy Players Directory*, however, that Henry Willson was not Williams' agent in the 1955–57 period (he would be a decade later, but briefly). In 1955, Williams was represented by his old friends at MCA Artists; he abandoned outside representation while under contract with U-I, then returned to MCA Artists in 1958. These facts cast significant doubt on the above reason for Williams' presence in *Written on the Wind*. In any event, the issue of Williams' representation is not a simple one, and will be discussed in Chapter 14.

---

139. "New Contract," *Des Moines (IA) Register*, July 31, 1955.

140. An early working title for *Four Girls in Town* (1957).

141. Thomas M. Pryor, "2 Fiction Works Acquired by Fox," article written on March 28, 1956 and published in *The New York Times* on March 29.

142. Robert Hofler, *The Man Who Invented Rock Hudson*, Carroll & Graf Publishers, 2005, 317. In a letter to me (June 2016), Hofler commented further: "Typical of Willson was that he would get minor clients put in Rock Hudson movies. He did that with several clients, Williams among them." (References to Hofler's book are cited in the text using the abbreviation RH.)

The Talk of the Town

Universal-International did not promote Grant Williams gossip aggressively; Warner Bros. would be more active on that front during his tenure with them. A few items, however, surfaced now and then in the syndicated or local news.

Two separate syndicated reports made the rounds of the press in October 1955, blowing the whistle on an alleged affair between Williams and Martha Hyer (who would co-star with Williams in *Red Sundown* and *Showdown at Abilene* the following year): one by columnist Harrison Carroll, laconic and innocuous,[143] and one by Walter Winchell, who remarked, in typical Winchellese: "Martha Hyer's hyer than a kite around Grant Williams."[144]

In August 1957, in his syndicated column "New York Confidential," Lee Mortimer, echoing Winchell's Winchellisms, reported: "Barbara Rush is getting the real rush from Grant Williams… ."[145]

Where Williams was concerned, Universal-International reached its promotional peak in 1956–1957, during the launch of *The Incredible Shrinking Man* (1957). Most of the articles that emerged at the time of such launch, for example those written by Rual Askew, Emily Belser, or Bob Thomas, were straightforwardly biographical rather than gossipy.

Debutante Balls

Universal-International was generous in arranging interviews and promotional tours for Williams, particularly in 1957. Personal appearances (at parties, for example), on the other hand, were rare. Aside from Williams' presence at the extravaganza organized by the studio for *Away All Boats* in June 1956 (more about that later), I could only find two events.

On February 24, 1955, the *Los Angeles Times*' James Copp wrote about a party involving Williams' agency, MCA. By this time, Williams was shooting television shows in the Los Angeles area and was about to sign with U-I.

---

143. Harrison Carroll, "Behind the Scenes in Hollywood," *Brazil (IN) Daily Times*, October 24, 1955.

144. Walter Winchell, "Winchell on Broadway," *Nevada State Journal* (Reno, NV), October 28, 1955.

145. Lee Mortimer, "New York Confidential," August 21, 1957.

MCA Transportation Manager Al Delgado pulled a birthday surprise (that worked, incidentally) on eyesome Marcell Smith and helping celebrate in Al's nifty B'Hills apartment were John Merrick, Pat Doyle, Eleanor Quinlan, Bob Hasha, Gene Corman with Nan Morris, Paul Miller. Grant Williams did a Johnnie Ray take-off, Ginny Glass acted as hostess and Saxon Rumwell missed the party (because he was bedded with pneumonia at St. Vincent's) but sent the honoree a huge box of carnations…[146]

Almost exactly a year later, a frivolous but charming photo spread appeared in the *Los Angeles Times*' Magazine Section. Williams and another U-I contract player, David Janssen, were depicted while playing inane society games with two buxom U-I contract beauties at an unnamed event. The beauties were Mara Corday and Hillevi Rombin (Miss Universe 1955). The title of the spread was "Bachelors."[147] On a separate page of the same section, the newspaper elaborated on the event in order to plant a promotional plug for Ms. Rombin:

Leap year is here and it's officially "open season" for the girls to do the courtin'.

Such a merry premise is the ideal springboard for a "turn-about" party where reverse etiquette is proclaimed standard procedure. Naturally, each girl must escort her date.

A game designed to get guests acquainted and the party spirit rolling calls for the girls to place their lipsticks in a basket. Then each boy selects a lipstick and tries to find the girl wearing the matching shade—she will be his partner for the next dance.

Hillevi Rombin, from Sweden, found this a delightful way to meet David Janssen, Mara Corday and Grant Williams.[148]

As illustrated by one of the photographs in the spread, Grant Williams found the girl wearing the matching shade to the lipstick he had picked— and got his dance with Ms. Rombin.

---

146. "Skylarking with James Copp," *Los Angeles Times*, February 24, 1955.

147. "Bachelors," *Los Angeles Times* Magazine Section, February 26, 1956, 32.

148. Ibid., 33

Back to School

Universal-International may not have been an aggressive gossip-mongering machine, but it was an important training camp for its contract players.

In a syndicated article dated August 1963, UPI Guest-Columnist Rock Hudson would lament the disappearance of the contract-player covenant in the changing studio system, looking back on his days at Universal's talent school:

> When I was signed by Universal, I joined a list of 43 contract players. Of that roster, 35 were relative beginners. We all were students in a $1,000,000-a-year talent school, going to classes daily to learn about our craft. The late Sophie Rosenstein, a marvelously gifted woman, imparted to us her great knowledge about acting. Trainer Frankie Van taught us body conditioning, muscle co-ordination and "action dramatics." We took dancing lessons just to learn posture and balance. We took singing lessons just to learn expression and voice control. We rode around the hill of Universal's mountainous back lot to learn horsemanship for possible western roles.
>
> Once a year we staged our own revue, demonstrating our acting wares in front of producers, directors and agents.
>
> [...] Many of us learned our first ropes in that Universal school—Jeff Chandler, Barbara Rush, Tony Curtis, Piper Laurie, John Saxon and others. From its alumni, ten became stars of a TV series—Hugh O'Brian, Jack Kelly, David Janssen, Dick Long, George Nader, Bill Reynolds, Grant Williams, John Russell, Clint Eastwood and Lori Nelson.
>
> No one major studio can afford to conduct a talent workshop like that today, but there is a crying need for one.[149]

All through 1955, American newspapers were brimming with plugs—large and small—for the Universal-International School for Actors or "College of Movie Knowledge," as it was sometimes called. Bob Thomas

---

149. Rock Hudson, "Hollywood" (UPI), *Childress (TX) Index*, August 18, 1963.

At the Universal-International School for Actors, Williams thrusts at John Agar (seated on the ground) during a fencing lesson, as instructor Jess Kimmel (far right) looks on. Next to Kimmel, a young Clint Eastwood. Photo: AP, 1955. Newspaper scan.

wrote an extended article about the school,[150] which was accompanied by a photograph of Grant Williams involved in a fencing lesson. (The photograph, which made the rounds of the press with or without Thomas's story, has unfortunately vanished from the AP archives; I am providing a scan from a newspaper.)

These articles dealt with the changes in the Hollywood system—changes that would yield their full thrust a decade later, and lead to the death of the traditional studios—but their surface topic was Universal-International and its careful training of young talent. One columnist called the new school "An experiment that other Hollywood studios [were] watching closely."[151] Such extensive coverage of the studio's training revealed, at a minimum, that the studio took its young actors seriously enough to make a sizeable investment in them. Whether it actually knew what to do with them once they were trained is another matter.

---

150. Bob Thomas (AP), "Hollywood 'Big Name' System in Eclipse," *Long Beach (CA) Press-Telegram*, July 1, 1955.

151. James Bacon (UP), "Movie Makers Looking About For New Faces," *Anderson (IN) Herald*, December 18, 1955.

Arthur Kennedy (1914–1990), co-founder of the Los Angeles theatrical company called Stage Society, had run a short-lived acting school of his own in Hollywood before signing with U-I in 1951. The experienced actor was full of praise for the studio's talent academy in an article about him from NANA:

> "[My school] died a slow and painful demise," [Kennedy] said. "Most of the youngsters who joined the classes didn't want to work, anyway. And those who did didn't know how. [...] They were trying to showcase themselves without qualifications. The real work behind the art of acting didn't interest them. They wanted to dress as actors, act like actors, and goof off while they were doing it. I gave the thing up as a bad job after about a year of it.
>
> "Two or three of the major studios now have their own talent-development schools where they really make the kids work," [Kennedy] says. "If they don't make the grade they might as well go back to the old home town and settle down."

Marlon Brando is the guest lecturer at the U-I talent school, 1955. Standing, back row, left to right: Karen Kadler, Leigh Snowden, Jess Kimmel (Director of school), Clint Eastwood, Floyd Simmons, Cathy Case, Grant Williams; seated, left to right: Dani Crayne, Colleen Miller, Mamie Van Doren, David Janssen, Marlon Brando, Barbara Rush, Gia Scala; seated on the floor: John Saxon. Photo: mptvimages.com.

Kennedy cites U-I's talent school as the best operated in the industry.

"They've taken raw youngsters [...] and have developed them into excellent performers," he says. "They worked 'em around the clock and gave them on-the-screen schooling no drama workshop around Hollywood has been able to do.

"Most of the movie schools fill 'em full of Stanislavsky," says Kennedy. "What they should do is teach 'em how to work!"[152]

A two-column UP article in July 1955 focused almost exclusively on the school's director, Jess Kimmel:

Only one lot still maintains an extensive training for future stars. That is Universal-International. The studio is even expanding its activities under the direction of Jess Kimmel, veteran of TV and stage associate of Jose Ferrer.

Kimmel, a strongly-built man who once studied to be an actor at NYU, proudly displayed the future facilities for U-I's talent program. Workmen have completed the foundation for what will be a 200-seat theater with rehearsal rooms.

"The theater will be just big enough with 200," Kimmel explained. "That will make it intimate enough to use movie acting technique. Anything larger would require too much projection."

The U-I training [...] has become so well-known that outsiders have tried to pay for the program. The studio has declined, limiting the curricula to its own young players. [...] A large part of the training is the day-in, day-out reading of parts. Kimmel believes in having the players study separately. Then they'll play the scenes over and over again with different students.

The youngsters are treated to occasional lectures by such visiting "professors" as Marlon Brando and Dan O'Herlihy. And they annually produce their own show, "Inside U-I."

152. "Youngsters Shun Work For Stage, Says Actor" (NANA), *Arizona Republic* (Phoenix, AZ), May 29, 1955.

The original caption for this press photo (© 1956, Universal Pictures Company, Inc.) reads: "Tony Curtis drops by for a chat with pal Grant Williams while Grant rehearses an outdoor scene for Universal-International's Technicolor-CinemaScope Hollywood love story, Four Girls in Town, which stars George Nader, Julie Adams, Marianne Cook, Elsa Martinelli, and Gia Scala." George Nader, standing far left, chats with Martinelli (back to camera).

Some flunk out, others may start the perilous path to stardom.[153]

In September, another short article from UP described the teachings of a gun expert hired to train actors in the art of shooting, and mentioned Williams:

Here's today's trade secret: Fred Carson is the gentleman who instructs our stars in the fancy art of how to handle their six-shooters like real cowboys. […] Carson's current pupil is Grant Williams, a recent import from Broadway, who plays a killer in

153. "Hollywood Star Situation Has Reached Critical Stage" (UP), *Asbury Park (NJ) Evening Press*, July 2, 1955.

"Red Sundown," a Universal-International adventure picture starring Rory Calhoun, Martha Hyer and Dean Jagger.[154]

Red Sundown

The earliest of Williams' pre-*Shrinking Man* roles at Universal was the character of hired gunslinger Chet Swann in Jack Arnold's Technicolor western *Red Sundown* (released stateside in March 1956).[155]

And a remarkable acting job it is, too. Williams, in a turn that Jack Arnold expert Dana M. Reemes calls a "bravura performance,"[156] creates an utterly original characterization for Swann, counteracting his slim build and blond good looks with a persistent grin (*very* friendly and *very* chilling) and a polite manner that make Swann the thug seem even more threatening. One could say that Williams effectively steals the show in his four brief but memorable scenes. His entrance occurs late in the film, at the fifty-minute mark, but it transforms the manner of the proceedings instantly. Swann's presence is a breath of fresh dramatic air that effortlessly wrests the tone of the film out of the other characters' hands.

Williams' characterization is a departure from many clichés of the period, and a curious peak of originality in an otherwise conventional— if efficiently realized—western. This departure from cliché demonstrates Williams' imagination as an actor, certainly; it also shows Jack Arnold's no-nonsense imagination as a director, a special talent that might bring to mind another "working-stiff" director with a knack for cliché-fighting choices for characters: Howard Hawks.[157]

---

154. "Fred Carson Teaches Movie Actors How To Handle Guns" (UP), *Arizona Republic* (Phoenix, AZ), September 11, 1955.

155. Early announcements for this film cited a different working title: *Decision at Durango* (*Los Angeles Times*, July 15, 1955).

156. Dana M. Reemes, *Directed by Jack Arnold*, McFarland & Company, Publishers, 1988, 85. Further quotations from Reemes's book are cited in the text using the abbreviation DMR.

157. The kinship between Arnold and Hawks was brought up explicitly by Williams' *Incredible Shrinking Man* co-star Randy Stuart in a 1996 interview. See Tom Weaver, *Science Fiction and Fantasy Flashbacks*, McFarland & Company, Inc., Publishers, 1998. (Further references to this work will be cited in the text using the abbreviation TW.)

Helen Brown (Mrs. Baldwin), Trevor Bardette (Mr. Baldwin), and Grant Williams
(Chet Swann) in a Universal production photo for Jack Arnold's *Red Sundown* (1956).
© 1956, Universal Pictures Company, Inc.

Swann's purpose in his introductory scene is to issue a threat to a family of peaceful settlers (Mr. and Mrs. Baldwin, played by Helen Brown and Trevor Bardette) on behalf of cattle baron Rufus Henshaw (Robert Middleton), in order to force them to abandon their land. When he appears at their door, Swann is the opposite of what one would expect from a hired thug. Slim, handsome, and clean-cut like the most innocent of boys-next-door, he is courteous and friendly, and smiles incessantly, even when he corroborates his threat by slashing Mrs. Baldwin's fine linen tablecloth with a knife and destroying all her finest china in one fell swoop. This last action elicits a little gurgle of a sob from Mrs. Baldwin; at this, Swann, who is standing absolutely still by the mayhem he has caused, smiles again, and his solar plexus is shaken by a single silent laugh that echoes her sob visually.

Williams is even given a great exit. His ultimatum issued *("Stay as long as you like: twenty-four hours at least.")*, his hat in hand, Swann stands by the front door and politely takes his leave from his hosts: *"Goodbye,*

Chet Swann (Grant Williams) smilingly admires Mrs. Baldwin's fine china before destroying it. Frame capture from *Red Sundown* (1956).

Mrs. Baldwin. Thank you for a wonderful dinner. Goodbye, Mr. Baldwin. It's been a pleasure." About to open the door, he stops, turns, and runs a hand through his hair as if confused by a thought: *"Oh. I—I forgot to introduce myself, didn't I?"* Still smiling, he faces the couple again, and adds: *"My name is Swann. Chet Swann."* And, smiling, he leaves.

Williams' gesture of running his hand through his hair may appear unimportant. It is a small gesture, it is true; but this character tic, which can also be glimpsed during Williams' introduction in his 1959 film *Lone Texan* (and then again in his appearance as "Patch" on *Bonanza* in 1965)

Chet Swann (Grant Williams) runs his hand through his hair, as if confused by a thought, before introducing himself. Frame capture from *Red Sundown* (1956).

is neither an expression of vanity on the part of the character nor an irrelevant action. The gesture calls our attention to the character's head, and hence to his thoughts; it subtly expresses a fleeting moment of introspection, of pensiveness—a private "inner" moment that concerns the character alone—through something exterior. In *Red Sundown* as in *Lone Texan* (and in all the best of his performances), Williams' subtlety and precision in coloring his character through these tiny touches are admirable. And all this without slowing down the pace of the scene.

That fleeting gesture in *Red Sundown* may be over almost before it begins, but it is an arresting interruption nonetheless, like a sudden orchestral color one did not expect or the addition of an extra measure that makes the rhythm of the piece irregular. That subtle confusion of Swann's confuses us too for a second. Both rhythmically and dramatically, it inserts a tiny caesura in the scene (separating the beginning of Swann's sentence, *"Oh, I..."* from the rest, *"I forgot to introduce myself, didn't I?"*) before allowing the normal flow of the line to resume.

That sudden confusion of Swann's, in Williams' hands, is not a pose; it is real. For a moment, Swann loses his icy cheer; the swagger temporarily goes out of his eyes, even while his smile remains frozen on his face. In that brief moment, we the audience may even be tempted to feel drawn to the character or to give him our sympathy. In the course of the scene, Swann has gone from boy-next-door to fiend; now, this moment of inconsequential doubt (about the fact that he has forgotten to introduce himself?) somehow swings the focus back on Swann as a person, as if we were glimpsing something deeply human about him. We are not sure exactly what we are glimpsing while he pauses by the door and makes that gesture: it may be nothing, but that nothing does not quite fit with what we have seen of him so far.

Williams (and Jack Arnold with him) dares to reverse the direction of what has come before and to look elsewhere; he dips his hands somewhere else in this man's inner world, and picks up something on the way back; that something he shows us. It is a puzzling fragment of information that he shows us, for it wrecks the smoothness of what we thought we understood, but gives us no certainty about the character. Technically, Swann's characterization in this scene has been a cliché-fighting dismantlement of the audience's expectations—a series of contradictions. With that gesture, Williams continues this series and adds yet another contradiction. With Pirandellian—or Brechtian—precision, he builds the scene by adding doubt to doubt rather than certainty to certainty. Humanly and dramaturgically, Swann is represented not as an exclamation point but as a question mark; his running his hand through his hair, too, is posed in the form of a question, figuratively and literally.

The entire scene from Swann's entrance to his exit only lasts a little over three minutes. In those three minutes, we see so many puzzling facets of his character that we cannot help but be a little curious about him. Now, by the door, Swann's moment of doubt again leaves us with an unsatisfied curiosity. What Williams has done in this scene is called fleshing out the character. The rest of the film does not allow his character exploration to continue (Swann is, after all, a secondary character, and becomes a more conventional, or functional, villain in his three remaining scenes), but the memory of that first scene is indelible. The puzzling, concentrated complexity of his character in that scene is the complexity of a potential protagonist. Imagine, if you will, Swann's first scene placed early in the first act of the film: the possibilities for development would be staggering.

Grinning villains have always been a dime a dozen. What is truly original, and exciting, about Williams' first scene is that he never lets the menace seep into his politeness, except fleetingly through his eyes. His smiles do not turn into snarls; there is no mustache twirling here. Swann appears to be a truly nice young man, his attitude running resolutely against the grain of his physical actions. Williams' other scenes in the film are more overtly sinister, and his smiles (or laughs) in them more overtly disturbing.

At the time of the film's release, most newspaper reviewers did not even mention Grant Williams' name, nor his role as villain in the film. A few did, such as the following writer in the *Shippensburg News-Chronicle* of Pennsylvania, who commented:

> Two sinister characters are strikingly played by Robert Middleton and Grant Williams, two actors who couldn't be more diverse in appearance. Huge, burly Middleton is a dominating figure as a greedy, crooked cattleman [...]. Comparatively slight Grant Williams, with his blond hair and pink cheeks, invests with chilling menace his role of a psychopathic killer hired to do away with Calhoun.[158]

158. *Shippensburg (PA) News-Chronicle*, June 28, 1956.

Variety too liked Williams, but telegraphically as usual: "[The Middleton character] is properly menacing, as is his hired killer, threateningly played by Grant Williams."[159]

Red Sundown marked the first pairing of Williams with Director Jack Arnold (1916–1992), arguably his biggest champion over the years, and a talented Hollywood professional. Arnold directed Williams in three films: *Red Sundown* (1956), *Outside the Law* (1956), and *The Incredible Shrinking Man* (1957).

Outside the Law

Williams' second film was *Outside the Law*, released in June of 1956. According to Peter Osteried, Director Jack Arnold had intended to assign the lead role to Williams, but Universal-International insisted on dark-haired Ray Danton, so Arnold did the next-best thing, and cast Williams as the villain.[160] (Perhaps coincidentally, British distributors of the film chose to display Williams rather than Danton on their "quad" posters.) Visually, the style is that of early-1940s gangster pictures.

Reemes, a supporter of the film, has written that *Outside the Law* "is like a clean, efficient, beautifully tooled little machine," and that "it is definitely a stand-out among Arnold's minor films." Reemes also opines that "the film seems a throwback to the program thrillers of a decade before," and that "[a]t a time when the "B" thriller was fast becoming extinct, Jack Arnold made a contribution to the genre that reflects the best of what the "B" thriller had been in its heyday." (DMR, 87)There is, however, something mechanical about the way the story is carried out, and something cold about the way the characters are developed. Danton's character, John Salvo, receives the most attention, if nothing else by dint of sheer quantity. He is in the vast majority of scenes, and here and there some character development slips by, but more as dutiful obligation than anything else. The balance of the storytelling leans heavily towards expository scenes that are both slow and dramatically inert: there is an awful lot of briefing and debriefing in this film, involving the Secret Service, the Treasury Department, and members of the law in general.

---

159. *Variety*, February 1, 1956.

160. Peter Osteried, *Jack Arnold, König des Phantastischen Films,* Medien Publikations- und Werbegesellschaft, *2012,* 178.

Grant Williams (left) and Ray Danton (right) symbolically demonstrate the criminal theme of Jack Arnold's *Outside the Law* (1956) in this publicity still. © 1956, Universal Pictures Company, Inc.

None of Arnold's Howard-Hawks-like originality is on display in such scenes, which drag on too long and neglect to add significant dramatic development. The intermittent presence of those information-giving scenes slows down the dramatic pace of the film, burdening it with a dull, gray-hued sameness. Some short vignettes involving secondary characters fare better, such as the early scenes involving Agent Phil Schwartz (prolific Character Actor Jack Kruschen) and his stomach problems.

The opposite problem occurs in the depiction of villain Don Kastner (Grant Williams), which is dramatically lively but much too fast and sketchy; Kastner's character arc is so hasty and schematic that it makes his psychotic bent appear simplistic and arbitrary. In theory, Kastner is the villain of the piece, but his objective seems utterly personal, and exclusively connected to his possessive attachment to secretary-slash-main-squeeze Maria Craven (Leigh Snowden). Hierarchically, Kastner is subordinate to another character, his boss Philip Bormann (Raymond Bailey), who pulls the strings of the counterfeiting ring; Williams thus finds himself relegated to a subplot. In Williams' interest at least, it might have been wise to merge the two villains and give Kastner power on both fronts.

With his elegant, measured acting style, Williams underplays his underwritten character (save in the action scenes, where his energy is volcanic), making him even more of a cypher than might have been intended. Still, the actor's presence is undeniable, and somewhat reminiscent of Alan Ladd's star-making turn as Raven in *This Gun for Hire* (1941).

There are some delightful touches in the writing here and there, admittedly, as in Chief Agent Alec Conrad's (Onslow Stevens, who would co-star with Williams six years later in *The Couch*) monologue illustrating the twenty-dollar bill under investigation, a monologue he delivers with wry, calibrated dryness:

> *All right, gentlemen: this is it. This is what we're looking for. This twenty-dollar note has had quite a history. We've been opponents for a long time. Now, a lasting association creates a certain amount of familiarity, so I've come to refer to our little friend here as "Willie," if you'll forgive the sentiment.* [He shows a schematic slide via a projector] *This, gentlemen, is Willie's birth cer-*

Leigh Snowden and an intense Grant Williams in a still for
Outside the Law (1956). Getty Images.

tificate. His father was a German named Emil Reinhardt. His mother was a set of hand-engraved steel plates, the most perfect ever made outside the US Mint. [...]

Variety liked the film well enough, but its only comment about the acting of the leads was: "[The film's story] gives further showcasing and experience to three of Universal's newer talents, [...] all of whom do ok by their lead assignments."[161]

The *Terre Haute Tribune-Star* of Indiana made one generous comment about Williams: "In what is his first important screen role, Grant Williams manages with great skill to create acceptance for an offbeat character, a fellow of angelic mien and satanic impulses."[162]

The *Greeley Tribune* film desk also had hopeful things to say about Williams, probably intended as a suggestion to U-I:

> Three attractive and talented young players, Ray Danton, Leigh Snowden and Grant Williams, do much to brighten Outside the Law, a well-paced, well-written and generally absorbing melodrama [...]. Williams has subtle good looks and a complex, fairly sinister personality projection that, properly showcased, may well turn him into one of Universal's best bets.[163]

Uncredited

Two uncredited jobs followed for Williams: as Lieutenant Steve Sherwood in the Technicolor war movie *Away All Boats* (released August 16, 1956) and as voice-over narrator Woodworth Clum in the western *Walk the Proud Land* (released in September 1956).

In *Away All Boats*, Williams' character has a name and a good military reputation (the other characters refer to him as a good officer and a born leader), but little else: his scant screen time is spread thin across the choral plot-based film and consequently Williams gets lost in a crowd of U-I male stars and would-be stars.

---

161. *Variety*, April 18, 1956.

162. *Terre Haute (IN) Tribune-Star*, July 15, 1956.

163. *Greeley (CO) Tribune*, September 25, 1956.

In June 1956, a large promotional and charitable event was organized by Universal-International to celebrate a special benefit screening of *Away All Boats,* designated as a premiere but taking place about two months before the film's official opening. The following piece was written by *Los Angeles Times* drama/film critic Edwin Schallert (father of William Schallert, the U-I character actor who would play small parts in *The Incredible Shrinking Man* and *The Monolith Monsters* in 1957) the day after the event:

> Unusual festivities and ceremonies last night surrounded a special benefit screening of "Away All Boats," Universal-International's wartime feature, at the Westwood Village and Bruin Theaters. Proceeds in an amount exceeding $13,000 net were tendered to the Navy Relief Society.
>
> The event was brilliantly attended by high-ranking Navy personnel, many socially prominent people and a sizeable professional group. […] Practically an entire two blocks in the vicinity of the two theaters in the center of Westwood Village was the setting for a Navy function, including renditions by Aircraft, Fleet Marine Force, Pacific Band, the raising and lowering of the colors, with special ceremonies to signalize Flag Day, and a spectacular drill demonstration by women Marines from El Toro Marine Base.
>
> A highlight of the festivities within the Weswood Village Theater, where the special benefit audience foregathered, was the presentation of an Honorary Admiral Award by Rear Adm. Robert L. Campbell, commander of the Los Angeles Naval Base and president of the Los Angeles chapter of the Navy Relief Society, to Edward Muhl, vice-president in charge of production at Universal-International.
>
> Jeff Chandler, star of the picture, attended with his wife and two daughters, while other players of the cast who were present included George Nader, accompanied by Martha Hyer, and Lex Barker with Lana Turner, Grant Williams with Lori Nelson. Other stars present included Esther Williams, Ernest Borgnine, Donna Reed, Robert Stack, Susan Hayward and Sidney Blackmer.[164]

164. Edwin Schallert, "Benefit 'Away All Boats' Showing Festive Affair," *Los Angeles Times*, June 15, 1956.

Grant Williams is a dour hand on deck in *Away All Boats* (1956).
Publicity still, © 1956, Universal Pictures Company, Inc.

Williams suffers an even worse fate in the Technicolor/CinemaScope western *Walk the Proud Land*. His voice-over narration, a far cry from his warm, beautiful storytelling in *The Incredible Shrinking Man*, disappears from the film after setting up the story in the first ten seconds.

Showdown at Abilene

Williams' role in *Showdown at Abilene*, released in October 1956, is sweet and poignant, but secondary. Williams plays Chip Tomlin, a nice young man on his way back home from fighting on the Union side of the Civil War. On the road, he runs into old friend Jim Trask (Jock Mahoney), who has fought on the Confederate side. The two rekindle their friendship and ride back to their native Abilene.

Chip has limited screen time, but is part of an important subplot: his death at the hands of the evil sheriff's men—virtually on the payroll of cattle baron Dave Mosely (Lyle Bettger), also a friend from Trask's younger days—is the catalyst for the titular showdown. Chip's character arc is simple, and Scriptwriter Berne Giler takes no pains to flesh it out— he even neglects to pay off a little character trait he sets up in an early scene, involving a portrait that Chip carries with him wherever he goes. Williams is warm and likeable, and plays an intense hospital-bed scene during Chip's recovery from the flogging he has endured, but his death happens off screen.

Bettger is good as Mosely the conflicted villain, and all hands are on deck for the character roles; the proceedings are, however, dominated by the stolid presence of protagonist Jock Mahoney and of the one lady in the picture, Martha Hyer, who does not seem to be trying very hard.

Written on the Wind

Williams' last film in 1956 was Douglas Sirk's *Written on the Wind*, released in December. While it was certainly a minor coup to be cast in a Technicolor melodrama directed by Sirk (and a rather splendid one at that),[165] Williams' role is a mere cameo, with just over ninety seconds of screen time; his character does deliver the final moral blow to oil tycoon Jasper Hadley's (Robert Keith) unhappy life, a blow that results in the old man's death from a heart attack; but the role is negligible, and Williams is justifiably forgettable in the film.

Four Girls in Town

Conversely, Williams is quite glamorous in the Technicolor/Cinema-Scope piffle *Four Girls in Town* (released on January 16, 1957), but glamorous in a male-pinup way. He plays millionaire's son Spencer Farrington Jr., the rich lothario with film-industry connections who sweeps starlet Maria Antonelli (Elsa Martinelli) off her feet in this romantic Universal-backlot

---

165. The film was, and is, well regarded. Philip K. Scheuer's review in the *Los Angeles Times* upon its release was glowing, calling the film "sensational" and "U-I's strongest film of the year." (Philip K. Scheuer, "'Written on Wind' Strong Sex Drama," *Los Angeles Times*, December 26, 1956.)

Millionaire Spencer Farrington Jr. (a very blond Grant Williams) turns serious with his conquest, Maria Antonelli (Elsa Martinelli), in this production still for *Four Girls in Town* (1957). © 1956, Universal Pictures Company, Inc.

spectacle. Williams is given the male-starlet treatment in *Four Girls in Town*, and is lit lovingly in warm, glowing Technicolor. He is very blond, very charming, and very thoughtful in his interpretation of a hollow, underwritten character; he wears nice outfits, and enacts some sexy dance moves for about a second, but the empty end result just makes one wish he were replacing Rock Hudson in *Written on the Wind* instead. Much of the same objectification is applied to the rest of the leads in the film: the girls are pretty, the boys handsome. Appropriately, one newspaper entitled its review of the film "Beauty Dominates in 'Four Girls in Town.'"[166]

166. *Battle Creek (MI) Enquirer and News*, January 6, 1957.

The film's story is split into four parallel, alternating subplots, with the four titular girls (Julie Adams, Marianne Koch, Elsa Martinelli, and Gia Scala) as aspiring Hollywood starlets competing for a talent search and the four boys (George Nader,[167] Sydney Chaplin, Grant Williams, and John Gavin) as the respective show-biz beaus who woo them. This splitting of the plot is the film's main problem, as it periodically sucks the life out of each individual story. Each of the four girls and four boys has a neat character arc, and Williams' playboy character even undergoes a neat final redemption by paying lip service to a mending of his ways; but the final effect is one of fragmentation. With more focus, any one of the four storylines might have been worthy of carrying the film by itself; multiplied by four, each of them ends up thin and weak. *Variety* agreed: "Where film comes up short mostly is spreading the interest among too many characters since there is bound to be a repetitive quality in dealing with four hopefuls in the same story."[168]

Though in all fairness Director Jack Sher and the film's undramatic dialogues do little to help the actors, one must admit that the acting in *Four Girls in Town*, especially by the four female leads, is for the most part atrocious. Thus, the better actors, mainly Adams and Williams, seem oddly out of place in their scenes. Abandoned both by their co-stars and by the writing, these better actors do what they can with the unsophisticated material, but fail to uplift the film.

In his static scenes with Elsa Martinelli, Williams—who behaves as if he were on a theater stage, his natural element—paints a deft, natural portrait of his little character with quick, decisive strokes, and devotedly pays attention to his co-star. In return, he gets nothing from Martinelli, who seems tone-deaf to both the style and the pace of what Williams is doing. Clearly uncomfortable with the English language, the Italian starlet awkwardly plays the repetitive drone of the one feeling she has picked for her character, line after uninteresting line, apparently oblivious to the rings Williams acts around her.

---

167. Syndicated Hollywood columnist Liza Wilson, in an improbable piece of hype concerning Nader's status as "Hollywood's Most Eligible Bachelor," (July 22, 1956) stated: "His friends are the Rock Hudsons, the Rory Calhouns, the Jock Mahoneys, Mara Corday, Grant Williams, Martha Hyer and Gia Scala." Nader was, in fact, a well-adjusted gay person, and enjoyed a fifty-year monogamous relationship with Mark Miller.

168. *Variety*, December 5, 1956.

Grant Williams watches his co-star Elsa Martinelli smoke a backstage
cigarette between scenes during the filming of *Four Girls in Town* (1957).
AP Photo/Harold Filan, April 24, 1956.

That is not all, however. In a grand gesture of self-sabotage, Writer-
Director Sher decides that the "fiction" the actors and actresses are to prepare and rehearse for the studio (the film-within-the-film) is a motion
picture entitled *The Story of Esther*, a solemn Biblical epic with some of
the dreariest, most stilted dialogues this side of Cecil B. de Mille, and
without the visual spectacle. Hence, the scenes on which these poor in-
experienced actresses are supposed to be tested seem designed to make
them fail, and to sink the film. If the four love stories (the substance of
the film) were sparkling and witty, the film might survive these dips into
mediocrity—much like Stanley Donen's *Singin' in the Rain* had done four
years earlier by ridiculing the badly written dialogues of silent cinema
and compensating with visual and verbal flair on the other hand. Instead,
the script of *Four Girls in Town* persists in being witless and sentimental
on both sides of the fence.

Los Angeles Times Reviewer Philip K. Scheuer was particularly dis-
pleased with the film. After entitling his review "One Long Test," he began
his first sentence with, "So is 'Four Girls in Town.'" This was his conclusion:

> The girls are good looking and certainly pleasing enough, but
> they don't justify the 85 minutes of minor escapades through

which they flounder [...] What Writer-Director Jack Sher gives us, in effect, is a naturalistic but paradoxically undramatic impression of life in a film studio.[169]

The Incredible Shrinking Man, the film for which Grant Williams is best remembered, was released in April 1957. It was the extraordinary result of a fortuitous confluence of eccentric talents, and its serendipitous intersection with Williams' career was one of those never-to-be-repeated happy accidents for which one should forever be grateful. The film merits an in-depth look, and is examined in the next two chapters, first from the point of view of its story and themes, then from the point of view of its promotion and reception.

169. Philip K. Scheuer, "Curtis' 'Mister Cory' Crashes High Society," *Los Angeles Times*, March 14, 1957.

Robert Scott Carey (Grant Williams) assesses his
measurements in this Universal-International publicity
still for *The Incredible Shrinking Man* (1957).
Photo: mptvimages.com.

5 The Incredible Shrinking Man: Music, Metamorphoses, and Metaphysics

MUSICAL STATEMENTS

It is the music that alerts us, during the main titles, as to the fundamental nature of the story we are about to see. After the appearance of the Universal logo and an initial rumble in which a succession of *fortissimo* orchestral chords is blared out in typical "Universal-monster" mode, the main theme of the film is stated by a solo trumpet accompanied by the string section and by the wordless harmonizations of a female vocalist. That theme, a plaintive, romantic siren song with a blues coloring to it, does not express the traditional threat and sensationalism of 50s Universal science fiction, but rather a potent feeling of longing and loss. That theme tells us that what we are about to see is a melancholy story.

Music is important in *The Incredible Shrinking Man*. More than half the intimate story of Robert Scott Carey (Grant Williams) is told without the benefit of dialogues: after the diminished protagonist finds himself stranded in his own basement, thirty-eight minutes into the eighty-one-minute film, his tale is carried out through music and wordless action, with the exception of his own voice-over narration, and of the brief appearance of two other characters. This means that much of the film's soundtrack is essentially a symphonic tone poem accompanying the visual storytelling. The symphonic style, too, is pure post-Wagnerian Richard Strauss *Tondichtung* with a fifties twist. Think *A Hero's Life* crossed with *Death and Transfiguration*. And, in more ways than one, *The Incredible Shrinking Man* is writer Richard Matheson's (1926–2013) answer to both those tone poems.

This solution endows the strange, solitary story of Robert Scott Carey with a musical lilt that sets the film apart from its contemporary genre counterparts, and wisely prepares its operatic, and effective, ending.

Richard Strauss's (1864–1949) *A Hero's Life* (*Ein Heldenleben*, 1898) tells the story of the titular hero (possibly the composer himself), of his achievements, of his fearless battles against a cruel world embodied by an army of hostile philistine critics, and of his eventual retreat to the contentment of serene contemplation. *Death and Transfiguration* (*Tod und Verklärung*, 1889) tells the story of a terminally-ill man, of his memories, of his anguish in leaving this world, and of his transfiguration as he achieves serenity and passes on to a different state of being. Both compositions (*A Hero's Life* in picaresque terms, *Death and Transfiguration* in existential terms) are about a state of conflict or torment being transformed into a state of serenity and acceptance.

These two elements, the heroic-picaresque and the tormented-existential, with their positive resolutions, are both present in Richard Matheson's novel, and in its film adaptation. The protagonist of *The Incredible Shrinking Man* is a well-adjusted advertising man who is forced to become a reluctant hero in a new, hostile environment (picaresque), but also a thoughtful man who is forced to come to terms with radical changes in his life and to revise his worldview before achieving a peculiar epiphany at the end of the story (existential). That positive epiphany constitutes one of the most original and poignant endings in Hollywood history, in any genre. In European non-genre cinema, a similarly existential, all-embracing epiphany would be achieved six years after this film by Guido (Marcello Mastroianni), the protagonist of Federico Fellini's *8 ½* (1963).

In his online column *DVD Savant*, Glenn Erickson makes a kindred parallel between *The Incredible Shrinking Man* and Fellini:

> Another movie from 1957 is about a woman of modest means, set in her ways, not too bright but with a good heart. Cheated and robbed, she loses her house, her possessions and her money, until at the end she's walking along with nothing, a total vagrant. All her material possessions are gone. In the last shot she looks at the camera and smiles. She's still there, she hasn't changed. Some human essence in her cannot be taken away. She breaks the barrier between the filmed story and the audi-

ence, and looks right into us. The movie is Federico Fellini's best [sic], *The Nights of Cabiria*, and it practically parallels *The Incredible Shrinking Man*.[170]

According to film-music expert David Schechter and to IMDb, the score for *The Incredible Shrinking Man* was a composite effort by three main (uncredited) composers active in those years at U-I's Music Department: Herman Stein (1915–2007), Irving Gertz (1915–2008), and Hans J. Salter (1896–1994). Lyricist Foster Carling and Composer Earl E. Lawrence contributed a song tune ("The Girl in the Lonely Room"), which formed the germ of the all-important main-title theme (to whose use the other three composers objected). The only person who did receive credit for his "music supervision," Joseph Gershenson (1904–1988), did not in fact write any music; he was simply the head of the Universal-International Music Department. Despite this patchwork approach to film scoring—a normal practice in those years, at Universal and at other studios—the score for *The Incredible Shrinking Man* achieves a surprising narrative seamlessness.

The Incredible Shrinking Man tone poem comes complete with the traditional leitmotif structure of the symphonic form, episodically developed. The main-title motif, for example, is initially associated with the radioactive mist that sets off Scott Carey's transformation; after its full enunciation during the main titles, it is cited during the opening scene by the electric organ, and has a mysterious, disquieting quality. It is then woven into the musical fabric of the film, before reaching its quiet climax in the final scene. It expresses, in effect, a mystery: the mystery of the unknown, perhaps, or of scientific progress and its dangerous consequences. By extension, it also expresses a deeper mystery, one having to do with the changes Scott must undergo and accept: the mystery of life and of the changes it brings with it, in one form or another, for all of us; the mystery of existence, of death, and of the universe. I am not overstating the issue: the importance of the motif is made clear by its constant presence, and by its final restatement during the philosophical closing scene, where it is tenderly hummed, not by the original female vocalist of the main titles, but by a male vocalist. I was not able to confirm this fact, and David

---

170. From Erickson's review of *The Incredible Shrinking Man*, 2006.

Role reversal: an imprisoned Scott Carey (Grant Williams) stares at a free bird from behind
the bars of his prison in this production still for *The Incredible Shrinking Man* (1957).
© 1957, Universal Pictures Company, Inc.

Schechter disagrees with me,[171] but, to my ears, it sounds like the vocalist humming that all-important motif might be none other than Grant Williams himself. Williams or not, that voice sounds like Scott Carey's voice.

The closing statement of the "mystery" motif (which overlaps with Scott's final voice-over narration) expresses, not the mystery of radioactivity or of biological hazards, but Scott Carey's own mystery, the one he strives to unravel in his closing scene. It expresses the acceptance of a change in perspective, and the sense of wonder towards a new world: Scott Carey's acceptance of a new point of view on existence, heralding new possibilities, and new wondrous mysteries.

It may not be by accident that when Ray Anthony and his orchestra extrapolated the main theme of *The Incredible Shrinking Man* for a 45-rpm recording released by Capitol Records,[172] they eliminated the strident, forceful elements present in the film's main title (even Anthony's

171. David Schechter, correspondence with the author, 2016.

172. Ray Anthony and His Orchestra, *The Incredible Shrinking Man*, Capitol Records, Inc., U.S.A., F-3676 (45-16602).

phrasing was more tender), and concentrated instead on the blues and on the magic. Without the aggressive, "shocker" component, this version tells the true story of the film.[173]

The film's commitment to its main character is absolute and earnest: he is in virtually every scene, and at no point does the film succumb to the temptation of camp. This is Scott Carey's story, a story whose weight he is allowed to carry on his shoulders, heroically. In a commercial genre film of this ilk, such an intimate and silent story setup is remarkable, and can be considered the closest thing to a serious exercise in character study. *The Incredible Shrinking Man* is, in fact, a character study masquerading as a genre piece. In order to please the genre audience, it has its share of genre thrills—the scientific mystery, the unexplained physical phenomenon, the battles with the giant cat and spider—but these thrills never clash with the intimate character study: nor do they merely complement the character study; they *are* the character study, in clever science-fiction garb.

It is as a character study that the music—especially in the second half, the cellar adventures—follows the main character's every action, as if narrating his story event by event, creating a counterpoint to Scott's vocal narration that resembles nothing so much as a dramatic variant of Carl Stalling's Warner Bros. cartoon commentaries.[174] Where Scott's voice leaves off, the music continues. In this capacity, the score intermittently abandons its leitmotif duty and concentrates on the narration of the action, using the instruments of the orchestra as incarnations of mood and action. Like the visual narration, the musical story unfolds with unfaltering dramatic commitment: Scott's tale is no laughing matter. One could say that the whole narration of the second half of the film is written and performed through three interwoven parts (as in musical part writing): Williams' voice-over, the action, and the music. In this respect, Williams' narration almost absolves the function of singing, threading itself through the musical discourse and the visual storytelling.

---

173. Universal never released a recording of the film's soundtrack; an independent label released excerpts years later (*The Classic Horror Music of Hans J. Salter,* coproduced by Salter Music Publishing Company and Tony Thomas Productions, TT-HS-4, undated).

174. Carl Stalling (1891–1972), composer, was the author of the witty orchestral scores to the best of the Warner Bros. golden-age *Looney Tunes* between 1936 and 1958.

The deuteragonist in the film's leitmotif family is the Spider motif, a brassy, dissonant theme shrieked by a group of trumpets and trombones accompanied by an ominous cymbal roll; this motif is made up of two sections: the first, which we might call "the spider menace," and the second, which we might call "the spider's walk." The spider-walk sub-motif is formed by two repeated notes, or, rather, by a repeated descending diminished-second interval. This sub-motif holds a peculiar kinship with the main-title "mystery" motif, or at least with part of it. The main melody of the "mystery" motif is composed of a series of descending seconds, and, in its re-appearances through the film, is often pared down to a descending second, sometimes diminished. This thematic interval is distinct from, but closely related to, the diminished-second interval associated with the spider. If the simplified "mystery" motif connotes the "menace from within," the "spider-walk" motif fragment connotes the "menace from without." Both motifs refer to Scott, and represent two aspects of the threat he is facing in his adventure.

In their pared-down form, these two leitmotifs slither through the film, creating a sonic background or aural environment: like the breathing of Scott Carey's new world. The plaintive "mystery" motif periodically injects its melancholy dirge into the story; the "spider-walk" motif in its simplified form becomes a transformed aural image of that same melancholia, tinted with fear. It is only in the closing scene that the full "mystery" theme reappears in its (male) vocal incarnation, and acquires a tender, consolatory tone: here the mystery no longer represents a threat or a diminution, but a conquest: a new understanding for the protagonist.

Metaphors and Transformations

The Chinese-box treasure of this understanding of Scott's is vibrantly incarnated in the closing scene by one of the most powerful images in the film, and in Hollywood history. Because Scott is continuing to shrink, the window screen that had barred his passage only hours before now lets him through: he is so small that he can slip through the holes of its net. What seemed a barrier is revealed to be a gateway, a medium for freedom. For Scott Carey, that net embodies a new concept now.

This image is missing from the novel (where it is never made explicit *how* Scott gets out into the open, save for several mentions of the fact that a window pane is missing), but there are inklings of the concept. Here is one from Chapter Three:

> But, somehow, days seemed longer now. It was as if hours were designed for normal people. For anyone smaller, the hours were proportionately magnified. It was an illusion, of course, but, in his tininess, he was plagued by manifold illusions; the illusion that he was not shrinking, but the world enlarging; the illusion that objects were what they were thought to be only when the person who thought of them was of normal size.[175]

Size aside, the paragraph hits upon a central idea: objects are thought to be what they are because a person thinks of them, because a person's perception of the world is imbued with thought, permeated by thought. As we look at an object, a being, or ourselves, our knowledge of that object, of that being, and of ourselves is a thinking knowledge. For everything we see, we have a concept: usually a subjective concept referred back to us, i.e. a representation, or occasionally a scientific concept. This applies to all objects, from the lowliest to the loftiest. Whether the object is a cup, a lamp, or a human being, we form our mental constructs (simple or complex as they may be) about it the moment we perceive it. The way we relate to the world, or the way we make the world relate to us, colors our perception of the world, often instantaneously, and often irreparably. Just as irreparably, we clash with the objects of the world when our concept of the world clashes with the reality of the world. In the course of our lives, we often have to revise our thoughts about the world (our worldview), whether voluntarily or forcedly. When we cannot perform such revision, the clash persists, and may become existential.

All stories are in some way metaphors, or allegories: in reading or viewing them, we must make them meaningful for ourselves. The protagonist is often an identification figure, a stand-in for Everyman, or for us. Fantasy, horror, and science fiction stories are more metaphorical than others: because of the fantastic, or preposterous, events described in them, their reality must often be "adapted" if it is to fit our own life in any meaningful way. In the case of the story under exam, we know that

---

175. Richard Matheson, *The Shrinking Man,* Fawcett Publications, Inc., 1956, 17.

no-one shrinks the way Scott Carey does; his plight has no relation to the reality of the world as we know it, and risks having no significance from a human or emotional standpoint, so a slight adaptation is necessary. This happens in steps, often simultaneous, and often unconscious. While we are aware that we are observing a preposterous conceit, we make an emotional reduction to a graspable common human denominator: ourselves. We observe our identification figure, Scott Carey, as we would ourselves in his shoes. This is the first step. The second step is to ask ourselves, "What does this mean for me?" Since we are not shrinking like Scott Carey, we take his plight as an allegory. It is like watching two parallel movies: on one track, the impossible fantasy of what is happening to Scott Carey, on the second, the closest equivalent to his plight in the world we know; an equivalent for which his plight becomes a stand-in. Each of us will choose the equivalent that is most resonant, for example aging, loss of self-esteem, or terminal illness. Scott Carey's worried look in the second scene of the film, when he notices that his shirt and pants no longer fit, is the same look we might display upon thinking we might have cancer.

We all shrink, one way or another. We shrink literally (after reaching maturity, or middle age), and figuratively. We lose our youth, we lose our loved ones, and we notice that our physical and mental capacities diminish; we lose money, we lose our homes, we lose control. We are all traveling to the same destination. Towards... what? As Scott Carey puts it at the beginning of his closing scene: *"I was continuing to shrink. To become—what? The infinitesimal? What was I? Still a human being? Or was I the man of the future?"*

The point is, life is a series of changes, whose causes and effects are often out of our hands; we can oppose those changes, or embrace them in some way. The road to acceptance is not an easy one.

Scott Carey undergoes many personal changes because of his biological predicament. He loses his job and his anonymity (he becomes famous); his relationship with his wife deteriorates; he is forced to fend for himself in an environment that becomes progressively more hostile, and more savage; he loses his will to live. With each change must come a new awareness, or a new personal elaboration of the facts of his life; with each change, Scott Carey must enact a different kind of transformation of himself in order to keep going, and make a new conscious decision to keep fighting.

While the window-screen image is the most powerful incarnation of this idea of a necessary change in perspective or point of view, the film is constellated by such changes. With each successive size, Scott must adapt to a new world: he must re-discover his world from another point of view. This idea becomes clearer and clearer as his size decreases: everyday objects such as chairs, tables, lamps, and pencils must be re-discovered by him. Finally, when he is at his smallest, in the cellar, Scott virtually re-invents his surroundings by adapting them to his state: a pin is no longer a pin but a spear or a grappling hook; thread is no longer thread but rope, etc. Scott must learn to find new concepts for the world and for himself, and the lesson keeps his mind agile.

Nature, God, and the Cosmos

The conceptual transformation of the window screen into a sudden portal to a different state triggers a moment of understanding for Scott; it opens his struggling mind to the acceptance of something beyond what is merely human, or merely terrestrial. If we, the audience, have enacted our personal adaptation of Scott Carey's story to our life and world, Scott's passing through the holes of the net into the outside world, where talk is made of God and stars and dimensions different from man's, can trigger a moment of understanding of our own; an emotional if not conceptual understanding. The music cue of Scott's last scene helps, too: a cue that David Schechter attributes to Herman Stein. This cue, all ethereal soaring strings and ringing tubular bells, is unmistakably mystical, and cannot but evoke (a) a different passage we must all face in our lives, and (b) an atmosphere of quietly joyful hopefulness. It therefore evokes the great beyond, or life after death. In Scott's case, life after his disappearance from the measurable physical plane; in our case, whatever we want to call that hopeful feeling that our lives are not ineluctably a series of measurable data, chemical reactions, and electrical impulses. In his 1975 *Cinefantastique* article about the film, John Hartl states:

> There is something undeniably ennobling and romantic about the mixture of [the final images of the film], Joseph Gershenson's [sic] religious [sic] music and Grant Williams' quite moving reading of the text. Perhaps this is why Matheson (whose

novel ends less expansively) has objected to the ending (which he claims he didn't write). It isn't difficult, in the midst of the emotions the scene evokes, to miss the point that Carey is talking about the acceptance of his own death.[176]

It might be, as is suggested by Matheson's abstention from any reference to God in the novel, that Scott Carey's passage is simply a descent into a subatomic or submicroscopic world, still within a material realm. However, this descent of an intelligent being into such world is in itself a magnificent travel to something unknown to today's man, or to something unknowable. Whether one takes the novel's route to a prudently materialistic definition or the film's route to a sentimentally metaphysical definition, whether one prefers a literal explanation or a metaphorical one, it cannot be denied that this ending deals with something extraordinary and unprecedented. In the film, our narrator adds:

So close, the infinitesimal and the infinite. But I suddenly knew they were really the two ends of the same concept. The unbelievably small and the unbelievably vast eventually meet, like the closing of a gigantic circle.

Scott pronounces these words just as he is slipping through the holes of the window screen net, and both images—and changes in conceptual view—spin the discourse into a vibrant symbolic direction absent (at least explicitly) from the novel. The shift in perspective, the sudden transformation of the prison into a means of escape, creates a curious conceptual enlargement, as if a series of mirrors facing each other were suddenly reflecting an idea and bouncing it off each other's surfaces ad infinitum. The reverberations of that simple image are dizzying. Two corollary concepts grow out of this reflective "spin" in the film: (a) the concept that the transformations inflicted by life can go hand in hand with a conceptual transformation of our worldview, and (b) the concept that, whether we believe in an intelligent Nature or in an intelligent Superior Entity, there is some mysterious logic tying everything together in the universe, or in the universes, and we can be part of that logic by embracing change. It is

176. John Hartl, "The Incredible Shrinking Man: To inherit the Universe, man must truly know what it is to be meek," in *Cinefantastique*, vol.4, n. 2, 1975.

not difficult to notice that there is a kinship between the concept embodied by Scott's passage through the window screen and, for example, certain Taoist aphorisms, such as those by Lao Tzu, paraphrased or quoted in later years by authors such as Richard Bach. The most appropriate of these aphorisms is the following: "What the caterpillar calls the end of the world, the Master calls butterfly."[177] Viewed from a different vantage point, what appears to be an end is not an end at all.

In both the novel and the film, Scott Carey's words question man's limited viewpoint and suggest the broadening of concepts such as "dimension," "universe," and "zero." In the novel, the impersonal narrator describes Scott's thoughts:

> He had always thought in terms of man's own world and man's own limited dimensions. He had presumed upon nature. For the inch was man's concept, not nature's. To a man, zero inches meant nothing. Zero meant nothing.
>
> But to nature there was no zero. Existence went on in endless cycles. It seemed so simple now. He would never disappear, because there was no point of non-existence in the universe.[178]

And here is Scott's narration in the film:

> *I looked up, as if somehow I would grasp the heavens. The Universe. Worlds without number, God's silver tapestry spread across the night. And in that moment I knew the answer to the riddle of the infinite. I had thought in terms of man's own limited dimension. I had presumed upon nature. That existence begins and ends is man's conception, not nature's. And I felt my body dwindling, melting, becoming nothing. My fears melted away, and in their place came acceptance. All this vast majesty of creation, it had to mean something. And then I meant something, too. Yes, smaller than the smallest, I meant something too. To God there is no zero. I still exist.*

---

177. Lao Tzu, *Tao Te Ching*, Macmillan, 1989; also, Richard Bach, *Illusions*, Delacorte Press, 1977. Reemes (DMR, 61) also mentions Lao Tzu in passing when discussing the film's ending.

178. Matheson (1956), op. cit., 192.

While it is true that God is never mentioned in the novel, nature itself acquires a status akin to God's, the status of a wise entity that governs the "endless cycles" of life and knows no dimensional limits. In both versions of this final rumination of Scott's, the key words and phrases are metaphysical.

In both novel and film (but more potently in the film) Scott receives an illumination: a light bulb goes on over his head, and he intuits something important. Just how important this illumination is, or how vast, will depend on our own conceptual view of things. The film pushes a more metaphysical interpretation,[179] whereas in his novel Matheson leaves the allegory open. It must be noted, however, that Matheson was an ardent student of metaphysics in general, and of the theosophical writings of Harold W. Percival (1868–1953) in particular. In the introduction to his book *The Path: a New Look at Reality*, Matheson writes: "I have used a number of metaphysical ideas in my stories, novels, and film and television scripts. But I always felt a need to express them directly and not through fiction."[180]

Though he later expanded his ideas beyond the confines of orthodox Theosophy, Percival was a member of the Theosophical Society, a creation of Helena Blavatsky (1831–1891), a Russian-born occultist and spiritualist. Far from being the paranormal charlatanry that common prejudice believes it to be, the original Theosophy of Blavatsky and its enlightened offshoot, the Anthroposophy of Rudolf Steiner (1861–1925), were philosophies of knowledge descending from a long lineage of esoteric thinkers and theologians (Plato, Pythagoras, Plotinus, St. Augustine, Christian Rosenkreuz, Antoine Fabre d'Olivet, Antonio Rosmini, etc.). Anthroposophy, for example, for all its colorful discussion of spiritual phenomena and celestial hierarchies, fundamentally stemmed from the basic Delphic tenet "Know Thyself," positing a "spiritual science" or inner investigation that could lead to the perception of the invisible makeup of the investigator and later to the knowledge of intelligible entities.

179. The shooting script, dated April 1956, pushes the metaphysical envelope even further than the finished film. As Scott ends his monologue, at the words "I still exist!" the script closes thus: "The MUSIC RISES TO A TRIUMPHANT CRESCENDO, then FADES and we HEAR the ETERNAL WIND. FADE OUT. THE END." Almost Fellinian.

180. Richard Matheson, *The Path: A New Look at Reality*, Tom Doherty Associates, 1999, 11.

Spiritual macrocosm aside, Theosophy and especially Anthroposophy put the human being at the center of such Delphic investigation. This inner research was a path towards self-knowledge, inner development, and transformation.

As for the relation of Theosophy and metaphysics to *The Incredible Shrinking Man,* with all due respect for Matheson's *The Path* and for the direct expression of such philosophy, Arnold's film gives its audience a chance to "feel" or intuit those ideas subliminally, without being forced to hear them explicitly. Laced discreetly through the film, those ideas, camouflaged or not, resonate plenty for anyone seeking a spiritual outlook on existence.

Narrative from the Great Beyond

Many changes were made in the transition between the novel *The Shrinking Man* and the screenplay *The Incredible Shrinking Man;* we are lucky that those changes were ultimately made (some of them reluctantly) by Richard Matheson himself and/or by uncredited co-Writer Richard Alan Simmons (1924–2004). Cuts aside, the most important were the change from a narrative structure built on flashbacks and on jumps back and forth in time (novel) to a linear chronological narrative (film); and the change from third-person narration (novel) to first-person voice-over narration (film). Matheson may have been reluctant to submit to the film studio's interference, but, in spite of the author's misgivings, the film arguably profited from both changes.

The novel's narrative alternates between Scott Carey's predicament as a tiny (two-sevenths of an inch) man in the cellar and his gradual shrinking after the boating incident. Each chapter contains a section concerning Scott's cellar adventures and a section concerning his gradual decrease in size: the headings of the latter sub-chapters represent measurements: for example, 68", 64", 49", and so forth, all the way to 7". This disjointed structure is certainly interesting, and was something of an avant-garde dare for a genre adventure yarn in a period when such formal experimentation (descending from illustrious precedents by authors such as Lawrence Sterne, Gertrud Stein, James Joyce, and John Dos Passos) was rare unless the writer's name was Samuel Beckett, Raymond Queneau, or Alain Robbe-Grillet.

While the brazen formal innovation of the novel is arresting, it also creates a coldness, or an irony: as we read, we sense the presence of an author who is drawing attention to his writing. The writing of *The Shrinking Man* is self-aware, and while this is commendable from the literary standpoint, it limits our emotional descent into the story to some extent, periodically yanking us away from one episode and into another. It forces us to cool off from the event we have been experiencing and shift our focus to another event that happened at a different point in time. This opinion was shared by Director Jack Arnold.[181]

By contrast, the film draws us into Robert Scott Carey's odyssey quietly and gradually, allowing its (and our) observation of the main character to grow slowly and organically. Slowly not in the sense that the pace of the story is slow, but in the sense that the film takes its time observing its main character. Pace never becomes an excuse to shift the focus away from the character (plot-based films often use that excuse). This is especially true of Scott's cellar adventures. However pared down these adventures are compared to the longer novel, the film never foreshortens the telling of events in the interest of speed. For example, Scott's building of his makeshift weapons (the bending of the pin to form a hook, the cutting of the thread to make a rope he can fasten to the hook, the climbing of a wall, etc.) is observed in believable real time (and in long takes), allowing the character to think between his actions.

This is especially remarkable, and is worth repeating: the character *is allowed to think* between one action and the next, and the camera *is allowed to watch* him while he thinks; this is done efficiently and economically, thus never giving the impression that the story's pace is being compromised, but it can be seen as a confirmation of the fact that *The Incredible Shrinking Man* is about the character *first*, and about the events involving the character *second*. This methodical style of filmmaking, perfectly in tune with the existential thematic current of the film, is carried out admirably by Jack Arnold, who proves himself a real humanist: he concentrates with great dedication on the man Scott Carey and on his thoughts and actions, one could say fearlessly (for a genre film).[182]

181. Jack Arnold interview, in *Hollywood Professional: Jack Arnold und seine Filme,* Robert Fischer, 1993, 74.

182. As we will see in the next chapter, this character-based style elicited some criticism from *Variety*'s reviewers.

It is not only in the above respect that the issue of third-person vs. first-person narrations is interesting. The film's first-person narration also adds a fascinating layer to a story already endowed with an ambitious metaphysical, or philosophical, bent; for, where is Scott Carey when he tells his story—in the past tense—and, above all, how, or what, is he? And whom is he addressing? The fact that Scott uses the past tense indicates that some time has passed since the events he describes, and the events he describes include the closing scene of the film, at which point Scott is so small as to merit the epithet "infinitesimal." Is he a floating soul speaking from another world? Is he a microorganism?

The dramatic device of someone narrating his story *after* his disappearance is so peculiar that it becomes interesting in and of itself, quite apart from the events that are presented. Likewise, Billy Wilder's extraordinary *Sunset Blvd.* (1950) is interesting for being narrated in the first person by a protagonist who is discovered dead in a swimming pool in the opening scene.[183] In both cases, we find ourselves in the realm of meta-literature, or meta-narration: in the realm of literature that is not to be taken literally as a narration of real-life events, but as self-aware comment on itself, as tragic irony, or as *pure allegory* exempt from logic. One might expect such daring deviation from realism and straightforwardness in quirky masterpieces by proven "masters" of cinema, or in postmodern independent films; one does not expect it in conventional 1950s science fiction. Far from being a liability (Matheson objected to it all his life),[184] the change from third-person narration to this particular first-person narration makes *The Incredible Shrinking Man* modern and brilliant: it allows the film to fly above its genre peers, and to transcend its genre roots—even to transcend its own source material.

Compare, if you will, these two opening sentences. Here is the novel:

First he thought it was a tidal wave. Then he saw that the sky

---

183. More recently, Sam Mendes' *American Beauty* (1999) used this device by having the story narrated by its protagonist after he has been shot to death.

184. "There is too much voice-over narration in it, a lot of which I didn't write. It was a bit overdone," complained Matheson in Paul M. Sammon's interview in *Midnight Graffiti*, Fall 1992.

and ocean were visible through it and it was a curtain of spray rushing at the boat.[185]

And here, the film:

> *The strange, almost unbelievable story of Robert Scott Carey began on a very ordinary summer day. I know this story better than anyone, because I am Robert Scott Carey.*

The novel begins with a straight narrative setup: the story is told by an impersonal narrator. Conversely, in the film's beginning the (shrunken) protagonist tells us that what will follow is a story, and that it is an unusual story; he tells us his name, and we hear his voice, thus, we begin a personal relationship with him. This introduction is both elegant and sophisticated, with the tiniest pinch of delicate melancholic irony. Robert Scott Carey narrates his story with a quiet, intimate tone, without emphasis— vocal emphasis and hyperbole being all too common in U-I's science-fiction films of the fifties. Scott's voice is the voice of a lonely man, of a man who is wiser (though not necessarily sadder) for what he has endured. Here, and throughout the film, Grant Williams delivers a sensitive, tender performance, and his attention to vocal poise and restraint is palpable.

The voice-over narration also acquires a musical quality—almost the quality of singing—in Grant Williams' delicate rendering, and it is in this musical sense that one particular change from novel to script might be explained. Matthew R. Bradley, in his *Richard Matheson on Screen*,[186] complains about the "inexplicable expansion of the protagonist's name" from Scott Carey to Robert Scott Carey in the opening narration. I believe this expansion may have been motivated by an aesthetic question of meter—of music—in that opening sentence. Try saying that opening paragraph without the "Robert" and you will see what I mean.

Whatever might have been lost in the transition from disjointed structure to linear structure is compensated, plentifully, by the transition from third-person narration to first-person narration. For, subtly but un-

---

185. Matheson (1956), op. cit., 7.

186. Matthew R. Bradley, *Richard Matheson on Screen*, McFarland & Company, Inc., Publishers, 2010.

settlingly, the intimate relationship established by the film's protagonist with the spectator is a paranormal, meta-narrative gesture from a dimension beyond reality: from the great beyond perhaps.

Metamorphoses

In terms of imagery, *The Incredible Shrinking Man* fits rather snugly in the literary tradition of mythical metamorphosis, a tradition that for the Western world begins with the seminal *Metamorphoses* (*Metamorphoseon*) by Ovid (Publius Ovidius Naso, 43BC–18AD) and continues through the modern era with iconic texts such as Lewis Carroll's *Alice's Adventures in Wonderland* (1866) and Franz Kafka's *The Metamorphosis* (*Die Verwandlung*, 1915), not to mention Italo Calvino's allegorical novels *Il visconte dimezzato* (1952) and *Il cavaliere inesistente* (1959).[187] Scott Carey may not be exactly a new Daphne[188] or Arachne,[189] but his predicament is certainly made of the stuff of transformational myths.

Ovid's transformations of human beings into vegetable, animal, or mineral entities often follow one of two patterns: the human is transformed either as punishment for defying or competing with a god, or as protection against the unwanted attentions of a god. In some cases (Hyacinth), the transformation is a redemption that the god enacts to remedy the human's death: the sorrow of the god resurrects him as, for example, a perennial flowering plant.

In any case—whether punishment or salvation—the person's transformation in these myths expresses the interaction between the human and the divine, or, taking the trope one step further into metaphor, the constant, mysterious flow of the invisible forces of nature and of the cosmos: the unending transformation of living forms into other living forms.

This same perennial metamorphosis was posited by German Poet and Philosopher Johann Wolfgang von Goethe (1749–1832) in his scientific/philosophical studies of botany, specifically in his essay on *The*

---

187. Published together in English as *The Nonexistent Knight, The Cloven Viscount*, Houghton Mifflin Harcourt, 1977.

188. Transformed into a laurel tree by the gods to allow her to escape from Apollo's sexual pursuit.

189. Transformed into a spider by Athena.

Metamorphosis of Plants (1790). Goethe noted that the transformational impulse in the vegetable kingdom was responsible for the creation of ever-new shapes through an archetypical process of perpetual germination (e.g. every constituent part of the plant is a transformed leaf). Whatever his point from a strictly botanical point of view, by extension the philosophical idea proclaimed a principle of transformational creation: nature is never still, never fixed, but modifies itself continuously, adapts itself continuously, and creates itself continuously. If there is something fixed, it is the invisible law or idea (the archetype) that governs such process, not the individual visible shapes.

In the film, Scott Carey says: *"That existence begins and ends is man's conception, not nature's,"* and this realization is in tune with both mythical metamorphosis and philosophical metamorphosis. Living beings— in our specific case Scott Carey—are part of an unending process, a process that is not finite, in spite of its finite forms. The individual forms may cease, but they make way for new forms. Under the influence of nature— or of God, or of nature and God, or of a theistic nature, or of celestial entities—creation flows into re-creation; creation *is* transformation, for nature (or God, etc.) will not be arrested. It can be thwarted, it can be violated, it can be paused, but it will not be annihilated.

In Ovid's *Metamorphoses*, Jupiter prevents the character of Arcas from killing his mother, who has been transformed into a bear by Jupiter's jealous wife and put in Arcas' path to kill him; instead, Jupiter transforms both characters into constellations, the Big Bear and the Little Bear, and places them in the heavens. One can see from this particular double transformation that the poetical metamorphoses enacted by the gods (by cosmic forces) in Ovid's work do not limit themselves to the earthly plane, but jump cosmically from realm to realm with great freedom of imagination.

It may be true that Scott Carey is about to descend into the submicroscopic realm at the end of *The Incredible Shrinking Man*. But, tellingly, the final image of his person becoming invisible amongst the garden leaves as the camera pulls back from him skyward—and as he pronounces the sentence, *"And I felt my body dwindling, melting, becoming nothing"*— fades into images of constellations and galaxies in the heavens. The unbelievably small and the unbelievably vast do meet: they are both part of the same process, the process of unending creation and transformation, with its multitudinous forms, whether visible or invisible.

Re-inventing the world from a new perspective: a tiny Scott Carey (Grant Williams) makes large weapons out of tiny household objects in this production still for *The Incredible Shrinking Man* (1957). © 1957, Universal Pictures Company, Inc.

Siegfried in the Cellar and Other Mythical Forms

Trapped in the cellar, Robert Scott Carey, size two inches or less, must face a new hostile environment: a barren, subhuman wasteland. Once he has procured water, weapons, shelter, and makeshift clothing for himself, he must also secure food; but the only food available is a slice of stale cake, guarded by Scott's new enemy: a common spider that appears gigantic and invincible to our shrunken hero.[190]

Scott resolves to dominate his environment "*as man had dominated the kingdom of the sun,*" and to engage the spider in battle. He resolves to be a hero.

The protagonist's confrontation with the oversized arachnid carries with it inevitable connotations of the medieval knight fighting a mythical creature. The spider may not fly or breathe fire, but, as Scott puts it:

---

190. A black widow in Matheson's novel; a tarantula standing in for a common house spider in Arnold's film.

My enemy seemed immortal; more than a spider, it was every unknown terror in the world, every fear fused into one hideous night-black horror.

The spider, then, is an allegorical spider, and Scott's battle an allegorical battle. It is also a mythical battle, reverberating with the memory of countless legendary confrontations with mythical creatures in countless epic poems and chivalric tales. That battle is an obligatory rite of passage in the hero's journey.

The spider guards a treasure—the cake that will be Scott's only nourishment—just as Fafner the dragon (himself metamorphosed magically from his earlier incarnation as a giant) guarded a treasure in the German Nibelung saga. In the original legends and in Wagner's music-drama *Siegfried* (1876), when Siegfried the hero slays the beast, its blood pours over his hands, magically enabling the hero to understand the language of the forest birds, or the true meaning hidden behind the words of treacherous humans.[191] Thus, the magical bodily fluid creates a revelation for the hero, or an ability to perceive the truth beyond its illusory manifestations. It allows him to commune with nature (or with God, in Jerome F. Shapiro's reading of Scott's ending).[192] Through contact with the spider's blood, Scott the hero begins another transformation: there are no forest birds or treacherous humans to be deciphered, but, as soon as Scott brings the coveted prize to his mouth to eat, his hunger is suddenly gone. In Scott's words: *"... Even as I touched the dry flaky crumbs of nourishment, it was as if my body had ceased to exist. There was no hunger; no longer the terrible fear of shrinking."*

Exhausted, Scott falls unconscious on the ground, and sleeps. Come nighttime, he wakes up and realizes he has continued to shrink, his tattered, now-oversized robes making him appear like a martyr of old, or

---

191. As Reemes (DMR, 59) rightly states in his excellent analysis, both Siegfried and Scott Carey are transformed by their exposure to the monster's blood; Siegfried, however (at least in Wagner's telling), is not made invincible by the ordeal (arguably, he was invincible from the start); rather, like Scott Carey, he graduates to a higher—more mature—level of perception, or understanding, of the world. From a naïve gullible child he becomes an attentive adult; this passage is then further symbolized and completed by his sexual awakening with Brünhilde the mortal demi-goddess.

192. Jerome F. Shapiro, *Atomic Bomb Cinema*, Routledge, 2001, p. 117.

Like lightning: the miniature hero uses fire in this production still for *The Incredible Shrinking Man* (1957). © 1957, Universal Pictures Company, Inc.

like some weary ascetic saint. He reaches the window screen, and passes through its net; he receives his revelation. The sacrificial blood of the mythical spider-dragon has worked its magic.

The Incredible Shrinking Man does not limit itself to these relatively obvious references to adventure tropes derived from myth; as Shapiro notes in his illuminating comments on the film, images from other myths abound. Shapiro mentions, for example, the basement flood in which "the miniature Scott, like Odysseus, is drawn into Charybdis (the whirlpool) and nearly drowned." He also mentions the Buddhist tradition, the symbolic meaning of the spider in some cultures, the myth of rebirth, and the Garden of Eden that the reborn Scott is able to enter after his revelation.[193] But one could also add the myths of St. George and the Dragon, of Lilliput, of Alice's fall into Wonderland, and—most famous of all—the myth of Christ and of his resurrection; not to mention veiled references to symbolic esoteric initiation trials, such as the trial by water, the trial by fire, and the trial by blood.

---

193. Ibid.

The cellar sequences are rife with these mythical and chivalric reverberations. The sight of Scott Carey striking a giant match to sever a rope by burning it in half could be something out of an epic poem or folk tale. The sudden blaze flashes white, overexposing the film and illuminating Scott like lightning, while harp glissandi and trumpet fanfares flourish heroically, and magically, in the film's orchestra (trumpets figure prominently in the score, starting with Ray Anthony's solo during the main titles).[194] The cellar itself acquires the look and connotation of a primeval forest or plain, and Scott's climbing of a gargantuan orange crate is the scaling of an Everest. And musically, much of the cellar-adventure tone poem uses a Wagnerian-Straussian voice, harking back to the adventurous sections of Wagner's *The Ring of the Nibelungs* (1876) or to the descriptive orchestral splendor of Strauss's *Eine Alpensinfonie* (1915).

Via Dolorosa: the Path of the Lonely Hero

Whatever else can be said about Robert Scott Carey's strange predicament, at the very least it is a monumental test of his patience and endurance. Like a cruel cosmic joke or a cleverly designed torture, Scott's plight makes him a new biblical Job: just about everything that could happen to him happens to him. His story might be a fairy tale, if it were not so relentlessly painful for him, or if he were magically allowed to revert to his normal size at the end. Instead, Matheson and Arnold uncompromisingly carry the initial premise to its ultimate conclusion, and subject their protagonist to the pounding of a lifetime—of more than one lifetime, arguably.[195]

The Incredible Shrinking Man (which, let us not forget, is a commercial horror/science-fiction product of one of the Hollywood "majors") is especially remarkable for this cruelty, and for its courageous, heartfelt focus on its lonely main character. The Universal-International 1957 pressbook defines the film "almost a one-man show" (ISM, 3); and, indeed, what is truly memorable about the film is the sense of unrelieved solitude

---

194. Ray Anthony (born 1922), bandleader and trumpeter, was a member of the Glenn Miller Orchestra; he was extremely popular in the 1950s and 1960s, and even branched out into songwriting and acting.

195. The *Variety* review, dated February 6, 1957, noted that "[…] while most science-fiction thrillers contrive a happy ending, there's no compromise here."

Like a martyr of old: the exhausted hero rests after climbing a man-made Everest in this production still for *The Incredible Shrinking Man* (1957). © 1957, Universal Pictures Company, Inc.

one breathes in it (a solitude that, during Scott's most depressive moments in the cellar, is accompanied by some of the most plaintive woodwind solos in orchestral literature).

In the second half of the story, Scott is literally alone in his new world; this loneliness, however, starts early, in the first half, and is characterized (a) by Scott's desolate mood and (b) by his progressive retreat from human companionship. The moment he looks in his bedroom mirror in the film's second scene and worries about his size loss, Scott begins spiraling into a depressive state (thereby glossing over the first three steps of the Kübler-Ross pattern of grief).[196]

In an early scene of the first act, after his diagnosis but while he is still of comparatively normal size, Scott even begins preparing his wife Louise for the inevitable: *"There's a limit to your obligation,"* he says to her in their parked car. She reassures him, saying that when she married him

---

196. Elisabeth Kübler-Ross, *On Death and Dying*, Macmillan, 1969. The five stages are: denial, anger, bargaining, depression, and acceptance.

A worried Scott Carey (Williams, middle) awaits confirmation from Dr. Bramson
(William Schallert, right) that he is getting smaller; his wife Louise (Randy Stuart, left)
lends moral support. Production still for *The Incredible Shrinking Man* (1957),
© 1957, Universal Pictures Company, Inc.

she meant what she said, and adding: *"As long as you've got that wedding
ring on, you've got me."* For a moment, Scott is consoled; then the writers
and director slap him in the face with a cruel irony: as he lets go of his
wife's hand to start the car, his wedding band falls off!

However loosely one wants to read the analogy, Scott's solitary odyssey appears to make some oblique reference to the figure of Christ and
his stations of the cross, or at the very least to figures of martyred saints.
A U-I production still depicts Scott in his final scene, having just exited
the cellar window screen, as he grasps the net behind him with his arms
stretched horizontally on either side, and the homage to the crucifixion is
unmistakable. That pose never appears in the actual film, but the message
is there nonetheless: this hero's journey is one of solitary—though fruit-
ful—grief. Director Jack Arnold, who re-tooled Scott's final monologue to
make it what it is in the film, definitely felt this likeness:

While we were shooting the ending, Grant began to look Christ-like to me. There was a certain mood and impact created as he climbed through this little grate he could not get through before; the whole atmosphere is religious—deliberately so. I decided I wanted a kind of metaphysical ending; it was based on my own personal religious feelings, my ideas about God and the universe. (DMR, 61–63)

Arnold fought the studio brass tooth and nail on the happy ending they demanded for the film, stating that, ultimately, the ending as it stands in

Christ-like: Scott Carey is now so small that he can escape from his prison and see the stars. Production still for *The Incredible Shrinking Man*, © 1957, Universal Pictures Company, Inc.

the film was his idea.[197] By this last statement Arnold meant, surely, that he took what was already in Matheson's novel and punched it into metaphysical overdrive. Arnold's ending is a poetical metamorphosis of an original that already contained those ideas, in prudent camouflage.[198] That Arnold knew what he was doing when intentionally tweaking Matheson's ideas is clear from the following statements he made to Reemes regarding the significance of the ending for Robert Scott Carey:

> It is a quest for the meaning and limits of human identity. Carey learns about himself, human nature, and the nature of the universe—and learns to accept his fate. As he dwindles almost to the size of an ameba, Carey begins to unlearn his past. [...] The tremendous irony of *The Incredible Shrinking Man* is that Carey's maturity comes only when he is reduced to the tiniest of creatures. To inherit the universe, he must know what it is to be *truly* meek.... (DMR, 63)

In terms of this particular hero's quest, an important idea correlates itself to such loneliness: the solution to the problem, the prize to be won, the Holy Grail to be found, lies *within* the protagonist, and not outside. Joseph Campbell expressed this idea in his most famous book, *The Hero with a Thousand Faces*:

> The passage of the mythological hero may be over-ground, incidentally; fundamentally it is inward—into depths where obscure resistances are overcome, and long lost, forgotten powers are revivified, to be made available for the transfiguration of the world.[199]

---

197. Bill Kelley, interview with Jack Arnold, in *Cinefantastique*, vol. 4, n. 2, 1975, 17–24.

198. This is also confirmed by Bradley, who states, "Aside from equating God with nature—hardly a herculean intellectual leap—Arnold's ending mirrors Matheson's quite closely, as a direct comparison reveals. [...] In short, story and ending are Matheson's alone, although admittedly they have been brilliantly realized on the screen by Jack Arnold." (Bradley 2010, op. cit., p. 15.) A middle ground between these positions is possible. The difference between the two endings, and between the closing narrations, is not so much one of substance, or of individual words or phrases, as one of tone and register. Arnold's ending is undoubtedly more hieratic, and more lilting; more musical, if you will.

199. Joseph Campbell, *The Hero with a Thousand Faces* [1949], New World Library,

After his victorious fight with the spider, Scott approaches the food he has conquered, but realizes his hunger has vanished. The illusory conquest, the material prize, is irrelevant: it does not satiate or quench. The affairs of this earth as we know them are indeed finished for Scott Carey. He is on his way to a different dimension, where hunger, thirst, and earthly survival may no longer be an issue.

Just as Dante Alighieri's *The Divine Comedy* can be read as a voyage within man's inner world, and as a gnoseological catalogue of the demons (or Capital Sins) that prey on humans on this earth, so Scott Carey's voyage can be read as a test of himself, as a non-literal voyage. He is alone because he has shrunk, but also because he *must* be alone to look inside himself and find that meekness to which Arnold referred. The trials of Scott's odyssey are, metaphorically, the trials of everyone's life; the burgeoning humility he finds in himself as, for example, he offers the cake crumbs to the bird in the garden from inside his prison is a step in his voyage of discovery. Scott Carey's misadventures are, in effect, metaphors for an esoteric voyage towards an illumination. The systematic dismantling (shrinking) of all that he was as a person is a necessary preparatory step to the process of rebuilding himself from scratch.

As he wakes up from his hero's sleep after the battle and approaches the transformed (for him) window screen, Scott is reborn—as Shapiro rightly points out—and is about to enter a new world, one that is not measurable by normal physical standards. He is about to shed his body as he has known it.

This idea of an inner solution to Scott's problem is foreshadowed before his fight with the mythical spider, when he says about himself: *"A strange calm possessed me: I thought more clearly than I had ever thought before, as if my mind were bathed in brilliant light."* And also: *"My legs trembled, not with fear but weakness; yet somehow I felt in myself a new source of power, a giant strength urging me to the death struggle."*

In order to live, and not merely survive, Scott must find a new source of power and a new calm within himself: a calm and a power that will allow him to find new meaning for his existence. But even after his physical victory over the arachnid, as he walks towards the cellar window—only to fall asleep and shrink some more—Scott is guided by a force that Mathe-

2008, 22.

son's narration inappropriately calls "instinct." The thing that drives Scott towards the night sky, towards the new outside world, is a feeling different from an instinct. Its fulfilment is not the satisfaction of a physical need, but a spiritual/mental revelation: an understanding, and a willingness to let go of fears and sorrows (*"My fears melted away"*) and to shed the physical body (*"And I felt my body dwindling, becoming... nothing."*).

The suffering Scott has had to endure in his strange adventure must ultimately be transcended and transformed, if he is to gain a new meaning for his existence, if he is to enact a poetical metamorphosis of his idea of nature, and of life. Even Matheson's novel, for all its prudent camouflage of metaphysics, makes it fairly clear that the conclusion of Scott Carey's story is both mysterious and uplifting: the last word of the last chapter is "searching."

Poetical Casting

The choice of Grant Williams for the role of Robert Scott Carey proves felicitous on more than one count.

On an elementary cinematic level, Williams' young-man-next-door good looks endow his character with a reassuring respectability and an attractiveness that help draw the audience towards him. His Scott Carey is clean-cut and seemingly well adjusted, and displays just enough subtle bossiness towards his wife Louise to be seen as a normal fifties square.[200] This mainstream manliness has two functions: it makes the character's cellar adventures believable, and it counteracts his sullen bitchiness during the deterioration of his relationship with his wife and with the world.

Williams was handsome but not particularly rugged, trim and fit but not particularly muscular. His Scott is not a man you would readily associate with life-threatening dangers, or with roughing it in the wild. Williams was six feet tall, but his shoulders were not particularly broad, and his bone structure tended to make him look slight. His blond blue-eyed

---

200. The shooting script, op. cit., describes Scott Carey thus: "A sensitive, intelligent man who suffers intensely with his plight. Despite this suffering, however, he is innately courageous and adaptive, and these qualities enable him to rise above the situation and conquer it. In a sense, then, his physical shrinking is his mental growth." An important nucleus of the film's meaning is expertly contained in this description.

beauty was a delicate one. This slim elegant beauty endows Scott with a boyish vulnerability that is perfect for eliciting feelings of protectiveness in an audience; Williams' Scott Carey is believably in dire danger in the course of this story, and can look truly haggard and puny (but still handsome, in a disheveled way) in his poignant closing scene. Even after proving his athletic worth in wall climbing, weapon making, and beast fighting, Williams' Scott is still a delicate flower of a man, his look that of a handsome fiancé for the ladies and of a sensitive younger brother for the gentlemen (or vice versa).

Williams was a city boy with a sensitive disposition, and—having spent a part of his childhood in his father's native Scotland—was endowed with an Old-World finesse, or world-weariness, that was in some ways un-American.

More importantly, there was something haunted, or somber, about Williams' disposition: he could "do" dash and confidence when a role required it, but his real-life smiles were often hesitant. An intense melancholy—or terrified wonder—lurked in his eyes. Once his character starts shrinking, the sadness in his gaze never quits for the remainder of the story. It is this sadness that gives Scott's harrowing odyssey, and his final realization (which is simultaneously joyous and frightening) a special heartrending quality.

Lastly, Williams' voice, a warm low tenor or high baritone, was a sensitive musical instrument; in this film, it achieves a meditative, understated delicacy that easily lulls us into a natural sympathy for his character.

Williams was a talented actor, but he was just another newcomer among U-I's roster of other newcomers being groomed for stardom when *The Incredible Shrinking Man* was made, and it is probably only because of Jack Arnold that the studio selected him as the lead in one of its strangest, biggest-budgeted genre films. On paper, Universal could have chosen any number of its darker, surlier players (of the John Agar ilk) or of its more muscular, broad-shouldered actors (of the Richard Denning or Rex Reason ilk).[201] This would naturally have put the accent on the adventurous

---

201. According to numerous reports and interviews (by Hedda Hopper, Bill Warren, Tom Weaver, and several others), actor Dan O'Herlihy had been offered the part of Scott Carey and turned it down. See for example: Hedda Hopper, "Grant Williams Gets Top Role in 'Incredible Shrunken Man,'" *Chicago Tribune*, March 29, 1956.

aspect of the film. Williams, however, incarnates the existential thematic aspect to perfection: he embodies the delicate, melancholy core of the film, the same core sung by that main-title music. Arguably, none of those other actors could have truly expressed the loneliness, vulnerability, and bewilderment of Robert Scott Carey, or the simple wonder and tenderness of his closing scene.

In his *Poseidon's Underworld* blog, Jon Vater colors his profile of Williams with a tragic-ironic reference to the film, by entitling it "The Incredible Shrinking Career."[202] This is a natural but pitiless way of looking at Williams' life and achievements.[203] One could posit reversing the operation: rather than coloring the person of Williams with the film, one might do the opposite. In hindsight, the melancholy, unresolved figure of Grant Williams himself adds another layer to *The Incredible Shrinking Man*. His delicacy, his core of sadness, his inability to establish himself, and his gradual losing his foothold on both his career and his personal life function as a powerful basis for his acting instrument, and for our experience of the film. Williams' emotional life, with all its flaws and virtues, paired with his Method technique, is what makes him capable of expressing Scott Carey the way few others could have. Those viewers who know or study Williams can read this nucleus between the lines of Scott Carey; others can perhaps feel it, subliminally, for there is always some truth mixed with man's expression of fiction.

---

202. *Poseidon's Underworld* blog, "The Incredible Shrinking Career," September 14, 2010.

203. The pitilessness is due to the blog's concentration on Williams' career rather than on his person. The "shrinking" of Williams' career was a symptom of a different deterioration: a human one, as we will see in the following chapters. Such deterioration should invite our compassion, not our irony.

6 The Incredible Shrinking Man: Production, Promotion, and Perception

TIE-INS AND PROMOTION: A WORLD OF POSSIBILITIES

At the time of its release,[204] *The Incredible Shrinking Man* was one of the biggest financial successes in Universal-International's history, creating unprecedented revenue for the studio. According to *Variety*, the film's initial domestic gross was $1.43 million.[205] In his book about Director Jack Arnold, Reemes states that the film grossed "over four million dollars in less than two months." (DMR, 88) According to U-I's pressbook for the film, the set the studio built was "the largest indoor set ever constructed for a motion picture as a background for scenes [...]." (ISM, 4) The estimated budget was a medium-sized $750,000.

In other words, the studio had poured a substantial amount of money into the film, placing it in a middle ground between A-list and B-list. Likewise, it poured a sizeable amount into the film's promotion. Orson Welles was hired to do the voice-over narrations for a series of advance radio and television spots,[206] and Welles' voice alone undoubtedly commanded attention.

---

204. In Los Angeles, the film opened at three cinemas (RKO Hillstreet, Ritz, New Fox Hollywood) and at eight Pacific Drive-Ins on March 27, 1957. Nationwide, the film had opened on various earlier March dates. In New York, it had premiered on February 22.

205. "Top Grosses of 1957," *Variety*, January 8, 1958.

206. While Orson Welles (1915–1985) was never a contract player at Universal, after his return to Hollywood from a self-imposed European exile (1948–1956), he worked in two Universal projects: Welles guest-starred in Jack Arnold's *Man in the Shadow* (1957) starring Jeff Chandler, and wrote, directed and co-starred in *Touch of Evil* (1958).

Humorous promotion: a shrunken Grant Williams exits the Universal-International studio gate while the amused guard signs him out. Publicity still for *The Incredible Shrinking Man* (1957). Photo: AF Archive/Alamy.

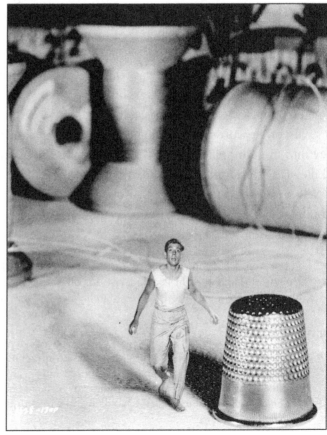

Thumbelino: Grant Williams, in costume, demonstrates his size in this publicity still for *The Incredible Shrinking Man* (1957). © 1957, Universal Pictures Company, Inc.

Universal went all out with paper advertising and product tie-ins. Posters of different sizes were produced: 24-sheets, six-sheets, three-sheets, one-sheets, 22x28's, window cards, lobby cards, heralds, and inserts. Some fifty-seven between "Mats" and "Ad Mats" of various sizes were issued, plus special advertising stills, composite mats, television "telops" and slides, banner accessories, fluorescent badges, and a mechanical display piece for theater lobbies or plazas. Day-Glo 24-sheet luminous billboards were prepared for at least 400 communities across the nation's highways and roads. (ISM, 2, 6–22) Capitol records issued a "Novelty Instrumental Tune" recording based on the theme music from the film, featuring Ray Anthony's trumpet playing. Fawcett Publications re-issued the paperback edition of Richard Matheson's novel. (ISM, 22)

An extensive nation-wide promotional tour was also organized for Grant Williams. An inkling of how grueling the tour must have been can be gleaned from the partial schedule Rual Askew provided in his profile of Williams for the *Dallas Morning News* on March 5, 1957:

He has been to New York, Baltimore,[207] Charlotte and Dallas, and leaves Tuesday for Houston, Boston and more New York before returning to West Coast assignments. (RA)

Many other cities were involved. For example, *The Indianapolis Star* mentioned Grant Williams' visit to their city in an article about *The Incredible Shrinking Man*: "Grant Williams, who was in Indianapolis Monday [March 18, 1957] to ballyhoo the picture, stars in what could be called the smallest role an actor ever had.[208]

With such an original film topic as *The Incredible Shrinking Man*, the press found fresh inspiration, and splashed tongue-in-cheek color all over its advance advertising. A syndicated item described the film shoot thus in a February 1957 spread:

207. R.H. Gardner, Columnist for the *Baltimore Sun*, interviewed Williams during his visit, but wrote a piece that dealt exclusively with the special effects of *The Incredible Shrinking Man* and not with Williams at all. Evidently, not all journalists cared to investigate Williams' life. (R.H. Gardner, "How The Horror Films Get That Way," *Baltimore Sun*, March 3, 1957.)

208. Polly Cochran, "Interest in Circle Movie Stretches With Shrinkage," *Indianapolis Star*, March 21, 1957.

Just when a big hunk of man—6-foot-2, to be exact, and hand-some, too—is getting well known around the Universal-International lot, what do the bigwigs do with him? They shrink him! Way down to one inch tall, no less! Grant Williams gets the squeeze in "The Incredible Shrinking Man," due for April release and presenting Williams in the title role. U-I pooled some of Hollywood's best technical brains to "put the shrink" on the tall Williams who plays the part of a man suffering from a mystery malady that shrinks away six feet of his six-one height and leaves him only the one inch. How they put the whammy on him—they have dubbed it "shrinkascope"—is interesting.[209]

Erskine Johnson, staff correspondent for the Newspaper Enterprise Association (NEA), visited the cellar set of *The Incredible Shrinking Man* during the film shoot in July 1956, and was impressed:

"Look, Ma, no starch!" Just call me the incredible shrinking columnist. No, not like a violet. Like Hollywood's newest movie hero who is only two inches tall.

It was a case of getting the lowdown on the latest science-fiction movie, "The Incredible Shrinking Man." So I let Hollywood magic shrink me, too. I got real low down, in fact. Right down to a two-inch size.

I simply opened a Universal-International sound stage door as a normal six-footer and immediately became a Lilliputian who could mistake Gary Cooper for the Empire State Building.

I was so little that a quart can of house paint looked the size of a two-story house; a kitchen match seemed to be at least six feet long and an ordinary lead pencil looked like a telephone pole?

LOOKED?

The can of paint was 16 feet high. The match was six feet long and the lead pencil, nine inches thick, measured 35 feet from lead point to eraser.

209. *Long Beach (CA) Independent Press-Telegram*, February 3, 1957. A July 1956 press release stated that *The Incredible Shrinking Man* was being filmed in "TeenyScope."

Like a child in a world of grown-ups, a somber Scott Carey (Grant Williams) works on the book that will tell the world about his existential predicament. Production still for *The Incredible Shrinking Man* (1957), © 1957, Universal Pictures Company, Inc.

[...] Art directors, special effects men and prop men like Eddie Keyes [the uncredited Prop Master for the film] are having a ball working on the film. Says Eddie: "I've been in the movie business 30 years, and I've never worked on a film so fascinating. There's a new challenge every day."[210]

Several props used in the film (in their new enlarged size) were advertised by U-I for tie-in campaigns: movie theater owners were encouraged to contact the representatives of the various companies whose products were featured in the film, and to display the items in their lobbies. The Superior Paint & Varnish Corporation, manufacturer of Nu-Enamel paint, was one such company. The Superior Paint cans on display were to be accompanied by a production still depicting a miniature Grant Williams

---

210. Erskine Johnson (NEA), "Use New Techniques To Film 'The Incredible Shrinking Man,'" *Santa Cruz (CA) Sentinel*, July 26, 1956.

Director Jack Arnold (back to camera, in chair) watches Grant Williams rehearse a scene
of *The Incredible Shrinking Man* in this production still. In the background, the giant
Nu-Enamel paint cans. © 1957, Universal Pictures Company, Inc.

sitting on an inclined giant paint stick during a scene in the film, with giant Nu-Enamel paint cans in the background. (ISM, 23)

Another ad campaign concerned the imported Captain's Chair distributed by Authentic Furniture Products. The chair could be displayed in a window of the movie theater together with a still depicting a medium-sized Grant Williams interacting with it in its larger incarnation. (ISM, 23)

Other curious lobby ideas proposed by U-I to theater managers had to do with size. In one ad, theater owners were encouraged to make an arrangement with local department stores or toy dealers for the loan of a doll house, to be used in the theater lobby with a display card reading: "Could you live in this house? But Scott Carey did." (ISM, 23)

Paint Cans, Metronomes, and Tamara the Spider

Over the years, viewers, reviewers and critics have been drawn to the technical aspects of *The Incredible Shrinking Man*, and with good reason.

A normal-sized Grant Williams amongst giant furnishings. In the background, the enlarged Captain's Chair. Production still for *The Incredible Shrinking Man,* © 1957, Universal Pictures Company, Inc.

Director Jack Arnold was justifiably proud of the inventive solutions—many of them without precedent—that he and the Universal-International technical departments had designed for the film.

The tale of the special effects of *The Incredible Shrinking Man* has been told countless times in reviews, interviews, and articles. Since the film's initial release, however, U-I's version of such tale has seldom, if ever, been seen in print. This version of the facts, told with the mixture of naïve enthusiasm and tongue-in-cheek irony typical of the publicity departments of the time, was by turns informative and fantastical, truthful and apocryphal. Most of this information was incorporated, verbatim, in the promotional articles and reviews published by the 1957 press.

Let us start with the production atmosphere:

> Actual production on "The Incredible Shrinking Man" began only after eight months of extensive tests with a revolutionary film process developed by the combined talents of U-I's cam-

era and special effects departments. Because the techniques were so novel, the picture was a top secret project from the very outset.

When actual production began, no one not directly connected with the filming of the picture, whether studio employee or visitor, was permitted on the set. The cast and crew members themselves were required to carry special passes to gain access to the set.

Among the things that U-I didn't want anyone to see were certain items—inconsequential in themselves—that had been sent to the construction department for duplication many weeks in advance of the start of filming. Some were recreated in their actual size, others were built 25 times as large as they were, and on a few the work order read: "Duplicate on scale 100:1."

As only one example, there is a 12-foot long common pin which Williams, supposedly only two inches himself in height, uses as a lance to kill a spider which attacks him. This is mentioned to indicate how one basic problem was solved for some of the scenes without involving any trick photography: since Williams himself couldn't be reduced in size, the same effect was achieved by increasing the size of every object he handled or against which he appeared [...], the enlargement being scaled to whatever size [Williams] was supposed to be at that point in the story. (ISM, 4)

Interesting details about set construction were also given, which are easily corroborated by production stills for the film:

The set representing the basement of Williams' home, for a long sequence during which he is two inches tall, was so large that it had to be distributed over nine separate sound stages. Had it been put together as a single unit it would have measured over a mile long and nearly three quarters of a mile wide.

To create such monstrosities as a paint can 55 feet high, a wedge of stale sponge cake 18 feet high, a pair of scissors 25 feet long and a three-penny nail that was seven feet long, and other oversized replicas of such ordinary objects U-I had to allot a budget to "The Incredible Shrinking Man" that was higher than any ever expended on a science-fiction thriller in the history of the studio. (ISM, 4)

The information thus far seems plausible enough, and is confirmed both by interviews with Arnold[211] and his cast (TW, 306–310) and by production photographs. The statements that follow are slightly more dubious.

The wardrobe department at Universal-International Studios set something of a record for costume duplication by making 22 versions of one outfit worn by Grant Williams in the title role [...].

The costumes, however, were far from identical in size. Scaled to represent the gradual diminution of the title character, the largest version was made to fit a six-foot tall man and the smallest a man less than an inch in height. This smallest version had to be put together and sewn with the aid of a magnifying glass. (ISM, 4)

Since, as Universal-International states on the same page of the pressbook, "Williams himself couldn't be reduced in size," the above costume duplication seems like a monumental waste of manpower, and is indubitably untrue.

Jack Arnold was famously involved in every aspect of the film, including the special effects; he drew extensive storyboards of the entire film, and collaborated closely with Clifford Stine (camera and special photography) on all process shots.

For the shots that required Williams to perform actions matching previously shot footage (for example his scenes with the spider), Arnold used a metronome. First he directed the spider, breaking down the action beat by beat and action by action. Then he directed Williams separately against a black background, using the metronome to count the beats corresponding to the original actions.

---

211. Kelley (1975), op. cit.

As for the spider itself, Arnold and his cast always insisted that, because regular tarantulas were not big enough to keep the camera in focus when they were being filmed, about sixty of the largest spiders available were flown in from Panama, and their movements were "directed" via air jets; many of these (interchangeable) spiders ended up being killed by the powerful studio lights while performing their acting duties.[212]

In its publicity phantasmagoria, however, U-I had other ideas as to how to spin the story. This fictional take on the spider facts appeared in their advance advertising, describing a fictitious "trained tarantula" named Tamara, allegedly the only trained spider in the world, and its proud owner Ralph Helfer.

Reception and Legacy

The Incredible Shrinking Man was received well enough by reviewers, and has acquired cult status with critics, viewers, and historians over the years. The film won the Hugo Award for Best Dramatic Presentation in the first year of the awards, 1958. In 2009, the Library of Congress named the film to the National Film Registry for being "culturally, historically, or aesthetically" significant.

In general, specialized critics have been more enthusiastic than newspaper reviewers. In his book *Science Fiction in the Cinema*, John Baxter calls the film "a fantasy that for intelligence and sophistication has few equals," and goes on to say: "[t]his film is the finest Arnold made and arguably the peak of SF film in its long history [...] [It] is Jack Arnold's masterpiece, interpreting Matheson's script with ferocious precision."[213]

In his seminal book *An Illustrated History of the Horror Film* (1967), Carlos Clarens has some reservations about the movie, but his conclusion is positive:

> The movie, directed with flat precision by Jack Arnold, had its quota of traditional adventure, as the hero becomes a tiny

212. Mark McGee and Susan Frank, interview with Jack Arnold, in *SPFX Special Effects Magazine* n.10, 2002; also in DMR, 66–68.

213. John Baxter, *Science Fiction in the Cinema: 1895-1970*, A.S. Barnes, 1970, 126–127.

> Robinson Crusoe in a world of threatening familiar things. The
> final effect, nevertheless, is hauntingly thoughtful.[214]

Clarens' reservations concern the ending, and they are rather curious:
"This disquieting ending was marred by an inopportune, uplifting comment to the effect that as far as God is concerned there is no zero."[215]

This last statement of Clarens' is particularly cynical, for it implies
that (a) an uplifting thought diminishes the value or intensity of personal
tragedy and/or (b) a wider perspective on man's existence has no legiti-
mate place in a genre yarn. In fact, for every positive statement he makes
about the film, Clarens feels obliged to swing in the opposite direction
and make a negative one. Though he admits that "the final effect [...] is
hauntingly thoughtful," and that the film "has become a sort of classic in
a remarkably short time," he also states that it has acquired such status "in
spite of lacking real excellence [...]."

Ivan Butler, in *Horror in the Cinema*, appraises the film thus:

> The fantastic story [...] is worked out with complete logic from
> its original premise. [...] Potentially ludicrous moments are
> rendered acceptable by restrained and sincere treatment [...].
> [All these details], aided by excellent trick photography, car-
> ry complete conviction, assuming, indeed, an epic quality of
> man's struggle for survival. The ending is uncompromising. A
> horror film with the courage of its conclusions.[216]

Leonard Maltin, in his *Movie Guide*, gives the film a rating of three-and-
a-half out of four stars, saying:

> Intelligent, serious approach, exceptional effects for the period,
> and a vigorous leading performance result in a genuine sci-fi

---

214. Carlos Clarens, *An Illustrated History of the Horror Film*, G.P. Putnam's Sons,
1967, 133. It is interesting to note that, while both Baxter and Clarens use the
noun "precision" to define Arnold's work, their choice of adjectives ("flat" for
Clarens, "ferocious" for Baxter) is different. I am inclined to agree with Baxter.

215. Ibid.

216. Ivan Butler, *Horror in the Cinema*, A. Zwemmer Limited/A.S. Barnes & Co,
1970, 168–169.

classic, unsurpassed by later attempts. [...] Director Arnold's best movie.[217]

Rob Craig defines *The Incredible Shrinking Man* as "one of the most profound movies of the [1950s];"[218] Shapiro insightfully calls it "one of the finest examples of the evocative symbolic expression of mystical experience,"[219] and Reemes considers it "a truly unique accomplishment in the history of film [...]." (DMR, 72)Bosley Crowther of *The New York Times* did not like the film when it advance-premiered at the Globe Theatre in New York on February 22, 1957. His main gripes, which in his wording appear to be both excessive and elliptical, seemed to concern the scientific credibility of the story and the philosophical finale:

> [... The] "incredible" of the title takes on an unintended meaning. For, unless a viewer is addicted to freakish ironies, the unlikely spectacle of Mr. Williams losing an inch of height each week, while his wife, Randy Stuart, looks on helplessly, will become tiresome before Universal has emptied its lab of science fiction clichés.
> [... Scott Carey's] last words en route to space are, "To God, there is no zero," which, like the rest of this adventure, manages to equate everything with nothing.[220]

Among the reviewers, *Variety* was a special case. Concerned as it always was with commercial viability and box-office returns, the magazine clung to a conception of the film that did not fully correspond to its intrinsic nature, then was disappointed when the film failed to deliver on such conception. *Variety*'s capsule definition of the movie was: "Science-fiction thriller for exploitation dates"; what follows is *Variety*'s commercial forecast:

217. Leonard Maltin, *2010 Movie Guide*, Signet, 2009.

218. Rob Craig, *It Came from 1957: A Critical Guide to the Year's Science Fiction, Fantasy and Horror Films*, McFarland & Company, Inc., Publishers, 2013, 105.

219. Shapiro (2001), op. cit., 117.

220. Bosley Crowther, "'Mister Cory'; 'Success Story' a la Hollywood Arrives," *New York Times*, February 23, 1957.

The exploitation market will find "The Incredible Shrinking Man" a handy subject for ballyhoo bills. Teamed with another science-fictioner or with a companion feature also having special appeal for the younger set, returns can be good.[221]

There is, of course, *some* truth to *Variety's* idea of the film, and the box-office results amply confirmed this. But here is the reviewer's complaint:

> While [the film's] release possibilities are obvious, film isn't thoroughly satisfactory chiller [...]. The unfoldment is inclined to slow down on occasion, resulting in flagging interest here and there [...].

In other words, *Variety* seemed to object precisely to that slow, methodical, melancholic observation that made the film unique among its peers and not a typical "handy subject for ballyhoo bills," nor one "having special appeal for the younger set."

The film's special nature as an existential, or humanist, musing on man's existence is what makes it unique; but, just as the composers of the music (and some music experts) were puzzled by the film's use of an "inappropriate" main musical theme, so *Variety* was puzzled by what "slowed down" its unfoldment. In this instance, *Variety* mistook a virtue for a limitation.

The standard labels of horror and science fiction just do not apply to *The Incredible Shrinking Man*. John Rosenfield,[222] the music and entertainment critic of *The Dallas Morning News* (and Rual Askew's boss), in covering a showing of *The Incredible Shrinking Man*, astutely remarked:

> This sort of thing is really the screen's heritage. It is mislabeled "science fiction" for the science is merely a blind for much free-wheeling invention, some of it as good as the Franken-

---

221. *Variety*, February 6, 1957.

222. John Rosenfield was a well-respected critic, who in 1956 won the award for outstanding critical writing given by the Screen Directors Guild.

stein Monster. [...] We submit that this is still the best escapism there is.[223]

There were some violently dissenting voices in the general chorus of approval in the press. The remarks of the few naysayers (including Mr. Crowther's), it must be said, mostly expressed unintelligent, uncircumstantiated dislike—hardly a basis for any serious revision of the consensus. Here is one particularly hateful reviewer:

> [... This film] makes the fatal mistake of taking itself seriously. [...] [T]o confuse the purposes of God with the obvious high jinks of photographic trickery seems a somewhat dubious inspiration. [... The few] moments of enjoyment become more and more scarce as the reels turn and the off-screen voice wallows more and more deeply into the depths of pseudo-philosophy. [...] While it gets nowhere philosophically, "The Incredible Shrinking Man" does make one thing abundantly clear. The big movie monsters are a lot more fun.[224]

Like Carlos Clarens, the above reviewer objected to the film's "philosophical" bent; but the wrath of his *kvetchy* pen did not spare Grant Williams: "Mr. Grant Williams, in the title role, proves to be quite an acrobat in the Douglas Fairbanks tradition. There is no way to judge his abilities as a dramatic actor."[225]

Such unfair dismissal of Williams has been rather common over the years. Even amongst generally glowing opinions about *The Incredible Shrinking Man*, Williams' contribution to the film has often been underrated or taken for granted, by critics and reviewers alike.

Variety was typically synthetic, but positive, in its appraisal of Williams: "[...] Williams does his role quite well."[226]

---

223. John Rosenfield, "The Passing Show: Screen's Heritage of Horror Pictures," *Dallas Morning News*, May 3, 1957.

224. Win Fanning, "New Film: 'The Incredible Shrinking Man' Comes to Fulton," *Pittsburgh (PA) Post-Gazette*, April 13, 1957.

225. Ibid.

226. *Variety*, February 6, 1957.

Philip K. Scheuer of the *Los Angeles Times* was also synthetic, almost noncommittal, about Williams in his otherwise positive review of the film (which he called "a fascinating exercise in imagination, as terrifying as it is funny")[227] upon its initial release: "While there is no time for much acting as such, Williams gives a realistically pained account of a chap in a plight without precedent."[228]

Most reviewers, at any rate, were too busy lavishing praise on the special effects to take any notice of Williams, and Scheuer was no exception. Only occasionally did such reviewers see something special in Williams' performance, as was the case with *The Philadelphia Inquirer*'s Mildred Martin (who detested the film's finale): "Big or little, Grant Williams is fine as the desperate hero [...]."[229]

If newspaper reviewers were tepid when it came to Grant Williams, critics and scholars (even when enthusiastic about the film) have not been much more flattering over the years.

Bill Warren, for example, admits Williams is "very good as Scott Carey, sustaining the film throughout and never losing our sympathy," but ends up sounding backhanded in his comments:

> His performance as Scott Carey is cautious and unsensational; [...] [i]t is not a star performance—he is not the thing we remember best from the film—but it is a competent and intelligent job of acting.[230]

Williams' performance is indeed unsensational (though not in the negative sense probably intended by Warren). It is not, however, cautious; it is thoughtful and measured. The actor's vocal delivery, velvety and understated, creates a warm foundation where Williams can navigate his character through a portrayal that is pointed inward; Jack Arnold's confident,

---

227. I wonder if by "funny" Scheuer meant strange, or humorous. I counted no laughs in the film.

228. Philip K. Scheuer, "'Shrinking Man' Film Frightening and Funny," *Los Angeles Times*, March 28, 1957, C13.

229. Mildred Martin, "Fox [Movie Theater] Offers Shocker in 'The Shrinking Man,'" *Philadelphia Inquirer*, March 22, 1957.

230. Bill Warren, *Keep Watching the Skies! American Science Fiction Movies of the Fifties*, vol.1, McFarland & Company, Publishers, 1982, 360.

economical storytelling does the rest. As for the performance being a star performance or not, given the outcome of Williams' career, the statement is a blow below the belt, and is irrelevant to the value of the film, for we know that stardom is not necessarily a reflection on talent, or on quality. Lastly, saying that Williams is not what we remember best from the film—a film that undividedly devotes its screen time to its protagonist, and never lets go of him throughout his harrowing ordeal—is curious to say the least.

Bradley, in his *Richard Matheson on Screen*, only goes so far as to say: "Although he never became a major star, Williams quite ably portrays the perplexity, bitterness, fear, frustration, and desperation of this slowly dwindling Everyman."[231]

These last two statements (by Warren and Bradley) bring up an important—one could say critical—point. For Bradley and many others (including members of Williams' audience and fan base), Williams' failure to achieve A-list stardom becomes an implicit parameter in judging his performances, while in fact the two things bear no intrinsic relation to each other. This intrusion of business factors into a discourse about artistic merit creates a contradiction in terms, unless one subscribes to the idea that success and art are inextricably conjoined. They may be conjoined to a certain extent for the people making the films, during the time the films are made; they should not be for the people judging or discussing the quality of those films after the fact.

Only Director Jack Arnold was always resolutely enthusiastic about Williams. Reemes—always a supporter of Jack Arnold's work and of his favorite actors—is positive about Williams, defining his work in the film a "bravura performance" and quoting Arnold as saying that, given the complex nature of the production and of its special effects, "a director's only insurance is an actor who is intelligent and knows his craft. [...] Grant gave a truly outstanding performance...." (DMR, 73)

The Human Element

That *The Incredible Shrinking Man* is a special-effects movie has been made abundantly clear by reviewers, critics and fans, and by a general enthusiasm for the clever solutions in optical trickery devised for the film.

---

231. Bradley (2010), op. cit., 12.

What is less explicit in the general perception (though some steps in the right direction have been made in recent years) is that the film is really a drama. Fantastical it certainly is, but the focus of its story is, first and foremost, on the human element. From the very first scenes, *The Incredible Shrinking Man*'s setup is that of a personal tragedy.

The novel, with its non-chronological structure, jumps from the initial incident on the boat—the spark that sets the events in motion—to the cellar scenes in which Scott Carey is less than an inch tall and has to defend himself against a giant spider. In other words, the move from the ordinary to the fantastical is made swiftly, quite early in the story.

In the film, the chronological order of the events dictates a gradual involvement of the viewer in the story—which is perforce a human involvement. The first act of Scott's "play" is a domestic drama, with an innocent setting that includes a cat drinking milk from a saucer, a married couple in their suburban home, and the protagonist getting dressed and having breakfast. Scott's discovery of his disease, the involvement of his wife Louise (Randy Stuart), and the deterioration of his mood and of his relationships are all played earnestly and believably, with dramatic truthfulness, against the 1950s kitchen-sink background. The genre antics are introduced unobtrusively, and the audience has to wait for them to ripen *through* the human story. From the point of view of acting and direction, *The Incredible Shrinking Man* is a place where the actors (and their characters) can thrive.

Randy Stuart, who played Scott's wife Louise, was certain of this from the start, as she told Tom Weaver:

> [Grant Williams and I] met before we started the film and we both agreed that we were either gonna believe it or we shouldn't do it. So we both went into it with that attitude, that we believed it was happening. [...] Grant and I came in and rehearsed, actually read lines together as we would if we were working on stage. (TW, 305–306)

According to Stuart's interview, this process involved long sessions with Arnold, Matheson, and the two leads (TW, 307). Stuart also had kind words to say about her co-star, both as an actor in the film and as a person:

[…] I'd never seen anybody work harder than Grant did in *Shrinking Man*, there was just a lot of stuff to be done. And you have to know that Grant personally was a very intense person.

[Grant's death] did really move me at the time. Toward the end, Grant had become—not a devoutly religious person, because what is religion?—but a devoutly good person who had accepted Christ as his savior. I was very pleased with that. (TW, 308–312)

Just how great the physical strain was for Williams became clear in Bob Thomas's article about Williams, which appeared in the syndicated press in February 1957:

Among Hollywood's new leading men, a notoriously nervous lot, Grant Williams is the exception. He can relate calmly how he was blinded for a week in a movie accident.

[…] Some of the scenes were shot against a burning arc lamp, and the glare erased his vision.

"For a week, I was completely blind," he said calmly. "But the doctors assured me it was just a temporary thing and my vision would return with exercise and massage of the eye muscles. I didn't do a thing in that time except receive treatments. After a week and a half, I began to see things, but it was three weeks before my vision was restored."

During the picture he also broke a vertebra in his neck and burned his shoulder.

Grant is now starring in another shocker, "Monolith" [sic] […]. I suggested that he might find himself the science fiction hero of Universal City. This would be a danger not only to his physical wellbeing, but to the longevity of his career.

"I think the bosses have more concern for my career than to let that happen," he said.[232]

And Emily Belser, in her 1956 on-set interview with Williams, commented:

---

232. Thomas (1957), op. cit.

Grant Williams, wearing his costume for *The Monolith Monsters* (1957), poses in front of an arc light just like the one responsible for his eye injury during the shooting of his previous picture, *The Incredible Shrinking Man* (1957). AP Photo/David F. Smith.

How'd you like to be one-inch tall battling for your life against a giant tarantula, caught in a rat-trap two-times your size and nearly drowned in four inches of water?

That's the fate of Grant Williams, a young new Hollywood actor with the daring of a Richard Halliburton and the luck of an Ernest Hemingway.

"I didn't know what I was getting into when I came to Hollywood," the young actor confessed, "but I must say it hasn't been dull."

[…] "If I survive this film," Williams laughed, "I can do anything." (EB)

The leads' commitment to their roles in *The Incredible Shrinking Man*, which was not only physical, is demonstrated by both their performances. The pressbook for the film defined Stuart's portrayal as "deeply moving," and Williams' as "inspired," which, for once, was no exaggeration.

This same dramatic commitment was certainly felt by Director Arnold, who directs the entire story absolutely straight: there is almost a documentary feel to many sequences of the film, particularly in the cellar half. Arnold's methodical approach to filmmaking may appear to some (such as Clarens) as "flat precision,"[233] but it is more than that. By pointing a magnifying glass to each micro-event in Scott Carey's miniature adventures, Arnold not only amplifies the events, he also amplifies the human being and makes him clearly visible.

Each Stanislavskian beat of Scott Carey's adventures is observed with scientific precision—with calm observation—and even the most inconsequential steps in Scott's progress (such as his looking at his chafed hands after his orange crate climb, or his making a mistake in throwing the grappling hook the first time, and his learning to do it right the second time) are depicted as logical moments in his inner life, which Williams is allowed to express. This precision is not limited to physical events but includes emotional events. Those reviewers (such as the *Variety* writer) who complained about the lagging of the film's pace perhaps mistook those emotional moments (such as the moment when Scott takes the time to interact with a garden bird from inside his prison) for an absence of plot. Given the nature of this peculiar inner story, quite the contrary is true: those infinitesimal events, those emotional instants, *are* the plot where Scott Carey's cellar story is concerned. And it is those precious inner instants that Director Arnold preserves for posterity with the rigor of a documentarist—which Arnold had been during World War II, Reemes tells us, by working as assistant to Robert Flaherty. (DMR, 9–10) Those instants allow us to watch the complete chronicle of this poor Everyman as he leaves our terrestrial dimension and proceeds to the next.

Godzilla (1954 or 1998) is a special effects movie. *The Incredible Shrinking Man* is an actor's movie. It is a movie about Everyman.

---

233. Clarens (1967), op. cit., 133.

7
Universal-International, 1957–1960

THE MONOLITH MONSTERS

Jack Arnold did not direct *The Monolith Monsters* (released in December 1957), but he did write the story for the film, and this fact, coupled with Grant Williams' presence as a protagonist, evokes Arnold in the film, as if the two artists were somehow connected spiritually after their previous three films together. Peter Osteried, in his overview of Arnold's career, goes so far as to say that *The Monolith Monsters* feels like a Jack Arnold film, even though it was directed by John Sherwood (1903–1959), who had previously made his living as an assistant director and had directed two films, *The Creature Walks Among Us* and *Raw Edge*, 1956).[234]

The Monolith Monsters benefits from four things: a "high-concept" script (minerals from outer space multiply when exposed to water and drain the life out of human beings); disciplined direction from Sherwood (with some lapses into sentimentality); beautiful chiaroscuro cinematography by Ellis W. Carter; and likeable performances from the cast. It is a pleasant genre film, but, unfortunately, not a great one.

In terms of acting, the best scenes in the film are the exchanges between Federal Geologist Dave Miller (Williams) and his mentor Professor Flanders (Trevor Bardette) as they study the mysterious rock, exchanges that lead to their accidental (and suspenseful) discovery of the mechanism that triggers its growth. These scenes achieve a relaxed,

---

234. Osteried (2012), op. cit.; IMDb.; incongruously (without further specifications), the Universal-International pressbook for *The Monolith Monsters* defined Sherwood as "Williams' close friend." (p. 2)

A candid photo of Grant Williams by his place of residence, circa 1958.
Courtesy of Nina Ingris' private collection.

natural conversational style in the midst of a very tense situation, and their Hitchcockian handling of suspense helps both the actors and the storytelling.

Coming as it does on the heels of his star-making turn in *The Incredible Shrinking Man*, Williams' role in *The Monolith Monsters* is necessarily anticlimactic. Emotionally and dramatically, the film is atmospheric but

With the help of the State Highway Patrol, Geologist Dave Miller (Grant Williams, right) gives urgent news from the town of San Angelo, California, while Journalist Martin Cochrane (Les Tremayne, standing extreme left) and Professor Arthur Flanders (Trevor Bardette, standing next to Tremayne) look on, in *The Monolith Monsters* (1957). Production still, © 1957, Universal Pictures Company, Inc.

William Flaherty, Grant Williams, and Trevor Bardette ponder the problem at hand in a production still for *The Monolith Monsters* (1957), © 1957, Universal Pictures Company, Inc.

innocuous, and is a mediocre showcase for Williams' talent, as well as a symptom of Universal-International's curious decision-making process. The early signs of a lurch in Williams' rise to fame are unmistakable.

Universal Limbo

Arnold and Williams remained friends for years; in the 1970s, Williams even invited Arnold to some of his acting classes.[235] Arnold was always ready to wax poetic about Williams' talent, often referring to him as a "favorite actor." Here is what he told Reemes about Williams' failure to achieve A-list stardom:

> Grant Williams was one of the best actors around. […] But the studio didn't give him the right parts and his career never quite took off. He had the wrong looks for the time and never caught on with the public. Hollywood wanted a Robert Taylor or Rock Hudson, not a blond guy with blue eyes. And he was a bit too pretty for character roles. (DMR, 85)

There might be some truth to Arnold's statements, even though the vagaries of taste and fashion make more sense in hindsight than they do in the thick of live history, and Arnold's belief that eye and hair color were the causes of Williams' professional downfall is particularly disheartening. Fashion, we have learned since, can be easily swayed by the appropriate hype or push; exceptions rather than rules determine swings in public opinion. Audience taste, for example, was swayed by atypical phenomena such as James Dean (slim and blond); this was probably because of Dean's talent, obviously, but also because of his eccentricity, and because of the exceptional projects in which he starred. Grant Williams may have been too square and too bland to go against the mainstream tide, but the reasons for Williams' permanence in second-tier stardom may simply lie in the quality of the projects that were selected for him.

In all likelihood, we are not dealing so much with audience taste as with the tastes of studio executives, agents, and producers, who evidently

---

235. Former acting student Ken Mulroney, conversation with the author, 2016. Further quotations from Mulroney are cited in the text using the abbreviation KM.

Grant Williams and Lola Albright are just terrified of *The Monolith Monsters* in
this publicity still, © 1957, Universal Pictures Company, Inc.; courtesy of
the C. Robert Rotter Collection.

were not able to see Williams' potential or were too conventional and
conservative to imagine any other path for their players but the most
beaten. In this respect, it is probably true that, in terms of leading men,
the 1950s were by and large a period of tall dark lugs. Perhaps, had Williams appeared on the Hollywood scene some ten years earlier, he could
have filled the spot of an Alan Ladd, of a Burt Lancaster, or of a William
Holden. One can certainly picture Williams feeding that kitten in Raven's
first scene in *This Gun for Hire* (1942), saying the line "*I did something
wrong... once,*" in the Swede's introduction in *The Killers* (1946), or edu-

cating Judy Holliday in *Born Yesterday* (1950). Williams' particular brand of melancholy and his delicate, underplayed comedic finesse would have been perfect fits for the *Zeitgeist* of the preceding decade.

In his brief career, Williams worked with excellent directors, such as Jack Arnold (*Red Sundown* and *Outside the Law*, 1956; *The Incredible Shrinking Man*, 1957), Douglas Sirk (*Written on the Wind*, 1956), Paul Landres (*Lone Texan*, 1959), James Sheldon ("Millionaire Gilbert Burton," *The Millionaire*, 1959), Robert Altman ("Brother's Keeper," *The Roaring 20's*, 1961), Delmer Daves (*Susan Slade*, 1961), and Charles R. Rondeau

Lola Albright relaxes with Williams on location while shooting *The Monolith Monsters*. © 1957, Universal Pictures Company, Inc.; courtesy of the C. Robert Rotter Collection.

("Nightmare in Paradise," *Hawaiian Eye*, 1962). But apparently nothing could save him from his fate once he had started down the slope, which was very early.

At the time of its release, *The Incredible Shrinking Man* was one of the biggest successes in Universal-International's history up to that point, and made a hefty profit. One would certainly expect such a hit (and such a performance) to have pushed Williams into a higher echelon at the studio. Yet a personal letter of Williams' immediately after the film's release finds him stalled:

> I'm going through one of those seemingly busy yet unproductive periods. I'm up for a lot of films which require seeing people and all but am not set for anything as yet. Heddy Lamar [sic] is not in town yet so we can't set "Hideaway House". She has final approval, of course.[236]

Williams was indeed up for *Hideaway House*, but, as one can read between the lines of Stephen Michael Shearer's biography of Hedy Lamarr (1914–2000), despite his recent notices, the actor was merely perceived (if he was perceived at all) as an indistinct entity within Universal's stable of interchangeable leading men. George Nader was eventually selected by Lamarr for the renamed *The Female Animal* (1958).

Variety reviewers had occasionally offered helpful hints to U-I about Williams; here is another one they planted in their review of *The Monolith Monsters*: "Williams makes a capable juve and should do better in more ambitious projects."[237]

It would seem, however, that no ambitious projects and no big promotions were forthcoming at Universal. If the parameter was to be beauty or beefiness, Williams had plenty of competition in his own court: as a contract player at the studio, he was just another number amongst a slew of lookers. His previous films had proven his worth as an actor, amply, but his acting made him competitive only if acting was the meter of judgment, which apparently it was not. In 1957, Universal-International was the domain of the Rory Calhouns, the Jeff Chandlers, the John Gavins,

236. Grant Williams, personal letter to L. Allan Smith, April 16, 1957.

237. *Variety*, October 23, 1957.

and the Rock Hudsons. It was also the extended domain of Henry Willson, who was not Williams' agent at this time but exercised some influence at Universal and had his own set of conflicts of interest. Managing as he did his male actors—many of whom were physically interchangeable with each other—in a very personal manner, Willson had his favorites. There was a definite hierarchy in his stable, with Rock Hudson squarely ensconced at the top. It would be an idle but fascinating exercise in visualization, for instance, to imagine what would have happened if all those Doris Day comedies—starting with U-I's *Pillow Talk* (1959)—and all those Douglas Sirk Technicolor melodramas—starting with *Magnificent Obsession* (1954)—had starred Grant Williams instead of Rock Hudson and John Gavin.

Failure to achieve A-list stardom and the wavering of the fickle affections of agents and executives were facts of life for many contract players, at Universal and at other studios: many actors suffered a fate similar to Williams' and remained trapped in a similar limbo. In Grant Williams' case, the reasons for this fate most definitely had nothing to do with lack of talent. It is possible, however, that, even at this early stage, some of the personality problems that would plague Williams later in his career were already rearing their ugly heads.

Williams was devoted to acting and to Method techniques, but his love for the craft and for quality did not prevent him from being ambitious as well. He wanted to be a good actor, but he also wanted to be a star. Here, in an interview he gave to Don Alpert of the *Los Angeles Times* in 1961, he explains what being a star meant to him in terms of his craft:

> Power is extremely important. What does 'star' mean to me? Power. I want to get to a position of power. I would say three quarters of the time I work with people who aren't well equipped to tell me what to do. I don't mean power in an ugly sense. Power breeds security and security makes you a damned happy individual. You have to be a star to be an actor in Hollywood. The star, meaning the power—or the power meaning the star—says "let's put our heads together" so someone will listen. The greatest directors I have worked with will listen to anybody.
>
> First of all the artist has to be true to his art and being true to it he causes good or bad. I would not appear in a lie—no

matter how beautifully presented. I turned down a Tennessee Williams play because of this.[238]

Though it is unclear exactly what point Williams is trying to make when he speaks of his refusal to appear "in a lie," one can infer from these last statements that Williams may have suffered from some degree of artistic vanity, or superiority. If this were true, such superiority might be factored into his industry downfall. If, for instance, this particular artistic hubris were added to Williams' alcohol addiction,[239] it might help us explain his alleged clashes with the studio brass and the brevity of both his studio contracts.

In all other respects, Williams' explanation of the meaning of power in Hollywood is more than reasonable. Being powerful meant carrying sufficient clout to have freedom of choice; it meant not being a mere executor of someone else's taste.

However, a deeper disquiet—having little or nothing to do with artistic standards—gnawed at Williams' heart, an incurable restlessness that all but pervaded his life.

The Leech Woman

Williams' last film with Universal-International, released in May 1960, after his contract had expired, was *The Leech Woman*.

The premise had potential, and some of the acting in the film is excellent, but it all goes to waste in a sluggish, ill-constructed script that cannot make up its mind who the protagonists are and exactly which story it is telling. For instance, Williams' character, initially secondary, becomes elevated to co-protagonist status—after disappearing from the story for more than thirty-five minutes.

The clumsiness of the script is perfectly illustrated by its awkward beginning, involving an overlong dialogue between the aging June Talbot (Coleen Gray) and her brutish husband Dr. Paul Talbot (Phillip Terry). The protracted scene, with its long pauses and sincere exchanges about

---

238. Grant Williams, in Don Alpert's "Have Psychiatrist, Will Act," *Los Angeles Times*, June 4, 1961.

239. See Chapter 14.

love, alcoholism, and age discrimination, sinks the film's opening into a quicksand of heartfelt drama that is both tedious and unexceptional.

The potential of the film suffers a fate much like that of Actress Estelle Hemsley and of her character, the wizened 152-year-old woman who lures Dr. Talbot to an African expedition with the promise of an elixir of youth. Hemsley (who was seventy-three when the film was made) was a wonderful actress, and her sad, world-weary eyes, her withered skin, and her vaguely ominous voice make her ancient woman a charismatic phantasm of a character. She is fantastic, even radiant, in her mummy-like spookiness. Then, as soon as the potion (distilled from a rare orchid and from a live man's pineal gland) works its magic and she is turned into a sinuous young woman (played by Kim Hamilton), all the life goes out of her character.

Much of this film behaves likewise: it sets up something interesting, then drains the life out of it. Never was a film title more appropriate.

Things get heated between Grant Williams and the titular Leech Woman (Coleen Gray) in this production still for the film, © 1960, Universal Pictures Company, Inc.; courtesy of the C. Robert Rotter Collection.

Grant Williams, in what could have been a protagonist role but is not, is fine. He is especially sensual in playing the sexual undercurrent of his scenes with the rejuvenated Mrs. Talbot (an attractive Coleen Gray). Their scenes together, especially their necking scene towards the end of the film, are particularly hormonal, and Williams' pear-shaped tones are caressingly seductive. As usual, however, every time something minimally interesting happens in this story, the script yanks us away from it and changes register. Which might be all right if the horror were frightening; instead, Gray's aging makeup is risible, and her vain character is impossible to root for. An inglorious end for Williams' association with Universal.

Variety summarized the film as follows: "Lower-berth horror item about a lady Ponce de Leon. Not horrible enough to be very potent." The magazine was, however, impressed with Hemsley:

> Coleen Gray plays the central character extremely well, sharing thespic honors with Estelle Hemsley who, as the aged leader of the tribe, reminds one vaguely of the late Mme. Ouspenskaya.[240]

Rosalind Russell and the Universal Joint

That Universal-International was not equally welcoming or supportive towards all its small- and medium-caliber contract players is not only logical (with so many hopefuls on staff, how could a big studio really decide whom to nurture?) but also supported by testimony.

Exhibit one: the TV movie *Allen in Movieland*, though an unofficial self-plug by the studio, was in fact filled with examples of cruelty—comical though they might have been—towards its guest star, Steve Allen.

Exhibit two: in her autobiography, Rosalind Russell, who briefly signed with Universal in the 1930s, entitles one of her chapters "Two Weeks Behind the Camera, or the Universal Joint." In it, she tells of her encounter with a Universal talent scout:

240. *Variety*, May 18, 1960. Russian Actress Maria Ouspenskaya (1876–1949) worked on stage and screen. She was trained by Konstantin Stanislavsky and worked at the Moscow Art Theatre before immigrating to the United States in 1922. In Hollywood, she became known for her portrayals of eccentric—or sinister—old women.

[...] I reported to a room in the same building that housed Radio City Music Hall and talked to a man from Universal Pictures. It developed that I wasn't the only genius who'd been spotted in Newark and environs; Universal had also sent for fifteen or twenty other actors. And what they were prepared to offer me was a really rotten contract—seven years of nothing.[241]

With sparkling irony, Russell then recounts the two weeks she spent in Los Angeles, first waiting, then begging, for her screen tests (which turned into a stint running lines behind the camera for other actors during *their* screen tests), then finally trying to extricate herself from the commitment she had hastily made to the studio. Russell ended up signing with MGM. Her tale of those Universal days is nothing short of horrific, and the contemptuous mistreatment she describes makes one's blood run cold (or hot, as hers did). Aside from the unpleasant personalities of the studio managers she depicts in her story, one gets the impression from her statements that Universal was simply too busy to care for any individual recruit, regardless of the recruit's talent. This may have been a real issue in the 1950s as well, and the curve of Grant Williams' career at U-I may be a symbol of it.

Signing, and training, too many actors indicated an ambition (one might call it a greedy ambition) on the part of the studio. It created an almost endless pool of talent, available at a moment's notice, to fill whatever casting gap occurred. The absence of a constructive, articulated career plan for most members of such pool, on the other hand, pitilessly revealed the flip side of the contract-player covenant: the studio did not *need* to nurture its players' careers, since those players were available anyway. There were too many wives in the sultan's harem, each with little or nothing to do.

---

241. Russell and Chase (1977), op. cit.

8 Ms. Karpuschkin and the Wonderful Fan Machine

IN 1956 AND 1957, Grant Williams was personally and enthusiastically involved (with the official title of Honorary President) in the planning and running of his newly created Grant Williams Fan Club. Like its brethren, the club was an unofficial cog in the publicity machine surrounding Williams, an independent entity with friendly ties to Universal-International's Publicity Department on the one hand and to the Hollywood press on the other.

Williams was a hands-on person, and did not delegate when it came to most personal and practical matters, even after hiring a secretary in the person of Nina Karpuschkin (who would later marry Composer/Explorer Eduard Ingris)[242] in 1958. Nina Ingris' main job from 1958 to 1965 was limited to taking care of club correspondence.

The information one can gather from two surviving personal letters[243] written by Williams (and not by a secretary) to the club president at the time, L. Allan Smith of Pittsfield, Massachusetts,[244] is certainly interesting from an archaeological point of view and as evidence of fan club mechanics, but not only: the letters also contain statements that subtly refer to Williams' personal feelings and private life.

---

242. Eduard Ingris (1905–1991) was a prolific composer (1000 works, including 48 operettas and one opera), conductor, photographer, documentarist, and explorer; twice he crossed the Pacific Ocean on a raft (the *Kantuta*) to help prove Thor Heyerdahl's migratory theories.

243. One (GW1) dated April 16, 1957, the other (GW2) July 31, 1957.

244. Other presidents would include one Linda Andersen and one Charles Thomas.

Here is a paragraph from Williams' letter dated April 1957:

> Your letter to Mr. Muhl was heartwarming. This may sound strange to you but to know that people as decent and as kind as you are, believe in me and want to help me fight, has been the one incentive over all to keep going. I'm not married as you know and have been quite alone most of my life. To live alone is sometimes pleasant, but to fight alone is terrifying. (GW1, 1)[245]

What is curious about Williams' above statements (aside from the touching mention of loneliness, which might confirm, if not the facts, at least Williams' *feelings* about the facts of his earlier family life and/or of his personal life at the time of writing) is his admission that he viewed his career as a fight, a fight he was not sure he wanted to continue—and this immediately after the release of *The Incredible Shrinking Man*. That word, "fight," certainly hints at the fact that something was awry in his relationship with U-I. Also, the involvement of Vice-President Muhl seems to indicate that the supplication written by L. Allan Smith concerned executive-level issues. Another sign that Williams' status at the studio was vacillating.

Here is Williams' assessment of the club's progress in April 1957:

> I will have Bruce [?] write you with a report on the quantity of answers to Muhl in response to your letter and forward his letter for the Journal. The memberships you have sent on have been recorded. By now Bruce must have sent the list of new members to you.
>
> I did not include the article on the "Marlon Brando" type for the Journal but replaced it with that little story about Okinawa. I think it would be more fitting for the first Journal.[246]

---

245. Edward Muhl (1907–2001) was Vice-President in Charge of Production at Universal Pictures from 1953 to 1973. According to Hofler, the closeted Muhl had a tempestuous sexual liaison with Rock Hudson in the 1950s (RH, 236–238).

246. Kadena Air Base, in the towns of Kadena and Chatan and the city of Okinawa, was instrumental as a base of operations in the Korean War. This is presumably the subject of the story to which Williams refers.

Edward Muhl, Vice-President in Charge of Production at Universal Pictures, signs Marianne Koch, aka Marianne Cook (Grant Williams' co-star in *Four Girls in Town*), in December 1955. Photo: UP.

A resume of the tour is enclosed.[247]

Thank you for getting us a club photographer.... Has she accepted and how do I reach her?

You can obtain a copy of the shot in Boston by calling Bucky Harris at the Universal Exchange there or the Boston

---

247. This might refer either to the tour in Korea during Williams' Air Force service or, simply, to the U-I promotional tour for *The Incredible Shrinking Man*.

Club.... He will put you in touch with the photographer. I don't
have another copy nor do I have the man's name. The Kriegsmann[248] shot is enclosed for your file and I will order a copy
of the publicity shot with Randy [Stuart]. I hope you kept the
extra copy of her bio or do you need one?

Application blanks are on the way to you, Mr. Kutzmer
[?] and Linda.[249] Please feel free (if you have the time) to run
off copies of the application blank at your end. Any cost will of
course be born [sic] by the club funds. It might be easier for
you to keep the East Coast supplied.

[...] Lilyan Miller[250] helped me prepare the letters to the
following magazines with extra "to whom it may concern" letters for anymore that pop up: International Fun Club League,
Filmland, Movie Stars Parade, and Hear. (GW1, 1–2)

Williams' practical involvement in the details of the Fan Club is outlined
by the statements he makes three months later, in his three-page July
1957 letter:

1.   The Journal was mailed yesterday finally—thank God
        and your sensational efforts. To list a few of the hold-
        ups; U.I. was supposed to be printing some of the pic-
        tures for me and then it turned out that the order wasn't
        approved, then the negatives were supposed to be filed

248. James J. Kriegsmann (1909–1994) was a famous theatrical photographer. Born
     in Vienna, he moved to New York City at the age of 20. He had a photography
     studio on West 46th Street for nearly four decades, and became one of America's
     foremost celebrity photographers, immortalizing among others Milton Berle,
     Cab Calloway, Sid Caesar, Sammy Davis Jr., Doris Day, Judy Garland, Benny
     Goodman, Eartha Kitt, Dean Martin, and Frank Sinatra. He was also the official
     in-house photographer of the Cotton Club. A trained musician, he wrote
     hundreds of songs for top recording artists of the day. (Sources: Wikipedia, and
     the article "Behind the Lens, Continuing a Legacy," by Vincent M. Mallozzi, *New
     York Times*, January 10, 2010.)

249. Presumably, the same Linda Andersen who would be President of the Fan Club
     after Smith.

250. Lilyan A. Miller worked in the Universal-International Fan Mail and Fan Club
     Department; she was President of the George Nader Club and a friend to many
     U-I stars.

This may well be the shot by celebrated Photographer James J. Kriegsmann to which Williams refers in his letter to L. Allan Smith. Notice the Kriegsmann logo in the lower right corner. Undated, circa 1957.

in N.Y. Finally in desperation, I went to a commercial house and had all the pictures printed myself—it came to $45.00. Wellman [?] took longer than he told us which also didn't help but anyway they are in the mail—Wellman's bill was $70.00 and the mailing charge was around $12.00. I must say it looks beautiful and everyone thinks it's the best Journal ever made. Naturally, the dues came nowhere near covering the bill so I paid for it... don't worry though or ball me out because....

2.   I have always known that my stepping into club activities as heavily as I have been was not wise and could

eventually lose prestige for the club and myself if I continued. Now, however, taking a good look at things and feeling very secure that I have the best club president in existence and wonderful friends like Lilyan and the other officers I think it is high time for me to bow out gracefully. As I told you some time ago I was concerned that if there was going to be a club I wanted to know that the club would not only be run right but serve a good purpose for everyone concerned with it. Thanks to you, it is not only run right but it is better in purpose than I ever dreamed. I am eternally grateful Allan.

3.   I have instructed Bruce to record applications so I have a record and then to send the application *with* dues on to you. I will have him continue to send the cards, picture and constitution from this end if you want or change this procedure if you would rather send them from your end or you can instruct Lilyan.

4.   I think that your cash book can start from zero since all dues taken in since the inception of the club have been spent and though some members from way back still owe us money, my investments will cover this and even everything up. Literally we now have 145 members 5 officers and 2 honoraries. If dues were all collected to the present from members, we should have at least $145.00 (at a 1.00) and a maximum of 156.25 (that is 100 members at (1.00) and 45 members at (1.25) Well, I have spent over $300. to the present time, so why don't we just scratch everything and begin our records with the dues Bruce sent the other day ($13.00 I think). O.K.?

5.   I have also told Bruce to send on to you complete, the letters of people who request starting chapters or inquiries into policy, club business etc. etc.

6.   I will personally forward any questionaires [sic] to you. The questionnaire you sent me I am going to include with this letter. May I suggest that you simply forward these people a copy of it since they are all basically alike,

then I won't have to keep on filling them out. I will make up a bio for you too.

7.   With my increase in activities, it is not only impossible for me to take care of club business, but also incorrect. Don't you agree.

8.   Is it possible for the Journal to be printed (mimeo, or multilith) in the East and mailed. By this I mean; do you have sufficient help, would it be cheaper, do you have the time etc.... or... would you like to deal with Wellman direct or through Lilyan and mailed from here?

9.   To answer a question you asked me in May... I think a Journal around Christmas would be wonderful but the timing of the Journal, its contents, newsletters, business etc will in future be strictly up to you... I promise!

10.   10. Naturally you may always count on my cooperation. [...]

P.P.S.   Do you have all the membership dates? Many renewals are due but I told Bruce to hold off until the Journal was mailed. All memberships began from last July (56) on. There are no dates before this since at that time everything was started anew. Bruce will send any information you want and please instruct him if you want cards etc. to go out from here; how to handle if you do etc. (GW2, 1–3)

It is obvious that Williams was overextending himself in the micro-management of his Fan Club. In any case, one gets the impression that, business or no business, club or no club, Williams was a courteous person, one who never forgot to add a tender personal touch to his missives. The post-scriptum (before the above post-post-scriptum) of the letter demonstrates this: "P.S. How has your mother been since the operation. My sincerest regards." (GW2, 3)Williams' eagerness to provide fresh personal news is demonstrated by the opening of his July letter, where the actor talks about houseguests (the Blackfriars managers,[251] Model/Actress Ellie Evers, a Dallas debutante/friend and her parents),[252] about his musical

---

251. See Chapter 2.

252. See Chapter 14.

Grant Williams
1314 North Hayworth Avenue
Hollywood 46, California

July 31st 1957

Dear Allan,

I am only too aware that this letter is long overdue, and can only ask your forgiveness. I have never been this tardy at answering mail and the reason very generally is that a constant flow of people from the East and a brand new interest - song writing - has kept me hopping.

Among those from the East were Fr. Robert A Morris who with a Fr. Carey, runs a theatre known as the Blackfriars Guild in New York on 57th St. I did a play there in 1953 which was very successful and which gave me a healthy shove in the business. Then Ellie Evers (my galfriend in N.Y.) was here for three weeks. I'm sure you know what it is to entertain 24 hours a day for weeks on end. I'd rather do a heavy days work. But I love these people.

Mary Anne West was here with her Mother and Father. I took them to dinner one night. They were very kind to me in Dallas.

I am back studying the piano very seriously since meeting Herman Wasserman. He was George Gershwin's teacher and is sensational. He concertized in the thirties himself and knew my aunt - Mary Garden - the opera star years ago.

I've also struck up a friendship with Leonard Pennario, one of the nicest people I have ever known. This is where the song writing comes in. We've finished one (a Concert Song) entitled "Search". I've finished the lyrics for a pop ballad and have started another. Of course I do the lyrics and Leonard, the music.

I was able to get a little vacation in with Leonard down at La Jolla for two weeks after Ellie returned to N.Y. and am presently feeling pretty good and very anxious to go to work.

I have so much to discuss with you that I think I'll just start listing points - a miserable way to write a letter?

1. The Journal was mailed yesterday finally - thank God and your sensational efforts. To list a few of the hold-ups; U.I. was supposed to be printing some of the pictures for me and then it turned out that the order wasn't approved, then the negatives were supposed to be filed in N.Y. Finally in desperation, I went to a commercial house and had all the pictures printed myself - it came to $45.00. Wellman took longer than he told us which also didn't help but anyway they are in the mail - Wellman's bill was $70.00 and the mailing charge was around $12.00. I must say it looks beautiful and everyone thinks it's the best Journal ever made. Naturally, the dues came nowhere near covering the bill so I paid for it.....don't worry though or ball me out because.........

First page of Williams' three-page letter to Fan Club President L. Allan Smith, dated July 31, 1957.

endeavors (piano playing, songwriting),[253] and about his personal doubts and feelings.[254] The same eagerness is again displayed in the final page of the letter, where Williams adds the following (unfortunately unverifiable) news:

14.   Did an interview with Donna Contant [?] last week. She's moving to Arizona and would like to start a new chapter there.

15.   Did a tape recording for Margaret Bell, Lilyan and Jack (Margaret's brother) Sunday. (GW2, 3)

The July letter proves one thing at least: though undoubtedly ambitious and concentrated on his career in the 1950s, Williams was not "all business"; he was a polite, personable man who knew how to write a gracious, friendly letter. The closing of the above July letter is also affectionate, but with a pinch of unexpected wit: "Can't think of another thing. It's quite late so will hang up now." (GW2, 3) Williams' Fan Club was still gestating through those first seven months of 1957. This is confirmed by the August issue of *Movie Stars Parade* magazine, where the Grant Williams Fan Club is listed in the "New Clubs" section of the Fan Club Corner.[255]

Williams' former Secretary Nina Ingris confirms that, by the time she met the actor and started lending a hand in 1958, the Fan Club was in place.

I had just arrived in Los Angeles from Brazil, where my parents and I had lived as Czechoslovakian refugees for twelve years. The United States had been our dream all along; they were certainly my dream. I was a big movie fan, and when I arrived in Los Angeles, I wanted to get close to the Hollywood dream factory somehow. I had no ambition to be an actress; I just wanted to be near the entertainment world.

I was a fan of George Nader at the time, and I somehow found the address of Lilyan A. Miller, who was President of the

---

253. See Chapter 13.

254. See Chapters 7, 13, and 14.

255. "Fan Club Corner," *Movie Stars Parade*, August 1957.

Grant Williams with Fan Club Secretary Nina Ingris, née Karpuschkin; undated, but circa 1961, most likely on the set of Williams' The Couch (1962).

George Nader Fan Club and was deeply involved in the fan-club business, especially around Universal-International. We met, and she introduced me to some friends who happened to be at her place, including Bill Singer and Grant Williams;[256]

256. William F. L. Singer, photographer and collector, was also involved in many a Fan Club in the 1950s. His life is lionized (rather hagiographically and ungrammatically) in Tony Bond, *Il Mondo: One Man's World*, AuthorHouse, 2012, where we find this passage: "[In 1957…] Bill had the pleasure of meeting Lilyan A. Miller, president of the George Nader Club and her guests, Grant

Grant needed someone to take care of his fan-club correspondence. I did not know shorthand or stenography, but I had learned something called speedwriting, which was similar; that was my one technical qualification, aside from my language skills (excellent English, German, and French); my enthusiasm did the rest. I was hired on the spot.

The Fan Club had already been set up when I volunteered; *The Incredible Shrinking Man* and *The Monolith Monsters* had been released. There were already several chapters all over the United States.

I was not paid for my work; I had a day job at Bank of America, and did my work for Grant out of love for the movies, and out of friendship. Being close to a movie star, and being invited to movie sets at the studios, was all the reward I needed.

I worked from my home, which during those last years of the 1950s was only blocks away from Grant's, on the same street;[257] Grant would set me up with stacks of photographs of different sizes (some already signed, some unsigned) and reams of his stationery. I received and sorted the fans' letters and requests, sometimes typed something in response to their queries if they wanted more than a photograph; then, about once a week, I would go to Grant's home and he would sign letters and photographs.

Grant was never lazy or jaded about this aspect of being a star; he was enthusiastic, and happy to give himself to the process and to his fans, adding something to the letters or making sure he personalized the photos' inscriptions. Grant never asked me to take care of his personal correspondence for him; he did that on his own. I don't remember there being any general assemblies or meetings of the fan clubs, so the club did not exist as a physical entity. There was only correspondence (NI).

An attempt to revive fan perception, and Williams' Fan Club, appeared in

---

Williams star of the *Incredible Shrinking Man*, and Rex Reason."

257. 1234 N. Hayworth Avenue (Williams' address was 1314 N. Hayworth Avenue).

newspapers in 1963, when Williams' career was faltering and the series *Hawaiian Eye* had just been canceled:

> Grant Williams doesn't believe in "letting George do it!" He does it himself.
>
> The star of ABC-TV's "Hawaiian Eye" series [...] has the courage of his convictions by enlisting his numerous fan clubs in the fight against juvenile delinquency.
>
> "We find responsible and mature leaders who'll work with youngsters in their towns. I get together with these groups whenever I can. We never lecture, but we attempt to foster good citizenship by placing the accent on dressing and behaving properly. We must set the example. I believe by using our influence in a constructive way, we can repay whatever gifts have been given us. With a little effort, we can make delinquents look like squares—which is what they really are!"[258]

This desire of Williams' to "set the example" is confirmed by other statements he made over the years. In a 1961 interview with the *Los Angeles Times'* Don Alpert, Williams lamented the fact that he was not a big star yet and imagined what kind of positive social influence he might exercise if he were to achieve that status:

> As a big star, I could certainly do a great deal to influence teenage thinking. I could scream my head off and it would be printed. I've got 2000 kids in a fan club who will do anything I tell them to do. You have no idea how frightening this is. It's the responsibility of the actor at a minimum not to do harm. And if he's a responsible and charitable human being, to do good, as well.
>
> I'm not moralizing. I'm not this square. I have a private life that I think is horrible. But my strict responsibility is not to influence wrongly.[259]

---

258. *Hazleton (PA) Standard-Speaker*, June 1, 1963.

259. Alpert (1961), op. cit.

Grant Williams with Secretary Nina Karpuschkin, probably on the set of
The Couch, circa 1961.

A curious report, indirectly connected to Williams' Fan Club, appeared
in the Illinois press on December 29, 1959. It concerned Chaw Mank
(Charles Mank Jr., 1902–1985), songwriter, band leader, record producer,
collector and fan-club operator,[260] who was a member of the Grant Williams Fan Club under acting President Charles Thomas between 1959
and 1960. Here is the frivolous tidbit from the *Edwardsville Intelligencer*
(Mank was a native of Staunton, Ill.):

---

260. From the blog *The World's Worst Records*: "seen any dead country stars recently?"
    posted on January 20, 2009.

Chaw Mank, song writer and orchestra leader, this year received over 50 Christmas cards from the famous stars of TV and radio. Total of cards, over thirteen hundred.

Some of the stars who sent cards were Elvis Presley, Jane Wyman, Lawrence Welk, Maureen O'Hara, Scott Brady, Pat Boone, Liberace, Hildegarde, Steve Rowland, Dick Jones, Jimmy Rodgers, Grant Williams, Carolyn Jones, Beverly Garland, Hugh O'Brian, Tod Andres, Minna Gombell.

Gifts were received from Liberace, Pat Boone.

Some of the cards and gifts came from Austria, England, Indonesia, Philippine Islands, Hawaii and France.[261]

261. "Receives Many Yule Cards," *Edwardsville (IL) Intelligencer*, December 29, 1959.

9

Television Work (and Some Radio), 1957–1965

THE 1957–1959 PERIOD, following the release of *The Monolith Monsters*, constituted a moment of transition for Grant Williams. Universal-International did not renew his contract upon its expiration, and Williams found himself between studios.[262] Television, however, was flourishing, and Williams continued his alternate career for the small screen during this period of transition as well as throughout his Warner Bros. tenure (1960–1963). On rare occasions, he made a radio appearance.

Matinee Theater II: "The- Flashing Stream"

On April 12, 1957, Williams appeared in the *Matinee Theater* color broadcast of the drama "The Flashing Stream." Here is a brief plot outline from the contemporary press:

> The first Broadway play[263] by Charles Morgan, well known author of *The Fountain*,[264] was adapted by Kathleen and Robert Howard Lindsay. It tells the story of a boy and girl, each bril-

---

262. The 1958 annual magazine *Who's Who in Hollywood* ended its bio of Williams with the sentence "[Williams is] now free-lancing." This would seem to indicate that his contract had expired in 1957. This is also confirmed by Lamparski (RL), who states Williams had been under contract to Universal for three years.

263. Charles Morgan, *The Flashing Stream*, Macmillan & Co. Ltd., 1939. Charles Langbridge Morgan (1894–1958) was a British novelist, playwright, and drama critic.

264. Charles Morgan, *The Fountain*, Macmillan, 1932.

liant young scientists, who are thrown together to develop a top secret project on a remote island.[265]

And here is a slightly contrasting synopsis: "Charles Morgan's drama of a dual relationship between a naval officer and a woman mathematician."[266]

Morgan's lengthy three-act play—about 220 pages in its published version—dealt with some Ibsenian conflicts between science and love, failure and hope, dominance and subservience, ambition and resignation, pure mind and bodily passion.

The London critics held Morgan's play in high regard, lavishing glowing adjectives on it during its successful Lyric Theatre engagement in 1938. Broadway audiences and American critics were much less enthusiastic: when the London production moved to New York's Biltmore Theater in April 1939, it was lambasted, closing after a week's run. Here is what the drama critic of *The Pittsburgh Press* concluded after seeing the play:

> Mr. Morgan, I fear, must grow less mathematical about his romance and less romantic about his mathematics if he is to be a successful dramatist in these parts. I wish he would grow less sacerdotal about sex, too.[267]

Lux Video Theatre III and IV: "Paris Calling" and "Barren Harvest"

A contemporary daily newspaper gives us at least a plot summary of the May 30, 1957 episode ("Paris Calling") of the television series *Lux Video Theatre*:

> Joanne Dru and Grant Williams [...] star in a drama of the French underground, "Paris Calling," also starring Jacques Aubuchon with Abraham Sofaer and Anne Seymour. Behind "Paris Calling," the code transmitter which threatened German security during the Nazi invasion of Paris, was the beautiful

---

265. *San Bernardino (CA) Daily Sun*, April 12, 1957.

266. *Melbourne Age*, September 26, 1957.

267. "London Drama Critic's Play, 'The Flashing Stream,' Considered Pompous Story of Love and Logarithms," *Pittsburgh (PA) Press*, April 16, 1939.

The caption for this photograph was the following when it appeared in *The Philadelphia Inquirer* on May 30, 1957: "Joanne Dru gets into trouble with the French Underground when she falls for suspected Gestapo agent Grant Williams in 'Paris Calling' On NBC's 'Lux Video Theater' at 10 tonight on Channel 3." Scan from newspaper.

Marianne (Miss Dru), who had joined the underground to retaliate for the tragedy in her family, caused by the Germans. Compassionately, she aids an injured soldier, Nick (Williams), who has lost his identification. Underground members, suspecting he belongs to the Gestapo, question Marianne's loyalty to their cause—and test her with an extremely dangerous assignment, on which the outcome of her life might depend.[268]

---

268. *San Bernardino (CA) Daily Sun*, May 30, 1957.

The August 8 episode of the same drama series, "Barren Harvest" (color, August 8, 1957), was based on a 1949 mystery novel by C.M. Nelson. A plot summary appeared nationwide on the day the episode aired:[269] "Color. 'Barren Harvest,' starring Grant Williams. A designing law clerk thinks he has committed the perfect crime but lives to learn there is no such thing, not in his case, at least."[270]

Here is more detail from another daily:

> Grant Williams is starred and Vaughn Taylor, Mabel Albertson and Audrey Dalton co-starred. The clerk ([Byron] Foulger) conceives the plan to murder his employer and enlists the aid of his employer's housekeeper.[271]

Yet another detail was added by *The Pittsburgh Press*: "A conniving law clerk murders his employer, and tries to pin the crime on the dead man's nephew.[272]

Judging from the original novel, Williams' character, David Forrest, the dead man's nephew, is the catalyst of the crime; envy and greed fuel the managing clerk's plan to murder his employer, Mr. Herbert Bayford, for fear that David, a promising Oxford student, might inherit his uncle's affections, his fortune, and a place in his law firm. David is also the falsely accused suspect and one of the investigators of the crime, not to mention the love interest of the female lead, so Williams is definitely the protagonist of the drama. He was certainly showcased as such in many newspapers of the time, which displayed a headshot of Williams next to the title of the show in their advertising. Nelson's novel can best be described as pleasant but contrived.[273]

---

269. And Williams himself, in his July 1957 letter, announces: "Before I forget—I will be on *Lux Video Theatre* starring in 'Barren Harvest' Thursday, August 8th (next week) channel 4 (check the time)" (GW2, 3).

270. *Eugene (OR) Guard*, August 8, 1957.

271. *Dover (OH) Daily Reporter*, August 8, 1957.

272. *Pittsburgh (PA) Press*, August 8, 1957.

273. C.M. Nelson, *Barren Harvest*, Crime Club/Doubleday, 1949. The *Pasadena Independent* referred to Nelson as "C.M. Nelson of Pasadena" ("Perfect Crime," *Pasadena Independent*, August 8, 1957).

Radio: *Family Theater*

An announcement of a rare radio appearance by Williams was published in the *Los Angeles Times* on September 11, 1957. The show was *Family Theater* (1947–1957), and the newspaper's comment was the following: "Grant Williams stars in the hilarious experiences of a haggard television writer who decides to 'rough it' on his summer vacation, in 'Roadshow.' Joan Leslie is tonight's hostess."[274]

The anthology radio show *Family Theater* was produced for the Mutual Broadcasting System (also called the Mutual Network) by Family Theater Productions, an extension of Father Patrick Payton's Family Rosary Crusade (whose iconic motto was, and is, "The family That Prays Together Stays Together"). The episode starring Grant Williams (number 540) was the show's last. *Family Theater*'s parallel television incarnation, entitled *Family Theatre*, which had debuted in 1951, would close in 1958.

While the episode in question[275] is not quite as hilarious as the *Los Angeles Times*' plug boasted but only mildly amusing, it provides further proof of Grant Williams' vocal versatility, this time in a lighthearted vein.

Williams' character, Charles L. Blackwell, is a successful television writer who desperately needs a break from show business and plans a weeklong family vacation to leave that world behind. His car trip from Los Angeles to San Francisco with his wife and daughter (with ill-fated stops in Bakersfield, Tulare, Sacramento, and Lake Tahoe) proves calamitous, with continuous mishaps along the way. Once in San Francisco, Charles discovers that, ironically, the parking attendant of the posh hotel where he and his family are staying desires nothing more than to discuss Charles's scripts and to write for television himself. Charles Blackwell does not shrink like Scott Carey, but his road trip—intended as a restful diversion—turns into a harrowing odyssey for him, one that leaves him exhausted and demoralized in the end.

The comedic episode is pleasant, but most of its gags are of middling quality. Two scenes stand out: the one in which Charles bickers with his wife about map-reading during the trip, and the one in which his tempo-

---

274. *Los Angeles Times*, radio listings, September 11, 1957.

275. At the time of writing, the episode was available for download from the website "Old Time Radio Downloads."

rary hearing loss (due to his infelicitous attempt at water-skiing) makes him an impossible interlocutor for his wife and daughter. These moments display Williams' secure command of pace and timing. This virtue notwithstanding, Williams was no comedian, and his readings are fundamentally dramatic.

That *Family Theater* was a show inclined towards mildness should not come as a surprise. The show's proclivities were clearly expressed in its introduction, spoken on this particular evening by Hostess Joan Leslie: "*Family Theater*'s only purpose is to bring to everyone's attention a practice that must become an important part of our lives, if we are to win peace for ourselves, peace for our families, and peace for the world. *Family Theater* urges you to pray, pray together as a family."

Grant Williams was not only a student of comparative religion but also a rather fervent catholic (in later years, this fervor would increase, as stated with satisfaction by his *Incredible Shrinking Man* co-star Randy Stuart),[276] and *Family Theater*'s religious inclination might have been a factor in Williams' decision to star in the show; he was, however, only the last of a long list of major and minor film and television performers to do likewise over its ten-year run. To name but a few: Lucille Ball, Jack Benny, Bing Crosby, Irene Dunne, Charlton Heston, Gregory Peck, James Stewart, and Jane Wyatt.

If one looks closely, one can discover that this episode subtly resonates with symbolic references to Williams' life and career. At the end of his Univeral-International tenure, only a few months after the release of *The Incredible Shrinking Man* and a few months before the release of *The Monolith Monsters*, it is not unlikely that Williams was able to recognize the warning signs (or the *fait accompli*) at U-I. On some level, Charles L. Blackwell's desperate flight from the television industry and his peremptory order to his family that, "*For the next seven days, no-one even mentions the words plot, story, character, or script,*" must have hit close to home for the Method actor saying those words.

Other actors in the cast included Lillian Buyeff and Howard McNear; the episode was scripted and directed by John T. Kelley.

---

276. See Chapter 6.

False Starts I: *Matinee Theater*: "The Little Minister"

Online databases such as IMDb or The Classic TV Archive do not mention Grant Williams' role in *Matinee Theater*'s episode "The Little Minister" (color, airdate December 26, 1957). As a matter of fact, they mention Ben Cooper as its protagonist. Most 1957 newspapers, on the other hand, only mentioned two names in their advance listings of the episode, Margaret O'Brien and Grant Williams, indicating that the two actors were the protagonists of the show.

Grant Williams was, in fact, slated for the titular role according to NBC's advertising for the drama; but something went wrong, as the *San Bernardino Daily Sun* reported on the day of the broadcast:

> Film actor Ben Cooper has been cast in the title role of today's drama, "The Little Minister," following withdrawal of Grant Williams from the role in the James M. Barrie classic.[277]

It is possible that Williams, miffed with Universal-International after their termination of his contract, was running low on patience and walked off the show for any number of petty reasons; or that, for the same reasons, he was fired.

Here is a plot outline from the *Statesman Journal* of Salem, Oregon: "This is the story of a young minister who risks the wrath of his mother and his congregation for the love of the beautiful but outcast gypsy girl."[278]

Jane Wyman Presents: "Tunnel Eight"

February 20, 1958 saw Williams starring with Preston Foster in the episode "Tunnel Eight" of the television drama series *Jane Wyman Presents* (also known as *The Fireside Theatre*, 1955–1958). The story involved railroad construction in the West, General Grant and the Army, a crooked crew member, and a brave construction engineer. Here is a plot summary from a daily newspaper:

---

277. *San Bernardino (CA) Daily Sun*, December 26, 1957.

278. *Salem (OR) Statesman Journal*, December 26, 1957.

General Grant is called upon to use the army in aiding construction of railroads west, a year after the Civil War, in "Tunnel Eight," starring Preston Foster and co-starring Grant Williams […].

Lt. Larry Dunham (Williams) is assigned by General Grant (Joseph Crehan) to bring construction engineer Dan McGann (Foster) to him to make sure that the railroads are built.

McGann's first assignment is with Central Pacific, the railroad that has bogged down at a point called Tunnel Eight, apparently because the builders can't make headway through the mountain.

Dan soon learns that the delay is deliberate and means big money to certain people—among them Roy Evans, the engineer of this section, and Boomer Doyle, who runs the place where supplies for the road are piled up and temptation waits to lure a man with sweet smells of wine and women.[279]

Radio: *Carr'l Righter*

On March 23, 1958, Williams was the featured guest on the half-hour FM-radio program *Carr'l Righter*, broadcast in the Los Angeles area by KRHM. Host Carroll Righter (1900–1988) was known as the "Astrologer to the Stars." The program was re-broadcast on March 30.

Matinee Theater III: "The End of a Season"

Grant Williams was a piano player in real life, and quite a good one. So good, that Columnist Rual Askew referred to him as a "concert pianist" and Williams described himself as "a student concert pianist." So good, that plans were made (but apparently never carried out) for his appearance at a Hollywood Symphony Orchestra concert as keyboard soloist.[280]

---

279. "Foster, Williams Co-Star In 'Jane Wyman Show,'" *Provo (UT) Daily Herald*, February 17, 1958.

280. See Chapter 13.

In view of this skill, it must have been a joy for Williams to play the role of a pianist in the *Matinee Theater* drama that was broadcast in color on June 3, 1958. The episode was entitled "The End of a Season." For additional connections between this episode and Williams' career, we might also point out that the concert pianist in question is blind (shades of Williams' scene in the 1955 TV movie *Allen in Movieland*). Several 1958 dailies mentioned Grant Williams as protagonist; on June 3, 1958, the *Long Beach Independent* of California published the following full cast list, headed by Grant Williams' name: Grant Williams, Mark Roberts, Julie Bennett, Nancy Hadley.

The story concerns Michael Lawrence, once a well-known concert pianist, who was blinded in an accident ten years ago and now lives a quiet life with his wife. Michael begins to entertain the hope that his eyesight might be restored when his wife's younger sister pays him a visit, bringing with her a famous eye surgeon. The surgeon proposes an operation, which Michael undergoes. The operation is successful, but happiness eludes him: his affections have meanwhile shifted from his wife to her sister, "with tragic results for the entire family."[281]

To date, no online resource (including IMDb) has mentioned Williams' participation in this episode. In contrast to the press of 1958, the Classic TV Archive (ctva.biz), the website tv.com, and IMDb all list the title of the episode as "The End of the Season."

Shirley Temple's Storybook; "The Wild Swans"

On September 7, 1958, Williams co-starred with Phyllis Love in the episode "The Wild Swans" of the TV series *Shirley Temple's Storybook* (1958–1961). A fellow Actors Studio alumna, Ms. Love was a native of Iowa; here is a blurb about the show from the *Des Moines Sunday Register*:

> Phyllis Love and Grant Williams, two promising young people who are comparatively new to TV, attain stardom on the medium Friday when they appear on "The Wild Swans" [...]
>
> Grant Williams, who will be seen as "King Julio" on "The Wild Swans," came to TV from the movies, where he was "The

---

281. *Arizona Republic* (Phoenix, AZ), television listings, June 3, 1958.

Incredible Shrinking Man." [...] A New Yorker, he served in the air force during the Korean War. He is 28 and a bachelor.[282]

The *Daily Herald* of Provo, Utah, helped with a plot summary on the occasion of a rerun:

> A wicked old queen and a kind young prince struggle for the life of a young princess (Phyllis Love) [...].
>
> With Miss Temple as hostess and narrator there is unfolded the story of the wicked queen Flavia (Olive Deering) who seeks the help of a witch (Anne O'Neal) in her plot to remove her stepchildren as heirs to the throne. The witch prepares a magic potion that will turn them into wild swans, legal prey for any hunter in the kingdom.
>
> Princess Elisa (Miss Love) is spirited from the castle and hidden in the forest. The Queen sends her soldiers after the princess who escapes with the help of Binky (Melville Cooper), faithful tutor at the court. Binky leads her to a magician (Joseph Wiseman), who reveals that her three brothers are now swans but can be brought back to manhood if she will perform a difficult and selfless task. Elisa vows to keep the silence imposed by the magician and to perform the task. She nearly falls when a young king (Grant Williams) falls in love with her and begs her to speak to him. She succeeds in freeing her brothers, then breaks the silence to express her love for the young king.[283]

"Better than usual," sentenced *The Arizona Republic* of Phoenix about the show on September 12.

Man with a Camera: "Another Barrier"

In November 1958, Williams played Major Sandy Dickson of the United States Air Force in the episode "Another Barrier" (airdate November 28, 1958) of the television series *Man with a Camera* (1958–1960),

---

282. *Des Moines (IA) Sunday Register*, September 7, 1958.

283. *Provo (UT) Daily Herald*, October 19, 1959.

starring Charles Bronson as the titular character, ersatz freelance Photographer Mike Kovac.

Major Dickson, of Edwards Air Force Base in California, is the subject of Kovac's photo spread on a new fighter jet, the X-2, and on its test flight piloted by Dickson. Williams is excellent in the role, but the dramatic balance of the episode is slanted in favor of the tedious hysterics of Dickson's anxious fiancée Liz (Norma Crane) and of her dark forebodings before and during his mission. When radio communication from the pilot is cut off in mid-flight, everyone fears the worst, and Liz's premature mourning and suicide attempt pull the focus of the denouement away from Dickson, engaging Kovac in her melodramatic rescue instead.

Still, the half-hour drama is conducted proficiently, and the delicate frisson created by the episode's relation to Williams' real-life Air Force service in Korea is certainly fascinating for anyone keeping track of Williams' personal history. Williams changes Air Force costumes several

Major Sandy Dickson (Grant Williams, right) reluctantly submits to being photographed in his long johns by the titular man with a camera (Charles Bronson, left) as he prepares for his test flight. Frame capture from "Another Barrier" (1958).

Shades of Korea: Grant Williams wearing full Air Force pilot gear in
"Another Barrier." Frame capture.

times in the show, going from coveralls to dress uniform to base casual to
long johns to full pilot gear and helmet.

Williams' relaxed, self-effacing acting is a pleasure to watch (it is ex-
quisitely natural and likeable in this episode), but the script cuts his involvement short in the second half of the show. Fortunately, the suspense
connected to Major Dickson's absence carries considerable tension: even
missing, Williams' character resonates through the episode, and his rescue comes as quite a relief, not only for his nervous fiancée.

Walt Disney Presents: "The Peter Tchaikovsky Story"

In some ways, the choice of Grant Williams for the role of Russian
Composer Pyotr Ilyich Tchaikovsky (1840–1893) in Walt Disney's half-
hour television special "The Peter Tchaikovsky Story" (filmed in color
and broadcast in black and white on January 30, 1959) was perfect casting. Williams' relationship with classical music was a life-long love affair; aside from playing the piano and being a concertgoer and operagoer,

he wrote song lyrics and occasionally participated in musical events as reader or guest speaker. According to those who had the privilege to hear him play, he was a gifted pianist.[284] One can catch a glimpse of this talent (mimed though it might have been to a certain extent for the benefit of filming) in Disney's half-hour biographical sketch.

Music and piano playing were not all that Williams and Tchaikovsky had in common. Both were undervalued for their work during their lifetimes; both suffered from some form of psychological/emotional unease, such as depression; and both died at the age of fifty-three. Both were also rumored to be gay, but, while in Tchaikovsky's case there is now definitive documental proof of such inclination,[285] in the case of Williams there is only uncorroborated (and controversial) hearsay.[286]

"The Peter Tchaikovsky Story" was intended as a tie-in to Walt Disney's theatrical release of the CinemaScope animated feature *Sleeping Beauty*, which premiered in Los Angeles on January 29 (the day before the broadcast). The feature film was entirely scored with adaptations of Tchaikovsky's music from his eponymous ballet; the television show paid biographical homage both to the Russian musical genius and to his compositions—particularly to the genesis of *Sleeping Beauty*.

The broadcast, which included the half-hour biography plus another thirty minutes of promotional footage focusing on Disney's feature film, came complete with instructions for obtaining a simulated stereophonic-sound effect at home. These instructions were attached to many of the newspaper announcements heralding the show on its airdate, and spoken by Walt Disney himself on the evening of the broadcast. Here is one such how-to scheme from the *Cincinnati Enquirer*:

> The program is presented in three-source sound. Two-way stereophonic sound may be heard by auditors seated at the point of a triangle four to six feet, center, away from a base of AM

---

284. On November 4, 1961, the *Hazleton (PA) Standard-Speaker* went so far as to write: "Grant Williams […] was a concert pianist in real life."

285. For further reading on Tchaikovsky's life, see for example: Leslie Kearney, *Tchaikovsky and His World*, Princeton University Press, 1998; Alexander Poznansky, ed., *Tchaikovsky Through Others' Eyes*, Indiana University Press, 1999.

286. See Chapter 14.

> radio and TV sets placed four to six feet apart. For three-way
> sound tonight by WCPO-TV put TV set center, FM radio left,
> and AM radio right. Sit center opposite TV set.[287]

The script of "The Peter Tchaikovsky Story" is maudlin and soft-hearted, spuriously based on Tchaikovsky's diaries. Even in Disney's edulcorated telling, however, Tchaikovsky is a tormented individual, and Williams is quite intense in expressing the composer's suffering and rage. What is special about the program is the constant presence of Tchaikovsky's music, some of it hauntingly beautiful—such as the lovely test theme the young composer receives from Conservatory Director Anton Rubinstein (Leon Askin) as an assignment for variation work. (Young Peter takes his assignment seriously, and writes 215 variations in one day.)

Disney's half-hour biopic, like many of his live-action television efforts, might seem naïve and syrupy today; in fact, it might have seemed old-fashioned to some even in 1959. Audience tastes were beginning to change, and demographically Disney's wares already appeared tailored for grandmothers, grandchildren, and few others. Even Disney's love for, and promotion of, classical music was destined to be inexorably outmoded in just a few years; in 1959, before the irreparable rift between pop/rock and classical, it still constituted mainstream entertainment.

In the three decades preceding "The Peter Tchaikovsky Story," the entertainment industry—films, radio, television, and animated cartoons—had been devoted to classical music, or had at least been liberal in its use. Films about composers and classical instrumentalists had been common in Hollywood; the film scores of composers like Max Steiner and Erich Wolfgang Korngold had been late-romantic symphonic compositions; and Carl Stalling's scores for Warner's *Looney Toones* had been brimming with music references—references that a large portion of the mainstream audience would probably have recognized. The music of Beethoven, of Grofé, of Lalo, of Rossini, of Johann Strauss Jr., of Von Suppé, and of Wagner—the alternative "Pops" of those decades— had been mother's milk to American audiences. After 1960, the fate of music, and of soundtracks, was destined to change. A film like Disney's *Fantasia*, for example, which had been a wonderful dare even in 1940,

---

287. *Cincinnati Enquirer*, January 30, 1959.

would have been a marketing nightmare in 1965 or 1970. This die-hard affection for classical music on Disney's part adds poignancy and charm to dated but heartwarming valentines such as "The Peter Tchaikovsky Story" and *Sleeping Beauty*.

So intense was Disney's love for music, that the premiere of *Sleeping Beauty* at the Fox Wilshire Theater (today the Saban Theater, 8440 Wilshire Boulevard, Beverly Hills) was preceded by Disney's thirty-minute wordless documentary film *Grand Canyon* (1958), photographed in Technicolor and CinemaScope by Ernst A. Heiniger, directed by James Algar, and set to the five-movement symphonic suite *Grand Canyon* by Composer Ferde Grofé (1892–1972). This Academy-Award-winning spectacle, more than the animated feature that followed it, elicited a rave from *Los Angeles Times* Reviewer Philip K. Scheuer.[288] Scheuer's enthusiasm was understandable: nineteen years after Disney's *Fantasia* and twenty-three years before Godfrey Reggio's *Koyannisqatsi* (1982), the film was a stunning, and charming, "pictorial interpretation" of music, which (like *Koyannisqatsi*) included time-lapse photography and a phenomenal use of visual rhythm.

The few reviews for "The Peter Tchaikovsky Story" were positive, though not without some reservations. The *Albuquerque Journal* had this to say:

> After your ears have been assaulted by three pronunciations of Tchaikovsky's name (only the actors get it right), a charming half-hour follows with a sensitive study of the brilliant composer's early years. His music forms an eloquent background, and the performances of Rex Hill (Peter the boy) and Grant Williams (Peter the man) are convincing. Just when your appetite has been thoroughly aroused, Disney stops short and spends the next half hour plugging his new movie. Too bad, particularly since Tchaikovsky's life is so much more dramatic.[289]

Some reviewers even started criticizing before the show aired:

---

288. Philip K. Scheuer, "'Sleeping Beauty' Is Typical Disney," *Los Angeles Times*, January 30, 1959.

289. *Albuquerque (NM) Journal*, January 30, 1959.

Composer Pyotr Ilyich Tchaikovsky (Grant Williams) receives a "Dear John" letter in Disney's "The Peter Tchaikovsky Story" (1959). Frame capture.

"DA – DA – DA – DUM!" I don't know what Walt Disney will come up with by way of a Tchaikovsky biography tonight on 9 at 8 o'clock. But the boys have some real good dramatic material going for them going in—provided they care to follow events in the life of Peter Ilyich instead of telling us a story based on a movie about the life of a famous Russian composer and entitled: "And Then I Wrote."

Press releases cause one to fear that the "And Then I Wrote" school of musical biography may prevails [sic]. A very popular magazine currently features a press department photograph of Grant Williams playing the piano while Narda Onyx sings. The caption reads: "Tchaikovsky accompanies his future wife Desiree Artot." Accompany her he did. But marry her he did not—not in this life, anyway.

[...] But no matter. If tonight's TV show has Tchaikovsky music (and it will have), there probably isn't a story in the world which can spoil the program.[290]

290. E.B. Radcliffe, "For Love Of Pete," *Cincinnati Enquirer*, January 30, 1959.

The above reviewer attacked Walt Disney for the inaccuracy of his press releases. Notwithstanding this warning, most newspaper television desks (including the *Cincinnati Enquirer*'s own) dutifully reproduced further inaccuracies from the studio without checking facts. Even AP Correspondent Charles Mercer, usually an accurate journalist, wrote: "The story follows the composer through his early disappointments to his first success, 'The Sleeping Beauty.'"[291]

Had those television-desk staffers bothered to check, they would have realized that Disney's press releases were wrong on more than one count. The ballet *Sleeping Beauty* was not Tchaikovsky's "first success," but a late work dated 1889 (four years before the composer's death), and it was only because of tie-in exigencies that it came to be the composer's "first success" in Disney's telling of Tchaikovsky's young years. Tchaikovsky's *Sleeping Beauty* was well received upon its premiere, but it was never a great success during the composer's lifetime; neither was his first ballet, *Swan Lake* (1877). In our perception more than a century later, of course, Tchaikovsky's *oeuvre* contains many "successes," most of them preceding *Sleeping Beauty*: for example, his overture *Romeo and Juliet* (1870), his Piano Concerto n. 1 (1875), his opera *Eugene Onegin* (1878), and his Serenade in C for Strings (1880).

Other inattentive journalists made mistakes of their own without Disney's help. *Sun-Herald* Columnist Valda Marshall of Sydney, Australia, in her advance announcement of the Australian broadcast of Disney's Tchaikovsky biography, wrote: "The Peter Tchaikovsky Story is a dramatisation of the boyhood and early manhood of the composer, with Guy Williams (star of the TV series Zorro) playing the title role."[292]

Yancy Derringer: "Longhair"

Williams' guest-starring role in the episode "Longhair" (airdate March 5, 1959) of the television series *Yancy Derringer* (1958–1959) was definitely a character turn.

---

291. Charles Mercer (AP), "Here Are Highlights Slated In Next Week on Television," *Circleville (OH) Herald*, January 30, 1959.

292. Valda Marshall, "Attlee and Evatt in panel show," *Sydney Sun-Herald*, November 22, 1958.

Grant Williams (right) plays General Custer and X Brands (left) Yancy Derringer's associate Pahoo-Ke-Ta-Wah in "Longhair" (1959). Frame capture.

General George Armstrong Custer (Grant Williams), on suspension from his Army post, pays a visit to an old acquaintance in New Orleans. As soon as he steps off the ship, he becomes the victim of a series of attacks on his life, seemingly of Comanche authorship. Only the quick reflexes of *bon-vivant* action man Yancy Derringer (series regular Jock Mahoney), who is in the welcoming committee, prevent Custer from being killed. The culprit turns out to be a disgruntled Army Captain seeking revenge for the demise of his Comanche wife, who died in one of Custer's unscrupulous raids.

Custer is not a sympathetic figure in this story. He is presented as an impulsive, irritable egotist, and as a vain fop. This enables Williams to pull out some comedy stops, which he does, but in a dignified manner, without resorting to any untoward shtick.

Custer's introduction takes place in his ship cabin; as the ship prepares for docking, he foppishly grooms his mustache while admiring himself in the mirror, Scarlet Pimpernel style, his curly hair flowing ele-

Vanity, thy name is George Armstrong Custer. This is the character's introduction in "Longhair." Frame capture.

gantly to his shoulders. It is a priceless intro for a character who becomes increasingly annoying as the episode progresses, and it is a pity that the creative team avoids a more comedic approach—probably in the interest of historical prudence, or in order not to alienate the action fans. Taken just one step further, the character of Custer would have made a great comic vignette, perhaps in the Yosemite Sam vein; instead, he is just irksome.

There are flickers of life in the episode in general, and in the rest of the cast (even Jock Mahoney is a little livelier than usual), but those germs are never developed. As for Custer, he was, after all, a hero of sorts, or at least an American legend, so the episode straddles the two registers of awe and irreverence until the end, when a farewell committee sees the General off at the docks and the episode closes on a semi-patriotic note.

Walt Disney Presents: Texas John Slaughter
"The Man from Bitter Creek" and "The Slaughter Trail"

Evidently, 1959 was a Disney year for Grant Williams (as well as one of his busiest: he appeared in one film and seven television episodes). After his starring role in "The Peter Tchaikovsky Story," Williams was assigned a sizeable guest-starring role in two episodes of Disney's western series *Texas John Slaughter* (1958–1961). Together, the two episodes, "The Man from Bitter Creek" (color, airdate March 6, 1959) and "The Slaughter Trail" (color, airdate March 20, 1959), advance the story of John Slaughter and of his pioneering creation of a new cattle trail through Comanche territory in New Mexico.

Williams' role is not huge in terms of screen time, but it is important in terms of story. Williams plays Mike Forbes, one of two brothers who befriend Slaughter and help him on his trailblazing adventures.

The episodes, and the series itself, are pleasant enough (though historically dubious); Williams' underwritten character is also a sympathetic one. Unfortunately for him, there are too many characters around, and too much plot, for his work to be memorable. A closer look, however, reveals a lively, committed performance and subtle, expert reactions to the other characters.

After three important roles in Disney's television shows, something was definitely brewing for Williams at Walt Disney Productions, as reported by some dailies in March 1959:

> Walt Disney is drawing up a chair at his "Swiss Family Robinson" feature-length movie dinner table for his TV contractee, Grant Williams—no relation to Walt's other TV star, Guy (Zorro) Williams.[293]

Unfortunately for Williams, and for us, that dinner table ultimately did not include Grant Williams.

The Millionaire: "Millionaire Gilbert Burton"

In April 1959, Williams played one of the most delightful roles of his career in the episode "Millionaire Gilbert Burton" (airdate April 29, 1959)

---

293. Mike Connolly, "Hollywood," *Pittsburgh (PA) Post-Gazette*, March 19, 1959.

of the television series *The Millionaire* (1955–1960). The premise of the series: an eccentric millionaire periodically donates a million dollars to a different deserving poor person, on condition of remaining anonymous. No other strings attached. Each half-hour episode traced the ripples such donation caused in the life of the recipient.

The donee of the week in this episode is Gilbert Burton (Carleton Carpenter), a likeable, gangly youth who works as a dishwasher at a New York nightclub. He has a crush on Margo (Dolores Donlon), the glamorous ballroom dancer who performs nightly at the club with her partner Maurice (Grant Williams). Once Gilbert becomes rich, he approaches the two and befriends them. The dancers, who are really Maggie Carter and her brother Mike, can spot a pigeon when they see one, and when Gilbert proposes that they use their two free weeks before a Chicago engagement to show him who's who and what's what in New York City, they jump on the bandwagon with enthusiasm.

Mike Carter is a swindler, but a likeable one, and there is an air of cheerful innocence about the story that prevents anyone from being too unpleasant or dangerous. Mike gladly takes money from his eager mark,

Grant Williams as Mike Carter in "Millionaire Gilbert Burton" (1959). Frame capture.

involving him in some misguided business propositions and in New York's glamorous night life.

Maggie, however, finds that she is enjoying Gilbert's company, and is having second thoughts; she is also worried that her brother might be taking the game too far, and tries to convince him to give some of the money back. What she does not know is that Gilbert is much less gullible than he appears, and has been aware of Mike's game all along; only, (a) he is in love with Maggie, and (b) he intends to keep an eye on Mike to help him go straight. Thus, it is with the unselfish excuse of "*getting a good brother-in-law for Mike*" that Maggie finally accepts Gilbert's proposal of marriage.

A triple moral victory ensues: Gilbert can love and marry Maggie for a good family cause, Maggie can watch over her brother with the help of a new ally, and Mike can be redeemed through his new guardian angels.

This charming, feather-light piece of entertainment is conducted with conviction and verve, and the acting by the three leads is lithe and polished. The dialogues are energetic, the characterizations convincing, and the story congenial and well written. Williams, his native New York

Williams with Carleton Carpenter in "Millionaire Gilbert Burton." Frame capture.

Mike Carter the small-time swindler (Grant Williams) with his sister Maggie (Dolores Donlon) in "Millionaire Gilbert Burton." Frame capture.

accent seeping into his performance, is adorable and full of youthful enthusiasm as Mike the small-time grifter, expertly balancing cynicism and likeability, greed and innocence. He also demonstrates considerable physical charm by sketching some new ballroom dance moves for Maggie.

"Millionaire Gilbert Burton" is a great, simple show, which once more proves just how underrated Williams was, and how talented; it also proves how much potential he had as a leading man given the right project.

One Step Beyond: "Dead Ringer"

The atmospheric episode "Dead Ringer" (airdate December 1, 1959) of the paranormal television series *One Step Beyond* (1959–1961) plunges Williams and his co-stars into quasi-nineteenth-century melodrama. It is full-blown, hand-wringing, scenery-chewing drama, especially for the character of Williams' wife, Esther (Norma Crane, who played the equally high-strung character of Williams' fiancée Liz in *Man with a Camera*). The topic: in the words of series host and episode Director John Newland,

Grant Williams with Norma Crane in "Dead Ringer" (1959). Frame capture.

bilocation, or ethereal doubles. Which means, ghosts from the past and split personality, or a mixture of all the above.

The dialogues, unfortunately, are weak and stereotyped, and their rendition is monotonously gloomy. Williams is intense but, thankfully, restrained compared to Ms. Crane; he adopts a classic mid-Atlantic theatrical accent to fit the stagey antics of the story, and conducts himself adequately, but there is a definite sense of *déjà vu* staleness to the proceedings. The more effective transitional scenes—away from the fist-biting—are eerily suspenseful, and could belong to a Victorian detective story. This is where the style is most grounded, and the melodramatics are left off screen.

Still, the final scene, where Williams' character returns home from an arson incident supposedly involving his wife's twin sister Emily and finds his wife Esther burnt in her bed, gives Williams the chance to indulge briefly in operatic overacting, and the result is not altogether unattractive. As a matter of fact, the entire venture demonstrates Williams' command of conventional high theatrics: his solid technique sustains him, allowing him to be elegantly intense in an outmoded style, without embarrassment.

Bill Quentin (Grant Williams in full melodrama mode) discovers his wife's disfigured
body in "Dead Ringer." Frame capture.

Villains and Quasi Villains: *Mr. Lucky, Bonanza, Gunsmoke*

Williams portrayed a number of villains or quasi villains in his television career. Two characters in particular stand out: Conrad, the deranged beatnik serial killer in the episode "Stacked Deck" (May 28, 1960) of the television series *Mr. Lucky* (1959–1960), and Lieutenant Paul Tyler in the episode "Escape to Ponderosa" (color, March 5, 1960) of the television series *Bonanza* (1959–1973).

Jack Arnold, who served as co-Producer on *Mr. Lucky* with Blake Edwards, directed "Stacked Deck" and fourteen other episodes of the series (*Mr. Lucky* only lasted two scant seasons, yielding a total of thirty-four episodes); Henry Mancini provided the theme music.

Director Arnold demonstrates his affection for Williams by allowing him to make eccentric choices for his characterization; Williams takes the opportunity and runs with it, flying far away from his normally understated persona. Bottle-thick horn-rim eyeglasses and flattened-out beatnik hair, his Conrad is a hissing snake of a character, an unhinged, paranoid, psychotic individual with a piercing gaze and a cool, curiously sexy undulating gait. He is a smart man with a demented theory for everything, who defines himself as follows: "*I am a network; a moving network of nerve endings.*" As in *Red Sundown*, Williams uses his smile as an offensive weapon, but it is more of a snarl in this case. It is clear that he relishes the part, and this relish gives us a rare opportunity to glimpse his own exposed nerve endings. Two years later, Williams would play a dramatic variation of this fundamentally comic derangement in the film *The Couch*.

Williams' character in the *Bonanza* episode is memorable for a different reason. Lieutenant Paul Tyler is introduced as a villain of sorts (an escaped convict and an army deserter), but matures to a full redemption in the end. Tyler is a remorseful, grief-stricken man, and Williams drenches him in sadness and in a tender, compassionate disposition. Tyler's tending to an ailing colt is especially touching. Despite this goodness, Williams' interpretation is far from staid or boring: his quick, intelligent reactions to other characters in his non-speaking moments clearly demonstrate that the actor is very much alive, and very much attentive.

Grant Williams (right) plays Conrad the murderous beatnik against John Vivyan's Mr. Lucky, in "Stacked Deck" (1960). Frame capture.

Grant Williams as Lieutenant Paul Tyler in "Escape to Ponderosa" (1960). Frame capture.

Williams appears to be building his character with loving care; this is revealed especially in the subtle but tormented soul work he weaves through his lines of dialogue: quite apart from the lines, it is Williams' face that is constantly alive. Tyler's guilt, for example, manifests itself in his reluctance to make direct eye contact with his interlocutors; in his confrontations, his gaze enacts an elaborate dance of shame to hide itself from the world.

No redemption is in sight for the villainous character Williams portrays in the episode "The Bear" (airdate February 28, 1959) of the television western series *Gunsmoke* (1955–1975). Williams plays the dastardly Joe Plummer, a jilted lover who does everything he can to ruin the impending wedding of his old flame, Tilda (Norma Crane again, in her third pairing with Williams), to Mike Blocker (Denver Pyle), the man nicknamed Bear (hence the episode title).

In the second of Williams' four scenes, in which his character corners his former lover alone in her room, one can feel the jealousy mounting in Plummer as he transitions from seductiveness to open threat to battery, and Williams' understated delivery contains just the right amount of lust and hatred—with a pinch of hurt as he tells her, *"Oh, that's not nice, Tilda."*

Williams is quite attractive, and plays the sexual undertones of the scene with quiet but seething intensity. It is because of this intensity, which is occasionally allowed to rise to the surface—or it may be because of that faint trace of New York one hears in his speech—that something distinctly Burt-Lancasterish emerges in Williams' performance. This occurs in his voice, primarily, but also in a certain hardening of his powerful gaze.

As in his best performances, here too Williams never succumbs to the temptation of mugging or of caricature, and builds a portrayal that is committedly on the character's side; one may disapprove of Joe Plummer but, Williams is telling us through his interpretation, one must understand him first. And understand him we do, for Williams makes us see what the character is thinking and feeling, clearly and lucidly. An old creative-writing adage instructs dramatic writers to fall in love with all their characters; the same piece of advice applies to the best actors, and

Grant Williams with Norma Crane in "The Bear" (1959). Frame capture.

Williams was one of them. In writing as in acting, only love can yield true knowledge.

Despite all their virtues, these television performances clearly show why Williams tended to be underrated as an actor. Williams' subtle, self-effacing style (together with minor roles and middling scripts) might be what barred his way to stardom, and sealed his fate as a repertory player. The failure on the part of those making decisions for him to recognize his untapped potential did the rest.

False Starts II: *The Iron Horseman*

In 1960, Mirisch Television and the National Broadcasting Company (NBC) produced a pilot for a proposed series; the title was *The Iron Horseman*. The series dealt with the adventures of a railroad detective in the Old West. The pilot was not bought, and the series fell through. Fred Danzig of United Press International (UPI) commented on this, and on other aborted television series, rather poignantly:

> At this sentimental time of year permit me to raise a toast to some special actors. They're not starring in the high, medium or low-rated TV series. I refer to "The Unaccountables," those players for whom the beginning of 1960 meant big things in TV. They were poised to star in new TV series. Production announcements were duly distributed. But after the publicity hoopla subsided and the new season started, they were among the missing. They didn't even get their turn at bat.
>
> [...] What happened? What went wrong? [...] Grant Williams and Barry Kelley were set for "The Iron Horsemen," a railroading series. [...]
>
> To these ballyhooed actors who didn't strut upon the TV stage this year, better luck next year. They are, after all, reminders of our own false starts, our own imperfections, the loser in all of us.[294]

---

294. Fred Danzig (UPI), "'Victory at Sea' Not Dimmed By Age, Still Drains Emotions," December 30, 1960.

With Barry Kelley in a promotional still (from the original negative) for the pilot episode of *The Iron Horseman* (1960).

The Roaring 20's: "Brother's Keeper"

If recent eyewitness reports about the extent of Williams' drinking problem are any indication,[295] his role in the episode "Brother's Keeper" (airdate November 19, 1960) of the television series *The Roaring 20's* (1960–1962) probably reverberated for him with secret connections to his private life; here is the plot as recounted in the *Indiana Gazette* of Pennsylvania.

---

295. See Chapter 14.

A comparatively new face appears on the scene tonight and it will be appearing more often from now on. It's a good looking face belonging to an actor named Grant Williams who will soon join "Hawaiian Eye" as a regular. Tonight he plays an alcoholic trying to drown a lot of memories. One of them is a girl-type memory, and she, too, is an alcoholic. Andrew Duggan plays Williams' brother, and Dianne Foster is the tipsy girl. Donald May and Dorothy Provine carry the banner on behalf of the show's regulars. For Drama Fans.[296]

The episode was directed by Robert Altman and was filmed on stage 17 of the Warner Bros. Burbank Studios. Another daily newspaper added some detail to the plot, and a comment about Williams' contract with Warner Bros.:

The Roaring 20's uncovers another of those wealthy families with a covey of skeletons in its luxurious closets. This banking clan has a drunken wife, a drunken and bitter brother, an old retainer who collapses when the examiners look over the books, and an attache case full of missing bonds. There's also a wooden leg and a desire to be the first man to fly the Atlantic solo somewhere in it. Grant Williams plays the wooden leg brother; he did so well the studio signed him for a movie lead.[297]

A contemporary review had this to say about the show:

Good show for this series. Up until the last act this is a rather absorbing tale, thanks to good performances by Andy Duggan, Grant Williams, and Diane [sic] Foster. After that it gets too hokey.[298]

296. *Indiana (PA) Gazette*, November 19, 1960.

297. *Abilene (TX) Reporter-News*, November 19, 1960.

298. *Bridgeport (CT) Post*, November 19, 1960.

Sufside 6: "Bride and Seek"

On December 26, 1960, Williams guest-starred in the episode "Bride and Seek" of the television series *Surfside 6*. Here is a plot summary (which actually sounds interesting) from a contemporary newspaper:

> Dave Thorne (Lee Patterson) is hired by a wealthy young heiress to find Frank Anders (Grant Williams), her husband of two days, who has mysteriously vanished in Miami [...]. The girl's grandmother, Mrs. Edward Clayborne (Louise Lorimer) flies from New York to Miami and confides to Dave that she believes Frank to be a hoodlum and hopes he is never found. She does want to see her grand-daughter, whom she loves, but when Dave sets up a meeting, and the girl arrives, Mrs. Clayborne has never laid eyes on her before![299]

Here's Hollywood

On August 11, 1961, the afternoon interview show *Here's Hollywood* (1960–1962) showcased two guests: Denise Darcel and Grant Williams.

The show, produced by Desilu Productions for NBC, was an interesting intrusion into the lives of film and television stars: each taped half-hour interview featured a visit either to the star's home or to one of the star's favorite haunts. It is a pity that the episode is not readily viewable, for it might give us valuable clues as to the private (though perhaps not authentic) Grant Williams.

In her Archive of American Television interview, the late Publicist/ Producer Esme Chandlee (1918–2012), who worked as Associate Producer and Talent Coordinator on *Here's Hollywood*, reminisced about the show's busy production schedule:

> Peer Oppenheimer, who was the producer and whose original idea *Here's Hollywood* was, had known me at MGM, because he was a fan-magazine writer originally. So when he was looking for someone to be an Associate Producer and Talent Coordi-

---

299. "Missing Groom Sought in 'Surfside 6' Show," *Provo (UT) Daily Herald*, December 19, 1960.

nator, he was looking for somebody whom he figured would know how to handle all the stars and get in touch with them and so on. So he came to me and said would I do it. It sounded interesting, [...] so I said yes.

[*Here's Hollywood*] was the first program to interview the stars. We had two mobile units; we went to two different locations every day. You did a star in the morning and a star in the afternoon, and usually in those days you went to their houses. And if you didn't, then you set up a place to take them to do the interview. It was the leading daytime show on all three networks for two years. Then for politics Peer lost [the show]. And it was too bad, because it was an interesting show, and it had an immense audience because nobody else was doing that.[300]

During its first season, *Here's Hollywood* was hosted by Dean Miller. With him—or sometimes in his stead—Actress Joanne Jordan often served as co-host. UPI Correspondent Vernon Scott wrote a syndicated piece in December 1960, some three months after the show's September premiere, showcasing Jordan as America's favorite (and most unknown) TV-commercial spokesperson. (According to Scott—but not to IMDb—Jordan made more than fifty different television commercials before breaking into film and television acting.) While plugging Jordan, Scott also described *Here's Hollywood*:

> Joanne's good looks and easy manner have brought her a regular show of her own—the five-days-a-week "Here's Hollywood" aired by the National Broadcasting Co.
>
> She and Dean Miller travel around Hollywood taping interviews with movie and TV celebrities, setting up shop in the stars' homes, in bowling alleys, golf courses, studios and wherever they can catch the pretty people at work or play.[301]

---

300. Esme Chandlee interview, Archive of American Television, conducted by Reba Merrill on February 21, 2001. Visit emmytvlegends.org for more information.

301. Vernon Scott, "Pitchgirl Joanne Jordan Nets Cool $200,000 a Year," *Ukiah (CA) Daily Journal*, December 6, 1960.

On the day in question, the topics of discussion were described as follows in a daily newspaper: "Denise Darcel recalls her Cinderella-like discovery; Grant Williams explains how psychoanalysis helped his career."[302] The latter topic was probably a plug for Williams' psychiatric investigation of his character in *The Couch* (1962).

Meet the Star

On October 8, 1961, Williams appeared as a guest on the short-lived (1961) television program *Meet the Star*. The half-hour interview show, which the press defined as "another Hollywood press conference series,"[303] had debuted in June. The format: Host Bill Bradley moderated a panel of entertainment reporters who could grill the daily guest with questions. A previous incarnation (1958–1960), called *Hollywood Diary*, had also been a talk show with a panel of columnists; Bill Bradley had alternated with, and then succeeded, Dave Willock as host. Syndicated Hollywood Columnist Vernon Scott (who wrote an article about Grant Williams in 1961) was a frequent guest on both programs.

Stump the Stars

On May 20, 1963, Williams appeared (as himself) in a television game show, originally called *Pantomime Quiz* (June 1949–October 1959) but renamed *Stump the Stars* in the early 1960s (September 1962–September 1963). The show—a game of charades played by celebrities—was produced and hosted by Mike Stokey.

The sentences/clues, suggested by viewers from around the country, were shown in secret to the contestants and appeared in large letters on the TV screen for home viewers, first in their entirety and then in sections. These sentences were often near-impossible charade assignments, and each contestant had a maximum of two minutes to make his or her team guess them. The program may have been a shameless promotional stint for whatever film or television series the guest team represented, but there was nonetheless an authentic sense of fun to the proceedings.

---

302. Rochester (NY) *Democrat and Chronicle*, television listings, August 6, 1961.

303. *Independent Press-Telegram*, June 11, 1961.

Host Mike Stokey (right) shows a dapper Grant Williams his clue for a charade in *Stump the Stars* (1963). Frame capture.

On this particular evening, Williams was on the *PT109* team with co-stars Robert Culp, James Gregory, and Ty Hardin.[304] The four team-mates played against show regulars Sebastian Cabot, Beverly Garland, Ross Martin, and Hans Conried. The men were all in black tie, Ms. Garland donned an evening gown; in glorious black-and-white, the show was definitely a throwback to the formal 1950s.

Grant Williams' sentence, suggested by one Mrs. Heath Thompson of Pittsfield, Massachusetts, was "Knock Knock! Who's there? Ostrich. Ostrich who? Ostrich in time saves nine." With frenzied energy, Williams gave his all to the task, awkwardly miming the absurd words and going so far as to impersonate an ostrich. Miraculously, Williams' team guessed the sentence in 101 seconds, but lost the contest in the end.

304. Williams, Hardin, and Gregory would make a return guest appearance on the game show on August 12; the fourth member of this second team was Roddy McDowall.

Grant Williams mimes a clue to teammate Ty Hardin (left, back to camera) in
Stump the Stars. Frame capture.

False Starts III

In January 1964, rumor had it that a new television serial was being
created, probably to cash in on the success of CBS's on-the-road series
Route 66 (1960–1964), which starred Martin Milner and George Maharis
and would be discontinued in March 1964. Here is the syndicated report
that appeared in American newspapers: "ABC is putting together an adventure series about a pair of touring golf pros. It's a sort of 'Route 66'
drive of the country's greens and fairways with Grant Williams as one
of the stars."[305] Just like *The Iron Horseman*, this untitled project too was
shelved.

The Munsters: "The Sleeping Cutie"

Williams' participation in the episode "The Sleeping Cutie" (airdate
December 10, 1964) of the television series *The Munsters* (1964–1966) is a

---

305. Hank Grant, "TV Specials Popular," *Decatur (IL) Herald*, January 14, 1964.

tepid thing. Williams plays a good-looking oil executive who is sent to obtain Grandpa Munster's (Al Lewis) signature on a contract, promising not to divulge or use a revolutionary formula he has invented, one that allows water to be transformed into gasoline (the oil company has checked: the formula works). Coincidentally, the Munsters are busy trying to break a spell that Grandpa has accidentally cast upon his pretty great-niece Marilyn (Beverley Owen). He was trying to cure her insomnia, but used the wrong potion (the "Sleeping Beauty" potion), and cannot wake her up; only a handsome prince can, by kissing her.

Sure enough, the name of the handsome executive who calls at the Munsters' house for that other industrial matter is Mr. Prince. Mr. Dick Prince. After some double takes and some perplexed looks at the eccentric family, Mr. Prince kisses Marilyn, and the spell is broken. All is well that ends well: Grandpa signs and Dick Prince asks Marilyn out on a date, much to everyone's merriment.

A few of Williams' double takes are amusing, but the whole amiable affair is deeply inconsequential and (despite the canned laughter) only mildly funny.

Regardless of what else might have been happening in Williams' private life, and regardless of what other problems he might have been suffering, the most awkward problem at this point in his career was the low quality of the roles he was being offered. Williams had not hit professional rock bottom yet, but he was on his way down, and fast. His lack of enthusiasm as he stoically plays his part by the numbers in "The Sleeping Cutie" is tangible.

Perry Mason I: "The Case of the Ruinous Road"

The episode "The Case of the Ruinous Road" (airdate December 31, 1964) of the television series *Perry Mason* turned out to be another middling affair, though Williams was assigned a sizeable role, that of Investigative Reporter/murderer Quincy Davis.

In his first scene, Williams plays a dialogue containing lines that are almost witty. Almost, but not quite. The same qualification can be made about the entire episode: it is almost good, but not quite; it is almost dramatic, but not quite. Like most *Perry Mason* ventures from the series' final seasons, the pace is slow—epitomized by Raymond Burr's lazy, inexpres-

Grant Williams in *Perry Mason*'s "The Case of the Ruinous Road" (1964). Frame capture.

sive deadpan and sluggish energy—and the story predictable and awkwardly blocked.

Williams—his hips and face showing signs of thickening and age, his hair no longer brilliant and flowing as in his early films, a deep sadness emanating from his eyes—is allowed to have some powerful bursts of dramatic energy in the climactic scenes; unfortunately, the whole package is ultimately anticlimactic, and so is Williams.

The Outer Limits: "The Brain of Colonel Barham"

In 1959, Roald Dahl published an original short story in his anthology *Kiss Kiss.* The story was entitled "William and Mary," and had to do with a daring experiment aimed at preserving the brain of a man after his death. The man in question is the titular William, Mary's controlling husband. Upon William's death, Mary receives a letter left with his solicitor in which her husband writes about the experiment and tells her where his brain—plus one eye to allow the brain to see—is being kept alive. Mary visits the facility and speaks to the doctor who performed the procedure. Initially, she appears to be fearful; but, in a wonderful ironic reversal (a typical Dahl sinister twist), as soon as she is in the presence of her husband's "seeing brain," she begins to enact a subtle but cruel revenge on him, by happily taking the domineering role in the relationship and doing everything, and anything, he condemned during his lifetime, such as cigarette smoking. The story ends with her telling the doctor, "Isn't he sweet? Isn't he heaven? I just can't wait to get him home," while puffing contentedly on a cigarette.

No such irony is present in the episode "The Brain of Colonel Barham" (airdate January 2, 1965) of the television series *The Outer Limits* (1963–1965), which casts Williams as a sort of protagonist. The organ being kept alive here is the brain of a brilliant but egotistic scientist, the titular Colonel (Williams' former *Hawaiian Eye* co-star Anthony Eisley). As soon as it is cut off from the ailing body of the dying scientist and connected to a computer, said brain begins to act out all its repressed delusions of grandeur and to develop superpowers.

Williams plays Major Douglas McKinnon, who is against the experiment from the start. His main job as military-base psychologist appears to consist in saving Colonel Barham's widow (Elizabeth Perry) from the homicidal clutches of her husband's vindictive brain.

The script and dialogues are conventional and drab, despite the series' cult status. Williams looks handsome in uniform, but appears tired and half-hearted, playing everything with massive doses of his customary self-effacement. There is little he can do to redeem the cliché-ridden material, and he does not try.

Bonanza II: "Patchwork Man"

No excuses need to be made for Williams' special-guest-starring participation in the episode "Patchwork Man" (color, airdate May 23, 1965) of the television series *Bonanza*. His role as Albert Saunders, aka "Patch," is a real treat: it dominates the episode (meriting visual credit in the main titles alongside the series regulars), drives its story and carries it to its conclusion, making changes in the life of one of the protagonists of the series, namely Hoss (Dan Blocker).

Even the character's introduction is distinctive. While he is cleaning old bricks in the main street of one of the ghost towns on the Ponderosa estate, Hoss smells something good; attracted by the scent, he follows it to the window sill of one of the abandoned houses, where a square pie tin is cooling. A hand appears and withdraws the tin; a male voice says *"Come on in, I'll cut you a slice. Should be cool enough now."* The hand and the voice belong to "Patch," a meek, mild-mannered young jack-of-all-trades who befriends Hoss but is full of melancholy warnings about himself: *"Life is kind of aimless and lonely anyway, no matter where you are,"* he says, and, *"You wouldn't want the likes of me around, 'cause I'm not worth a buck nickel."*

Patch is a courageous turn for Williams. His introduction is almost feminine: after serving his guest, he launches into a detailed description of the recipe for the pie he has just baked (a mock-apple pie he calls "pan pie"), much to the embarrassment of manly Hoss. Williams imbues his character with a self-deprecating sadness that is quite moving. In the following scenes, we gradually discover that what Patch is saying about himself is true: he is a coward. We also learn that this fearfulness is the result of trauma, for Patch witnessed the killing of his brother and of his best friends twelve years earlier, and was almost killed himself. But before this explana-

Grant Williams as "Patch" in *Bonanza*'s "Patchwork Man" (1965). Frame capture.

Grant Williams expresses his character's self-loathing in "Patchwork Man." Frame capture.

tion, which is given by Patch about forty minutes into the one-hour episode (through flashbacks and a heartfelt monologue that is like something out of a play), we have to suffer the sight of his character being ridiculed, threatened, beaten, and humiliated by various thugs, and it is a painful sight.

Williams goes all out in expressing Patch's fear—fearlessly—and takes a sizeable risk: he does not make Patch's cowardice attractive, nor dignified. Confronted by violence, the character cowers, whines, and whimpers like an old aunt. This is as far as you can get from a star performance.

On the one hand, we might feel tempted to interpret this self-destructive, sad theme between the lines of truth and fiction, and to correlate it meta-textually with Williams himself, or at least with his melancholy disposition as a person: symbolically, and in hindsight, Williams *is* Patch. On the other hand, this kind of role gives Williams great freedom: freedom from the obligation to be a star and to deliver star-like performances (with all the stifling conventions attached to such obligation), and freedom to explore character, creatively and truthfully. Like most freedoms, this one too is a double-edged sword.

A *noir*-lit Grant Williams looks guilty but is not, in *Perry Mason*'s "The Case of the Baffling Bug" (1965). Frame capture.

Williams' character is clearly delineated, with a powerful arc carrying him all the way to his redemption and transformation. Patch finally takes control of his life without resorting to gunfire, regains all the inner power he had lost, and becomes a man again through the call of friendship: it is to save Hoss's life that he pulls himself together. The transformation makes for a rewarding dramatic experience, for the audience as well as for Williams.

The *Sunday Express and News* of San Antonio, Texas, approved:

> More cowards on *Bonanza*. Grant Williams gives a very sympathetic performance as a "Patchwork Man," who prefers to live in a ghost town than to face the fact of his cowardice. But he can bake a mean pie, which makes him friends with Hoss, just as the Cartwrights have to prove their ownership to a piece of property on which a dirty-cut has started an hydraulic mine.[306]

---

306. *San Antonio (TX) Sunday Express and News*, May 23, 1965.

The Pittsburgh *Post-Gazette* was also happy with the show: "Good episode. [...] Grant Williams is fine as the coward and Dan Blocker carries the load for the family this week."[307]

Perry Mason II: "The Case of the Baffling Bug"

Williams had a role of some import in his second appearance on the *Perry Mason* television series. The episode, "The Case of the Baffling Bug" (airdate December 12, 1965), was part of the ninth—and final—season.

The context: industrial espionage; Williams plays murder suspect and courtroom defendant Dr. Todd Meade, who is also suspected of being the leak inside the company that is developing a very, very secret McGuffin.

Honest but conservative, Williams' performance is honorable enough, and is lit beautifully in at least one scene, but the context around him is pure rote, and cannot be called thrilling. It is safe sailing for everyone involved, and Williams is no exception.

---

307. *Pittsburgh (PA) Post-Gazette*, May 22, 1965.

10 Twentieth Century Fox, 1959–1960

DURING THE TRANSITION between Universal-International and Warner Bros., Williams made two films with Robert L. Lippert's Associated Producers Incorporated (API)—or, to be more precise, one with API and one with its former incarnation, Regal Pictures—the company that produced low-budget features for Twentieth Century Fox.

Lone Texan

The result in the case of Regal Pictures was the remarkable *Lone Texan* (March 1, 1959), a western "programmer" starring Willard Parker and skillfully scripted by James Landis and Jack Thomas after Landis' novel. Here is the plot as described by a contemporary daily:

> The picture tells of a former Union cavalry officer who returns to his Texas home following the Civil War to find his younger brother has become the virtually undisputed ruler of the area.
>
> Branded a turncoat by the citizens, he suddenly finds that he alone is strong enough to face the ever mounting terrorism of his brother's reign. Strong by virtue of being the only man in the territory fast enough with a gun to face the brother.
>
> How the "Lone Texan" resolves his problem of brother against brother only to be drawn into a fateful meeting through no effort of his own, makes for a suspenseful and exciting story.[308]

---

308. *Anniston (AL) Star*, March 8, 1959.

Variety showed its appreciation for the original thought that had gone into the dramatic construction of the film by revealing specific details about the finale:

> [The] younger brother (Williams) has taken over as sheriff and as judge, jury and executioner as well. He and his young hoodlum deputies terrorize the town, and Parker's return makes a showdown inevitable. When it finally comes, the off-beat finish has Williams reaching for a gun to shoot a deputy about to plug Parker in the back and Parker, thinking his brother is drawing on him, shooting his brother first and accurately, thus restoring ye olde law and order.

For once, *Variety* also showed some explicit enthusiasm for Williams' work: "Parker and Williams are excellent as the brothers, with [Douglas] Kennedy turning in a fine performance as a lawyer." In fact, *Variety* was uncharacteristically warm about the film as a whole:

> Regal Films makes a regal farewell with "Lone Texan," last of 42 low-budget features it has turned out for 20th-Fox in the past two years. Skillfully scripted by James Landis and Jack Thomas, it's a strikingly good film [...].
> Producer Jack Leewood made good use of all his assets, casting well [...]. Paul Landres' direction moves the brother-versus-brother battle in taut fashion, ably mirroring the conflict in his other players.[309]

Variety was impressed, and rightly so. The film achieves a dynamic synthesis of pace, poise, intelligence, and character development that is quite extraordinary for a B-western.

Already during the main titles, the music makes it clear that what we are about to see is not an action film but a humane drama. Composer Paul Dunlap writes sensitive, poetic music in the style of Aaron Copland's *Appalachian Spring* (1944), with yearning strings and tender, unresolved harmonies.

---

309. *Variety*, February 11, 1959.

Williams' character, Greg Banister, benefits from a protracted setup before his entrance about twenty minutes into the film: other characters talk about him, establishing important facts about him before his appearance. This frees Williams from the obligation of expository dialogue, and leaves him free to concentrate on his character emotionally and physically.

Greg Banister is wound up tight from the very start: brooding and unsmiling, he carries a heavy weight on his shoulders, like the tragic character he is. Sibling rivalry, an inferiority complex, an ideological conflict, a feeling of revenge against the world: all these things, and others besides them, are boiling inside the character. Wisely, Williams lets the tragic nature of his character transpire between the lines of his villainous plot activities, in fleeting moments of introspective pause.

During his first scene, when he and his snarling deputies storm into the sheriff's office with some prisoners, Williams takes every opportunity to isolate his character from the commotion that surrounds him; with quick strokes he establishes Greg's brooding, nervous disposition—beginning with the practical gesture (similar to the one he made in Chet Swann's first scene in *Red Sundown*) of running his hand through his hair after taking off his hat. Here, the gesture draws our attention to Greg's furrowed brow as he examines the contents of a bag he has just deposited on

Tragic character's entrance: Greg Banister's (Grant Williams) practical reason for running his hand through his hair in *Lone Texan* (1959) is that he has just taken off his cowboy hat. For other, less practical, reasons, see Chet Swann's identical gesture in *Red Sundown* (1956). Frame capture.

the table before him. During that brief pause, as in several other brief moments in this and in later scenes, Greg stops reacting to what is happening around him, and is essentially alone even when surrounded by people.

The film allows the two Banister brothers to express their tragic conflict in short but vibrant exchanges. It also allows something important to happen to the character of the "evil" brother: the dawning of self-doubt. In an early scene with his fiancée Florrie (June Blair), before his first meeting with the brother he has believed dead, Greg confesses: *"Now that he's alive, I don't know how I feel."* There is nothing Manichaean or simplistic about this story, despite the thuggish Confederate-Union conflict of sympathies coursing through the Texan town that forms its setting. The quiet scene that precedes the brothers' climactic showdown, where Greg, alone in a room, is pondering his next move, is loaded with tragic foreboding and conflicted self-hatred. If Greg is to fulfill the "evil" karmic mechanism he has set in motion, he must kill his brother, or be killed; the thought does not make him happy. And all this without sentimentalism.

Outwardly, Greg Banister appears to be his brother Clint's opposite. Greg Banister is young, Clint middle-aged; Greg is irascible and dynamic, Clint slow-paced and moderate; Greg speaks in a high-baritone voice, Clint is a bass; Greg is the incarnation of power-hungry ambition, Clint is a spokesman for justice; Greg is tall, Clint taller. Incidentally, the difference in age and stature between Clint and Greg makes their scenes together look like dialogues between a father and a rebellious son (*"Like my old man,"* intones Greg's deputy Jesse while making a comparison between Greg's relationship with his brother and his own conflictual relationship with his late father).

While this outward opposition—fueled by the political/ideological conflict which, as *Variety* stated, is mirrored in many of the surrounding characters—creates the outer storyline of the film, Landis and Thomas's script never forgets to keep the deeper, inner conflict between the two brothers in focus, thus creating a parallel storyline dealing with conflicted brotherly love. In other words, the outer events in the plot never obscure the characters because they stem from the characters.

The writers also do something else: they create a polarity between Greg's animal-like deputies and a curious figure among them. Three of the four men are like rabid dogs growling at each other and picking fights with anyone they encounter, while also incarnating the ideas involved in the chauvinistic conflict triggered by Clint Banister's arrival in town; but the fourth man, Jesse (Dick Monaghan), serves a different purpose. Of the four hoodlums, he is the least unsympathetic, and—although weaker than the others, and less educated—the most moderate. In fact, Jesse is a feeble voice of reason among the dogs as well as Greg's own private Greek chorus.

In an early scene, Jesse comments on Greg's conundrum with exquisite intuitive insight, revealing Greg's thoughts to him as the latter is brooding about his brother's return to town after the war (and once again freeing Williams' character from the burden of excessive expository dialogue):

> *Jesse (coming closer and sitting on Greg's desk): I understand how you feel, Greg. You're bound to love 'im 'cause he's your brother; and you're bound to hate 'im 'cause of what he stands fer. Just like my old man: you know, he treated ma real good, and I liked him for it. But when he'd slap me around and yell at me to fetch the chicken and fetch the water and fetch the firewood, I'd hate 'im. That's all I was good for, fetching! When he died I didn't know to cry or be glad. And it gets you all mixed up inside.*
>
> *Greg: Yeah. Clint taught me everything I know: how to use a gun, how to fight, how to do everything he wanted me to. But it was always his way. I was always second-best.*

Greg Banister (Grant Williams) and his personal Greek chorus, Jesse the insightful Deputy (Dick Monaghan), in *Lone Texan* (1959). Frame capture.

Jesse: You ain't second-best now, Greg. You're the best! There ain't nobody that can stand up to you.

(A pause, then Greg snaps out of his brooding and slaps Jesse's knee enthusiastically.)

Strangely, this use of Jesse's character as a chorus feels neither arbitrary nor contrived: it feels clean and organic, though stylized. (Greg's fiancée Florrie, played by June Blair, fulfills a similar role in her scenes with Greg.) This device entails two important things: (1) the writers do not shy away from introspection, and develop the characters' psychologies through honest, explicit dialogues about them, and (2) they allow Greg to embody this introspection dramatically and physically rather than verbally.

Importantly, Jesse—Greek chorus or voice of conscience—does not stop being a real character; and it is as a real character that he becomes the indirect cause of Greg's death when he tries to intervene in the imminent

Greg Banister with his other Greek chorus, fiancée Florrie Stuart (June Blair), in a production still for *Lone Texan*.

showdown between the two brothers, for he must take Greg's side in the conflict and protect his hero (*"If you get killed, what will I do? I ain't got no place to go,"* he confesses to him in an exchange).

Just about all the characters in this piece, even the smallest, have their day in court, through vignettes that are imaginatively written and performed. Comedienne Barbara Heller, for example, shines as Amy Todd the town gossip, spewing forth rivers of words at breakneck speed. Like most if not all the actors in the film, she neither underplays nor overplays her role but carefully weighs equal portions of natural realism and understated theatrical style while expertly sustaining the energy and pace of her character from within—another sign of the wisdom of the outstanding talents contributing to the end result.

In a wonderful piece of tragic irony, it is Greg's own inner voice, or Greek chorus, that triggers his impulse to save his brother's life instead of ending it, in what appears to be an inevitable showdown between the siblings. Just before this incident, Greg had been softening in response to Clint's plea to end the conflict:

> *Clint: What's happened to us, Greg? In the old days we used to talk things over.*
> *Greg: Too late for that now.*
> *Clint: No, it's not too late. There's time for both of us, believe me!*
> *(Pause. Greg is thinking; he lowers his gaze, his hat throwing a deep shadow across his face; Jesse appears behind a porch, ready to shoot Clint in the back; Greg looks at Clint again, and—stammering—says:)*
> *Greg: Uh—Maybe if—*

Greg then sees what Jesse is about to do, so he draws his gun to shoot him; Clint mistakenly thinks Greg is about to kill *him,* and shoots Greg. It all happens very fast, which makes the event all the more powerful, and all the more stirring, like an ineluctable series of Freudian reflexes (if Clint is Greg's father figure, Greg is Jesse's). Those reflexes stem organically and logically from the characters and, in that sudden flurry of action, the logical pieces that have flowered from the characters' nuclei all fall into place, as if by magnetic attraction.

Alone in a crowd of actors and extras, a pensive Grant Williams (second from left, standing) enjoys a moment off duty on the set of *Lone Texan* (1959) in this behind-the-scenes photo.

As Clint leans over his fatally wounded brother, Greg pleads: *"Clint, I..."* and dies. A poignant, unresolved ending, the scene is a powerful symbolic reminder of the things that are left unsaid between people who love each other but are hampered by ideology, fear, jealousy, or envy. The final shots of the film come a bit too abruptly after this, as does the title announcing the end; nevertheless, story-wise, the dramatic denouement is brilliantly, pithily complex—and reveals a warm, unsentimental humanistic bent in the writers.

Speculating about an intimate connection between certain aspects of *Lone Texan* and Williams' private life might be a stretch; however, there was reportedly a significant amount of unresolved sibling rivalry between the Williams brothers,[310] and Grant Williams was, after all, an actor devoted to the Method. It is not unlikely that, had Williams been searching in his emotional baggage for ways to express Greg Banister's dilemma truthfully, he would have stumbled on his feelings towards his brother Robert.

---

310. See Chapter 14.

13 Fighting Men

Williams' second film for Twentieth Century Fox was *13 Fighting Men* (1960), another Civil-War "programmer" taking place immediately after the end of the hostilities. In contrast to *Lone Texan*, this film is tedious and uninspired, and no flourish of imagination comes to its rescue either from its writers (Robert Hamner and Jack W. Thomas) or from its director (Harry Gerstad). The story is honest but plodding and static, with Williams' Union soldiers holed up in a civilian home for three days while the unit of a rebel Confederate Major (Brad Dexter) holds siege outside in the hope of seizing a shipment of gold.

Weighed down by the tedium of the indifferent writing and direction, the actors inevitably flounder. The film, shot in CinemaScope and in rather plain black and white (no masterly chiaroscuro here, such as the one created by Ellis W. Carter for *The Incredible Shrinking Man* and *The Monolith Monsters*), provides no spectacular visuals to compensate for its lack of dramatic verve. *13 Fighting Men* feels and looks like a B-picture, and makes its actors feel and look like B-actors. Williams, who is the protagonist, tries nothing daring and honestly complies with the uninspiring

Grant Williams with Brad Dexter (left) in *13 Fighting Men* (1960). Production still.

task for which he has signed. He looks good in uniform and sideburns, and does what he can with the inept script, but only ends up delivering a dutiful rendition of nothing. *Variety* acknowledged that the leads went "through their paces well" but concluded: "The characters are one-dimensional, and Director Harry Gerstad isn't able to pierce the surface to offer much insight into them."[311]

---

311. *Variety*, March 23, 1960

11

Warner Bros., 1960–1963

In Sickness and in Health

In 1960, Williams' new contract with Warner Bros. may or may not have felt to him like a promotion compared to his pact with Universal-International, a studio that had given up on him after *The Incredible Shrinking Man*. Warner's promotional stories about Williams after the signing—stories that included extensive interviews—seem to suggest that he considered his new situation a step in the right direction.

We will probably never know the true reasons for U-I's abandonment, but it is possible that Williams himself, restless creature that he was, had been aching for a change. This need for change was implied in the statements reported by Central Press Association Correspondent Armand Archerd in August 1961:

> It's obvious that the fired up thespian hopes for a long, interesting, and it is to be assumed profitable, career as an actor. However, he turned down several fat contracts along the way to a major studio pact. Why?
>
> "Most of the deals I was offered," Williams claims, "were to appear in one series, or one show. I didn't want to be fenced in at this stage of my career. I wanted the chance to get lots of experience. And I can tell you I needed the money when some of these deals were offered me."
>
> Williams feels it's short sighted for an actor to focus on a weekly paycheck. It's the long haul that makes an actor a suc-

cess—he must have opportunities to learn, experiment, or in other words, he must have a chance to act.

"Otherwise," he laughed, "it will be a short and not so merry professional life. I signed with Warners knowing they have a big list of TV shows always before the cameras. With all those shows going I figured to get the chance to work in plenty of different roles—westerns, costumes, cops-and-robbers, comedy, almost anything.

"I figured if they had me under contract they'd want to get their money's worth out of me just like I'd be getting my experience's worth from them. And, let's face it, I also know they make movies, and chances were that something would come along for me in them, too.

"For once, I guessed right on both counts," he laughed. "I've been busy ever since the ink dried on the contract!"[312]

An early mention of Williams' contract with Warner Bros. appeared in November 1960:

Warner Bros. has signed handsome Grant Williams to a term contract. The young actor has already appeared in two of the studio's television series: "Brother's Keeper" segment of "The Roaring 20's" and "Par-A-Kee" in "Surfside 6."[313]

A strange bit of fluff regarding Williams' new contract with the studio was written by Columnist Harrison Carroll in October 1960. Whether there was any truth to this alarming piece of news or not, the report might have been intended as a veiled reference to Williams' drinking problem:[314] "Grant Williams was lucky to be able to report to Warners on the first day of his new contract. His car skidded in a sudden downpour, crashed into a house at Pacific Palisades... ."[315]

---

312. Archerd (1961), op. cit.

313. Syndicated press release, *Sandusky (OH) Register*, November 11, 1960.

314. See Chapter 14.

315. Harrison Carroll, "Behind the Scenes in Hollywood," *Greenwood (SC) Index-Journal*, October 21, 1960.

Columnist Harrison Carroll in a 1942 press photo. International News Photos.

Either Harrison Carroll had a propensity for chronicling accidents when it came to Williams, or Williams was prone to them (or Carroll was trying to hint at something), for the columnist reported other similar occurrences during the same period. On March 14, 1961, Williams allegedly chipped a bone in his hip while doing his own stunt work;[316] on March 31 of the same year, he accidentally jammed an ice pick into the palm of his hand while shooting *The Couch* and had to be medicated.[317] And here

316. Harrison Carroll, "Behind the Scenes in Hollywood," *Greenwood (SC) Index-Journal*, March 14, 1961.

317. Harrison Carroll, "Behind the Scenes in Hollywood," *Greenwood (SC) Index-*

is another item from Carroll in June: "Grant Williams didn't tell Warners, but he was under sedation for two days after being hit by a car near
the Ambassador Hotel...."[318] Carroll's final Williams catastrophe of 1961,
published the following month, was an item connected to the aftermath
of Williams's work on *Bonanza*'s "Escape to Ponderosa" (1960):

> Grant Williams, a hit in Warner's "Hawaiian Eye" TV series,
> enters St. Joseph's Hospital for surgery on the back of his neck.
>   It's the result of a freak accident a year ago on a "Bonanza"
> TV segment. A blank cartridge exploded too close to Grant. A
> piece of the shell was imbedded in his neck. Doctors thought
> it would work its way to the surface, but it hasn't, so Grant is
> having it removed.
>   Ironically, during the Korean war, Grant was hospitalized
> by an exploding enemy shell.[319]

Kiss Kiss

It was clear from the outset that Warner's publicity had a different
hue from Universal-International's, and that Williams was complying
with Warner's rumor spreading. Which could mean one of three things:
a) Warner Bros. was more forceful in its policy, b) Williams felt that the
augmented publicity was beneficial, or c) Williams had been thoroughly
domesticated by his test run at Universal-International and by its disap-
pointing outcomes. Williams had, after all, worked as a publicist himself
in younger days, and knew the value of publicity.

The fact remains that, between 1960 and 1963, America's daily newspapers were suddenly crowded with all sorts of news about Williams and
his work with his new studio. Sometimes, these plugs were playful, ironic
stories about the hard, hard life of a star, as in Columnist Hank Grant's
report about the star's holiday chores:

Journal, March 31, 1961.

318. Harrison Carroll, "Behind the Scenes in Hollywood," *Tyrone (PA) Daily Herald*,
    June 17, 1961.

319. Harrison Carroll, "Behind the Scenes in Hollywood," *Tyrone (PA) Daily Herald*,
    July 20, 1961.

No one is happier than Grant Williams that the Christmas season is over. Since Thanksgiving, he'd doubled from "Surf Side 6" chores to ride in a total of 18 Christmas and New Year's parades![320]

Mostly, however, the items consisted of reports linking Williams romantically with several women—something to which Universal had seldom resorted. Among the gals who were allegedly dating Williams during his three-year Warner Bros. tenure were Cathy Case,[321] Cathy Crosby,[322] Dolores Donlon,[323] Gloria Grey,[324] Anne Helm,[325] Wanda Hendrix,[326] Connie Stevens,[327] and Romney Tree.[328]

Indomitable smear artist Harrison Carroll indulged in a minor piece of gossip concerning Donlon (who had just co-starred with Williams in

320. Hank Grant, "Miss Montgomery Rejects Shows to Be With Husband," *Asbury Park (NJ) Press*, January 9, 1962.

321. Lee Mortimer, "In Hollywood," *Lancaster (OH) Eagle-Gazette*, January 23, 1960. In another column by Harrison Carroll ("In Hollywood," *Lancaster (OH) Eagle-Gazette*, February 6, 1960), a rumor of Williams' engagement to Case was squelched.

322. Lee Mortimer, "New York Confidential," *Logansport (OH) Pharos-Tribune*, December 8, 1960.

323. Harrison Carroll, "Behind the Scenes in Hollywood," *Greenwood (SC) Index-Journal*, November 9, 1960; also, same column, November 17, 1960.

324. Harrison Carroll, "Behind the Scenes in Hollywood," *Greenwood (SC) Index-Journal*, January 26, 1961.

325. "Connie Stevens and Anne Helm have Grant Williams sitting on a fence," declared Lee Mortimer in his "New York Confidential" column on March 18, 1961.

326. Lee Mortimer, *Logansport (OH) Pharos-Tribune*, December 27, 1960; also, Louella O. Parsons, *Anderson (IN) Daily Bulletin*, December 12, 1960.

327. Lee Mortimer, "Behind the Scenes in Hollywood," *Greenwood (SC) Index-Journal*, December 30, 1960. In December 1960 the couple was spotted by Columnist Harrison Carroll at the historic Italian-American restaurant Little Joe's at 904 North Broadway, Los Angeles (1928–1998), or at the adjacent Italian grocery store, it is not clear which (Harrison Carroll, "Behind the Scenes in Hollywood," *Greenwood (SC) Index-Journal*, December 30, 1960). On October 20, 1963, Vernon Scott (UPI) reported that Williams was among the invited guests at Connie Stevens' wedding.

328. Lee Mortimer, "New York Confidential," *Pocono Daily Record* (Stroudsburg, PA), February 13, 1961.

The Millionaire and was finishing an Italian movie in Rome),[329] Crosby,
and Williams:

> In the middle of a party at the Excelsior Hotel in Rome, Do-
> lores Donlon called boyfriend Grant Williams in Hollywood.
> They gave each other permission to date others while Dolores
> is in Europe. Dolores confided that the party was being given
> in her honor by actor Peter Dane. Grant said it was ok, that he
> had taken Cathy Crosby to dinner at Chianti's....[330]

The episode seemed like an elegant way of putting an end to what had
probably been a fictitious affair, and a brief one at that. The attentions
of the press for the Williams-Donlon couple, which Carroll had termed
the "most romantic twosome in town,"[331] ceased almost before they began.

The most oddly persistent of the dates attributed to Williams was
first reported by Lee Mortimer in his "New York Confidential" column: "Grant Williams persuaded Warners to screen test his gal, May
Heatherly, the femme bullfighter."[332] The next mention of the Williams-
Heatherly couple appeared in Harrison Carroll's "Behind the Scenes in
Hollywood" column on August 31, 1961: "The beauty who met Grant
Williams at the airport at 4 a.m. was May Heatherly." The romance was
taken one step further in 1962; the first mention of serious intentions
was printed in July, Dean Gautschy substituting for a vacationing Harrison Carroll:

> Before Grant Williams starts "PT 109," he's flying to Spain to
> ask May Heatherly, who fights bulls for real, to marry him. He

---

329. The film was *Odissea nuda*, starring Enrico Maria Salerno and directed by
Franco Rossi. It was released in Italy in April 1961 and in America in October
1962 as *Nude Odyssey*. Donlon was billed as Patricia Dolores Donlon.

330. Harrison Carroll, "Behind the Scenes in Hollywood," *Greenwood (SC) Index-
Journal*, November 17, 1960.

331. Harrison Carroll, "Behind the Scenes in Hollywood," *Greenwood (SC) Index-
Journal*, November 9, 1960.

332. Lee Mortimer, "New York Confidential," *Terre Haute (IN) Tribune-Star*, March
30, 1961; another rumor about the couple had appeared in his Feb. 3 column.

has asked her before, but she couldn't tear herself away from the arena.[333]

The affair ripened in October, this time Harrison Carroll "reporting":

> When Mae Heatherly, female bullfighter turned actress, finishes that picture in Spain, Grant Williams will try to put a wedding band on her finger. He's already bought a house, in case she accepts. He'd like to tie the knot before the "Hawaiian Eye" company goes to Honolulu on location in mid-November.[334]

Columnist Mike Connolly, however, contradicted the above progression on July 28, when he stated: "Grant Williams switched his romantic, roving 'Hawaiian Eye' from May Heatherly to Rosemary Moody."[335]

To complicate matters, or should we say to clear them up, Columnist Louella Parsons had already paired Williams with Ms. Moody at the very height of the alleged Williams-Heatherly affair. Here is Parsons, going into considerable detail about the new duo in December 1961:

> What's this about Grant Williams, one of the stars of the "Hawaiian Eye" TV series, and Rosemary Moody, New York model? Grant went to Dallas to spend the holidays with her at her parents' home, and immediately after she flew to New York to spend New Year's with his family.
>
> Grant met Miss Moody last spring while he was in Honolulu on location. To add to the puzzlement, Grant has bought a family sized house with a swimming pool on King's Road [in West Hollywood], so it looks like there will be wedding bells for them.[336]

333. Dean Gautschy, "Behind the Scenes in Hollywood," *Valparaiso (IN) Vidette-Messenger*, July 9, 1962.

334. Harrison Carroll, "Behind the Scenes in Hollywood," *Greenwood (SC) Index-Journal*, October 23, 1962.

335. Mike Connolly, "In Hollywood," *Pittsburgh (PA) Post-Gazette*, July 28, 1962.

336. Louella O. Parsons, "Janet Leigh Has Femme Star Role In 'Bye, Bye Birdie,'" *Anderson (IN) Daily Bulletin*, December 28, 1961.

May Heatherly and Grant Williams at an undetermined event; undated, but circa 1962.

In case anyone is keeping score, the purchase of a new house mentioned by Carroll in October 1962 would have been Grant Williams' third in just over two years. The first, as we will read below, allegedly occurred in the fall of 1960, before the Williams-Heatherly romance even began, while the second (in honor of Williams' possible nuptials with Ms. Moody) was reported by Parsons in December 1961. Williams' former secretary Nina Ingris, who was working for the actor in that period, has no memory of any of those purchases. It is therefore reasonable to assume that either the romances or the real-estate investments (or both) were fabrications. It is also reasonable to assume that Warner Bros. wanted their new contract player to appear to be moving up the social ladder after signing with them, and to flaunt his new status by giving the impression that he was spending money and settling down.

From what we have learned, Williams was actually a melancholy loner, and his lifestyle was in all likelihood a solitary one, which was a problem for the busy folks at the Warner Bros. Publicity Department and for those eager columnists. What better way to solve the problem than to invent news?

Not that all the news was necessarily fabricated. Williams—whether in the interest of his career or to fight his inclination towards solitude—was probably making an effort to be social. He was fundamentally a likeable person, and the role of the sociable actor was probably not a difficult one for him to play.

The most eccentric reports of dates in the early sixties did not originate with Warner Bros. but with the person doing the dating, who in this particular case was also the reporter doing the reporting. In a rather brazen gesture of self-promotion, Hollywood Columnist Lorraine Gauguin began planting news of her own outings with Williams in the column she wrote for the Sioux Falls *Argus-Leader*.

Here is the first plant in September 1961:

> Swingin' on the Sunset Strip.... Grant Williams took me to Cyrano's after the preview of "The Young Doctors." Met Shirley Knight and her husband. Shirley is starring in "Sweet Bird of Youth" at MGM. Perhaps this year she will win the Academy Award. She costars with Grant in "The Couch" to be released soon. All we could do was rave about "Doctors."[337]

Three months later, another rendezvous with Williams:

> Somebody fouled up my tickets for "Flower Drum Song." They never arrived. Was my face red. I had already invited Grant Williams who took me to dinner instead. Nice to know these good-looking actors.[338]

The following year, the two met again for an evening at the movies:

> Grant Williams took me to the opening of "Two for the Seasaw" [sic] with Shirley MacLaine and Robert Mitchum. The

---

337. Lorraine Gauguin, "Hollywood Callboard," *Sioux Falls (SD) Argus-Leader*, September 10, 1961.

338. Lorraine Gauguin, "Hollywood Callboard," *Sioux Falls (SD) Argus-Leader*, December 10, 1961.

theater was jammed, people were standing and sitting in the aisle. The picture is excellent, but sad. Shirley is the adorable Jewish beatnik, Gittel Mosca is a nut.[339]

One gets the distinct feeling that these outings (if they existed) were not romantic in nature, but merely friendly. Let us then hypothesize a friendship between this star-struck columnist and one of the good-looking actors she knew. The most charming of these friendly meetings was reported at the end of 1962:

> We had a merry Christmas at our house. Dick Chamberlain (Dr. Kildare) dropped by en route to the airport to visit his folks in San Francisco. My house seemed to be the stopping off place for the airport as Grant Williams, of Hawaiian Eye, carrying his bag, was on his way to New York and his folks.[340]

Something had definitely soured in the friendship by 1964, or it may simply be that Grant Williams' being out of work after the expiration of his Warner Bros. contract and the cancellation of *Hawaiian Eye* the previous year had made him an embarrassing commodity. Here is the last of those friendly meetings:

> I moved this week and didn't make my usual rounds to the studios. Had countless phone calls from out-of-work actors who wanted to help. Called it off the second day after James Drury (The Virginian) , Richard Rust, Grant Williams, Rex Reason and Marlon Brando—if you please—filled up the kitchen all day drinking coffee, telling lies, using the telephone, eating sandwiches, playing the bongos while the movers (at $18 per hour) tried to move furniture around them. These big helpers made more mess, caused more trouble and more breakage than a group of chimpanzees. Finally chased them all away

---

339. Lorraine Gauguin, "Hollywood Callboard," *Sioux Falls (SD) Argus-Leader*, October 21, 1962.

340. Lorraine Gauguin, "Hollywood Callboard," *Sioux Falls (SD) Argus-Leader*, December 28, 1962.

and after three days of back-breaking work it looks as though I made it.[341]

Gauguin aside, many tidbits appeared in the mainstream Hollywood press during Williams' Warner Bros. tenure. More often than not, these were not full articles but tiny humorous reminders to the public that Williams existed.

The mythology of the film star would not have been complete without one particular item: the luxury car. In the case of Grant Williams, the lonely artist with sophisticated tastes, the car in question could not be something as commonplace as the sports car. The press (or Williams) came up with two solutions. Here is the first:

> Grant Williams, the "Hawaiian (Private) Eye," traded off his '61 chariot for a 1929 Lincoln, which doesn't sound like a particularly sound business deal unless you know that the vintage clunk may have belonged to the late, unlamented Legs Diamond. Anyway, it has the bullet-proof glass and portable bar of that car. So Williams figures that it will increase in value at the rate of $250 a year as an antique, while his new car would depreciate about $1000 a year.[342]

For the second solution two years later, the press (or Williams) went back to the old reliable cliché, the sports car, but from England, if you please, and from an illustrious relative:

> Grant Williams, between a couple of fast hands of bezique while waiting for his "Hawaiian Eye" set-ups, assembled the sports-car his aunt shipped him from England—complete with a bar in the rear. His aunt is the 86-year-young Mary Garden.[343]

---

341. Lorraine Gauguin, "Hollywood Callboard," *Sioux Falls (SD) Argus-Leader*, March 29, 1964

342. "Trading Down?," *Cincinnati Enquirer*, October 11, 1961.

343. *Philadelphia Inquirer*, March 31, 1963. Garden was actually 89.

A star must have a Hollywood Hills home, according to the mythology. Sure enough, Williams' alleged "new house" that popped up intermittently in the Hollywood press followed the tradition perfectly: it was in the Hollywood Hills. A minor disaster at the new Williams homestead was reported, somewhat irrelevantly (by itself and without a context) but with a touch of irony, in March 1962: "Grant Williams can walk across his swimming pool. Recent heavy rains in Hollywood caved in a hillside behind his new home and filled the pool with rocks and mud."[344]

An item correlating this "new-house" thread with—wait for it—Mary Garden had appeared in November 1960 in Hedda Hopper's *Los Angeles Times* column:

> Mary Garden's nephew Grant Williams bought a Hollywood Hills home to celebrate his Warner Bros. contract. He's invited auntie over from Scotland for the holidays. "Who knows," he said, "perhaps I can persuade her to stay; she could have a new career in TV." Grant is given a star spot in the Hawaiian Eye series, and has a top role in "Susan Slade."[345]

Williams and his famous operatic aunt were paired again in another charming piece of journalistic fluff published in November 1962:

> Grant Williams, currently working in Warner Bros.' thriller "The Couch," received a prize collection of records dating back to 1917 from his great aunt in Scotland, opera star Mary Garden.
> Grant explained, however, that his birthday is August 18—and the prized recordings were lost in transit since the middle of last year, and only recently located and delivered.[346]

The above fact may or may not have been true; if it was, here is a detail from Garden's 1951 autobiography (where she never mentions any American relatives) that tints her alleged gift to Williams with a note of

---

344. *Abilene (TX) Reporter-News*, March 17, 1962.

345. Hedda Hopper, "Sam Spiegel Signs Horst Buchholz," *Los Angeles Times*, November 5, 1960.

346. "Grant Williams Gets Old Records," *San Bernardino (CA) Daily Sun*, November 17, 1962.

sarcasm: "I feel the same way about my disks; I just loathe them. I can't bear it when someone plays a trick on me and turns them on."[347]

The most curious non-romantic piece of publicity—through the Associated Press—concerned Director Michael Curtiz testing Grant Williams for the role of St. Francis of Assisi in a new film. The year was 1960. The actor was described as follows: "[Williams is] a former minister turned actor. He once was the star of 'The Incredible Shrinking Man' and other science fiction and horror movies."[348] The role of St. Francis in the Twentieth Century Fox film *Francis of Assisi* (1961) eventually went to Bradford Dillman.

Where exactly the Associated Press got the idea that Grant Williams had been a minister, we do not know, but it would be natural to think that this reference had something to do with Williams' interest in religious studies. It probably did not: coincidentally, there was a minister by the name of Grant Williams in California. This particular Williams was the Chaplain (and later Commander) at Post 64 of the American Legion in Santa Cruz. Newspaper photographs confirm that this was indeed a different Grant Williams.[349]

The problem of homonymy is an annoying one when researching Grant Williams. In the 1950s and '60s, American newspapers were filled with Grant Williamses. Aside from the operatic tenor discussed in Chapter 13, there were: an all-star football player in Panama City, Florida; an organist in Ogden, Utah; a Baptist minister from Eau Claire, Wisconsin; a popular car dealer in Austin, Minnesota; a forest ranger in Panguitch, Utah; and several socialites by the name of "Mrs. Grant Williams," for example in Shamokin, Pennsylvania.

At any rate, Warner's initial attitude towards Williams was quite friendly. The press that the studio devoted to its new star was not merely cheerful; it was glowing. In terms of feature-film work, Williams may have been relegated to secondary roles (until *The Couch*), but his regular participation in the *Hawaiian Eye* television series elicited enthusiastic tongue-in-cheek promotion from the Warner Bros. press crew.

---

347. Garden and Biancolli (1951), op. cit., 233.

348. Associated Press, "St. Francis Role Stirs Woes," *Salt Lake (UT) Tribune*, June 19, 1960.

349. For example, see *Santa Cruz (CA) Sentinel*, May 27, 1957, or June 24, 1959.

Williams himself appears to have been happy with the attention, or at least with the opportunities that came with it. Columnist Eve Starr[350] was certainly convinced that this was the case after her conversation with him (a conversation that yielded a rather insightful profile of Williams):

> Williams has, among other things, a keen appreciation of publicity and a keen sense of having lacked it during the three years he was under contract to U-I.[351]

In any event, Williams' name was bouncing around the nation's newspapers on a regular basis: Williams was a weekly concern for journalists. Here is an item about teaching:

> Grant Williams, who plays Greg MacKenzie on Hawaiian Eye, has organized some acting classes in which he coaches young hopefuls. One former pupil, who got a small role in a show, called Grant for some last minute coaching.
>
> She later had much trouble explaining to her jealous boy friend (who was threatening to punch MacKenzie in the nose) that the date was really and truly only business.[352]

Another delightful bit concerning Williams' attachment to his role on the series appeared in April 1962: "Grant Williams likes his long-running stellar role in Warner Bros.' *Hawaiian Eye* to such an extent that he has installed a door bell in his home which chimes the show's theme song."[353]

---

350. Eve Starr's column "Inside Television" was a fixture of several successive dailies from 1953 to 1966. Before settling on the catch phrase "Hollywood–Starr Report" as an intro, Starr had begun her columns with different phrases, such as "Hollywood–Starr Talk," "Hollywood–Teletorial," or "Hollywood–Starr Digest."

351. Eve Starr, "Inside Television," *Pottstown (PA) Mercury*, August 12, 1961.

352. In "TV Scout Reports," *Abilene (TX) Reporter-News*, July 13, 1962.

353. *La Crosse (WI) Tribune*, April 28, 1962.

Social Seasons

Warner Bros. occasionally encouraged Williams to make public appearances in the Los Angeles area, but these appearances were of a different ilk from those initiated by Universal-International in the 1950s. Six years, and the reign of television as a competitor with cinema, had contributed to quite a change in public taste. Silly and contrived those 1950s social parties and gala premieres in which Williams had participated for U-I might have been, but they were still more dignified than most of his studio-imposed appearances in the 1960s. Some examples follow.

Only the first event, a Hollywood gathering of publicists, actors, and directors, sounds remotely interesting. It was reported by Columnist Lorraine Gauguin on November 27, 1960, eleven days after Clark Gable's death on November 16. Gable's ghost haunted the entire column.

> Helen Heigh and Bill Dodge, publicists, had an interesting crowd gather at Helen's for brunch. Director Tay Garnett and his lovely actress wife Mari Aldon brought their six year old daughter, Teala, to meet Casey Tibbs, the world's champion cowboy. Casey, his wife and Arthur O'Connell came in western garb. Arthur said he attended mass in the outfit and the REAL cowboy, Casey said he put on his cowboy costume after they left church. Warner Brothers actor Grant Williams (is he a handsome one!) said he had had a premonition of Clark Gable's death in a dream and he was all shaken up.[354]

On February 1, 1961, Williams was on call as "star of *Hawaiian Eye*" at the Glendale, CA, branch of Sears, Roebuck & Co., paired with Beatrice Kay, star of Columbia Pictures' neo-*noir* film *Underworld U.S.A.*, about to be released (May 1961). A full-page advertisement in the *Los Angeles Times* on that day urged the public to "Join the Stars" and celebrate the department store's diamond jubilee, with different (minor) stars of film, radio, or television appearing at each of the eleven Greater L.A. branches. Bozo the Clown was on call at the Inglewood branch.

In April 1961 (possibly April 2 according to the planned schedule for the event), Williams served on the jury of a beauty contest. The venue was

---

354. Lorraine Gauguin, "Hollywood Callboard," *Sioux Falls (SD) Argus-Leader*, November 27, 1960.

Villa Frascati, a restaurant located at 8117 Sunset Boulevard on the Sunset Strip of Los Angeles (and only a few blocks away from Williams' first West-Coast home on North Hayworth Avenue). The *Los Angeles Times* wrote about the outcome after the fact:

> Italian starlet Ondine Coryell copped the $500 prize in the Villa Frascati Dining Beauty Contest. She won a Don Loper gown and fetching coif by Flaire. Judges consisted of casting director Jerry Bloom, fashion expert Caroline Leonetti, actress Jayne Mansfield, actor Grant Williams, newspaperman Neil Rau and Bob Turnbull.[355]

On February 8, 1962, the *Los Angeles Times* announced a parade by the Beverly Hills Girl Scouts for their annual two-week cookie sale. The Wilshire Boulevard parade was to start on Saturday, February 10, at 9:45 a.m. The film and television stars participating in the event included Grant Williams, Bobby Diamond (who, in his years as young-adult television performer, bore something of a resemblance to Williams), Robert Denver (of *Gilligan's Island*), and Shelley Fabares (of *The Donna Reed Show*).[356]

And, finally: on February 20, 1963, the Reseda Theatre in Reseda, California, re-opened after major renovations. The gala evening included a special preview of Walt Disney Pictures' *Son of Flubber*, with celebrities in attendance. Among the celebrities, Grant Williams, Stubby Kaye, Roger Smith of *77 Sunset Strip*, and Williams' *Hawaiian Eye* co-star Doug Mossman.[357]

Susan Slade

Susan Slade (1961) was the first of Williams' three feature films with Warner Bros. It is definitely a product of its age (or, better, a belated product of the late fifties): it is typically melodramatic, typically slick, and typically as removed from reality as human drama can be, while pretending

---

355. Joan Winchell, "Around Town," *Los Angeles Times*, April 30, 1961.

356. "West Girl Scouts to Launch Cooky Drive," *Los Angeles Times*, February 8, 1962.

357. "Reseda Re-opens to Throng," *Van Nuys (CA) News*, February 28, 1963

Grant Williams and Connie Stevens brace themselves for the future on a windy ship deck in this publicity still for *Susan Slade* (1960). © 1960, Warner Bros.

to say something progressive about the fears of mainstream 1950s society. The film gives lip service to non-conventionality, but plays into the squarest assumptions of middle-class morality, in glorious Technicolor.

Like the sentimental Harlequin-novel fable that it is,[358] *Susan Slade* (based on a novel by Doris Hume) is populated by cardboard fairy-tale types. There is a well-meaning but glacially society-conscious mother; there is a mountain-climbing Prince Charming who woos and conquers the vestal-virgin protagonist; and there is a handsome stable hand who consoles Susan and stands by her in her hour of disgrace after the Prince's death. In glorious Technicolor.

358. *Variety* called the film a "contrived soaper-meller." October 4, 1961.

Grant Williams and Connie Stevens in a guilty moment of *Susan Slade*.
Production still, © 1960, Warner Bros.

Grant Williams plays Prince Charming, aka Conn White, a hand-some, rich, sensitive loafer who climbs mountains compulsively and finds love at first sight when he meets Susan. Susan is not very good at kissing—she has led a very sheltered, rich life, you see—but she would like to learn. Conn easily overcomes her initial diffidence, and teaches her. On an ocean liner, and in glorious Technicolor.

Conn (great name, and a pun waiting to happen) is presented as a seductive but ambiguous figure.[359] Is he too good to be true? Is he after easy adventure? Is he lying when he claims he wants to do good by Susan and marry her when he comes back from his climbing expedition in Alaska? These are the questions the audience is invited to ask. Actually, the answers to those questions are no, no, and no. Conn is sincere in his affections, but he is also what you would call a free spirit: the mountain-climbing expedition he has organized comes first, with Susan a close second.

---

359. Some contemporary reviews dubbed the character "what you might call a villain." For example, Boyd Martin in "Boyd Martin's Show Talk," December 6, 1961.

Back at the ranch (a Carmel ocean-view home that an architect has just completed for Susan's rich family), Susan waits for Conn's letters from the mountains of Alaska, but they do not come. She begins to think he has forgotten her, until she learns that he has not, and has desperately been trying to phone her, but too late. Reached by phone, Conn's father tells Susan how much his son talked about his love for her; he also tells her that Conn has just died while climbing that far-away mountain. Susan is devastated, and pregnant. What to do? Mom has a solution: claim that she herself is with child, and take Susan away on a long European cruise before the truth begins to show so people will not talk.

Connie Stevens and Grant Williams kiss on deck in this publicity still for *Susan Slade*. © 1960, Warner Bros.

The acting is good all around (Dorothy McGuire is wonderful as usual as the mom), the story is enjoyable, Max Steiner's score is romantic, Lucien Ballard's Technicolor is glorious. Even the set decoration by William L. Kuehl is grand: according to contemporary reports, the photographs of Chile gracing the walls of the living room of Dorothy McGuire's character were prize-winning shots taken by McGuire's real-life husband, photographer John Swope.[360]

Grant Williams is dangerously sweet as the prince-tempter, but has little to do except be charming and seductive, and disappear from the film early on (*Variety* called him "good-looking and adequate in the role").[361] The *Los Angeles Times'* Philip K. Scheuer called the film a "feeble 'family' drama."[362]

The Couch: Preparation

The Couch (1962) was an important break for Grant Williams, and his biggest, though not necessarily greatest, starring vehicle after *The Incredible Shrinking Man*.

With the blessing of Warner Bros., Williams' preparation for the role of Charles Campbell the disturbed serial killer dug deep into the Method techniques, as Columnist Boyd Martin explained in an article:

> Away from the camera, Williams spent many hours with a real psychiatrist, Dr. Leland Johnson, Van Nuys, Cal.[363]
>
> "I wanted to understand as fully as possible the fictitious person I portray," Williams explains. "I figured it would help if I were analyzed as Campbell. In the real-life sessions I was able

---

360. Leonard Lyons, "Lyons Den," *Post Standard* (Syracuse, NY), December 29, 1960.

361. *Variety*, October 4, 1961.

362. Philip K. Scheuer, "'Susan Slade' Proves Feeble 'Family' Drama," *Los Angeles Times*, November 9, 1961.

363. On November 3, 1957, the *Van Nuys News* of Van Nuys, California offered the following bio of Dr. Johnson on the day of a parent-teacher meeting for Bethel Lutheran Church School: "Dr. Leland Johnson of the Medical Evangelists College will speak on 'Retaining Good Mental Health.' Dr. Johnson received his PhD at USC and spent five years as school psychologist for the Los Angeles City Schools."

Grant Williams as Charles Campbell in a Warner Bros. production still for
The Couch (1962). © 1962, Warner Bros.

to probe Campbell's character with the help of Dr. Johnson. I
learned how he would act in various instances, how he might
walk, why he behaved as he did.

Williams came to the sound stage with an elaborately documented case history of Campbell when filming began on "The
Couch." All spaces of the analyst's questionnaire were filled in
with comments on the patient's chief complaint, his attitude,
his progress record, his social status, and his surface character-
istics. A notebook was crammed with information on similar

cases, and on the pages of his script Williams has written his imagined reactions of Campbell to what others were saying and doing. Consequently, Williams has become a booster of the value of psychiatric treatments.

"You don't have to be mentally ill to be helped by a practicing analyst," he says. "Anybody with a specific problem may find a solution by talking it over with a good psychiatrist."[364]

In a conversation with Columnist Vernon Scott, Williams elaborated both on this preparation process and on its impact on him:

Grant was so impressed [by the work he did with the analyst] that he is having his own psyche investigated. With luck the young actor (best known for his detective role in TV's "Hawaiian Eye") may be able to play himself as convincingly as he does a paranoid in the new movie.

"I had no idea how to play the role, so I went to the psychiatrist to find out about him," Williams said in all seriousness. Grant, a tall, handsome blond young man spent four weeks tattling on the id of a fictitious nut.

"We developed an entire past for the character," he explained, "based on what we know of him from the script. The doctor asked me questions which I answered based on my own interpretations of the man, taking each scene and situation in sequence. "I feel as if we created a real human being. It was my idea and I think it worked out beautifully."

According to Grant this is method acting raised to its zenith.

"I know Charles Campbell (the character) as well as I know myself. I could predict his behavior under any conditions," he boasted.

Evidently he knows Charlie better than himself. Much as he knows about good old paranoiac Charlie, Grant isn't exactly sure what he hopes to find out about himself on the couch.[365]

---

364. "Boyd Martin's Show Talk," *Louisville (KY) Courier-Journal*, December 6, 1961.

365. Vernon Scott, "Hollywood," *New Philadelphia (OH) Daily Times*, April 8, 1961.

Grant Williams and co-star Shirley Knight strike a dramatic pose in this
Warner Bros. publicity still for *The Couch* (1962). © 1962, Warner Bros.

There were those who believed that this psychiatric preparation was
only a promotional ploy, and Williams promptly defended himself from
such accusations in an article written by Columnist Harold Heffernan
(NANA):

> "Some folks claim I'm only trying to hunt some publicity
> gravy," said Williams, whose regular duties at Warners center
> mostly around the weekly 'Hawaiian Eye' TV series, "but they
> don't know how wrong they are. I've always been interested in
> mental theories."

Grant Williams dredges up his ferocious side—courtesy of Lee Strasberg's emotional memory—as he practices stabbing in a scene of *The Couch*. Frame capture.

> [...] Williams has had calls from a number of actors about
> to embark on similarly complex film roles, with all expressing
> avid interest and seeking operational information.[366]

Amusingly, this prolonged therapy qualified Williams as an expert of sorts in psychiatric matters, at least on Warner's television sets. A short article about an episode of *Surfside 6* involving a psychiatrist mentioned Williams in an unusual capacity: "Grant Williams of Hawaiian Eye, who underwent an eight-month session with a psychiatrist, acted as technical adviser on this show."[367]

Speaking of Williams' preparation work, a curious piece of information appeared on October 21, 1962:

> Grant Williams, who stars in the forthcoming Warner Bros.'
> "The Couch," said that recalling the memory of his feelings
> when he stabbed a poisonous snake to death in the Philippines

366. Harold Heffernan (NANA), "Afreud of The Couch?" in the *Baltimore Sun*, June 4, 1961.

367. *Willoughby (OH) News-Herald*, December 4, 1961.

The iconic Warner Bros. logo is superimposed over the *noir* imagery of the opening sequence of *The Couch*. Frame capture.

helped him register emotion for a scene in the picture in which he stabs a man.[368]

Which is plausible enough, as is the following research task: "Grant Williams has bought the complete works of Sigmund [sic] Freud as 'homework' for his role […]."[369]

The Couch: Outcomes

Visually, *The Couch* introduces itself through *noir* imagery: after a short teaser in which a young man (whose face we do not see) makes a call from an indoor public telephone—shades of *Dial M for Murder* (1954)—announcing that he will murder someone at seven o'clock sharp (right before his regular appointment with a psychiatrist), we are taken outside, in the streets of Los Angeles. As the man strolls down the urban landscape, photographed in contrasted black and white and accompanied by jazzy music, the Warner Bros. logo appears. These urban main-title

368. *San Bernardino (CA) Daily Sun*, October 21, 1962.

369. *San Bernardino (CA) Daily Sun*, June 23, 1962.

shots are a rare opportunity to glimpse Downtown Los Angeles as it was in 1961, and a homage to latter-day *noir* films such as *Sweet Smell of Success* (1957). *Sweet Smell of Success* this film is not, but there is a gritty atmospheric hardness to its chiaroscuro cinematography, and it is a pity that dramatically the film decides to take the road of melodrama rather than that of *noir* sharpness.

The Warner Bros. pressbook for the film reported a flattering (for Williams) incident that occurred while shooting those opening shots:

> Grant Williams is now resigned to the fact that an actor who appears frequently on TV can't remain anonymous.
>
> Producer-director Owen Crump wanted to "steal" newsreel-type documentary footage on the downtown streets of Los Angeles for sequences in [*The Couch*]. He instructed Williams to forego makeup so that he could mingle with the rush hour crowd unrecognized.
>
> Crump's plan was to photograph Grant as he walked through the crowds with a camera concealed in a moving car. And the idea worked well for just about three minutes. But then a couple of girls spotted the actor and squealed, "There's Grant Williams from 'Hawaiian Eye.' Let's get his autograph."
>
> Crump took over quickly and promised the actor would send them autographed photos if they'd just disappear and permit filming to resume (WBC, 18).

Variety had this to say about the film's main character:

> The killer (Grant Williams) employs the melodramatically advantageous technique of phoning in his immediate homicidal intentions to the local police authorities. Otherwise he is a singularly uninteresting lad, one for whom the audience can feel no genuine compassion. [...] The motivations for his mental disarray are illustrated via through-the-eyeball scenes on the analyst's couch, but the history of his case never comes into dimensional focus.[370]

---

370. *Variety*, February 21, 1962.

In *Variety*'s view, "Williams delivers an agitated, menacing, appropriately unstable portrayal [...]." Frame capture from *The Couch* (1962).

The film's main gimmick, and probably its biggest flaw, is its concentration on the technical/psychiatric search for Charles Campbell's motivations. Rather than focusing on the "fun-ride" aspect of a killer's derangement, as Scriptwriter Joe Stefano and Director Alfred Hitchcock had in re-tooling Robert Bloch's telling of *Psycho* (1960), here Bloch himself writes a script[371] that aspires to some kind of psychiatric rigor. Arguably, the weakest and most tedious scenes in *Psycho* are those in which a psychiatrist explains Norman Bates' psyche; in *The Couch*, Bloch treats Charles Campbell's entire tale like a case history, and therefore tends to explain rather than to dramatize. Thus, the protagonist's story becomes tiresome for two reasons: first, the investigative process of psychoanalysis, or psychiatry, is interesting for the subject of that investigation but not necessarily for an external observer; second, explanations are expository, and exposition is fundamentally undramatic.

Williams' scenes away from the analyst's couch—for example his scenes with his quasi girlfriend, Terry (Shirley Knight)—are both more effective and more interesting from the point of view of acting. In these scenes, the oscillating tension that Williams establishes between a relaxed Charles and

371. The script was based on an original story by Blake Edwards and Producer-Director Owen Crump.

a nervous Charles is a fascinating exercise in emotional mobility, or fluidity. As he had done in *Allen in Movieland* (1955), Williams demonstrates his skill in subtle emotional transitions, by continuously shifting the register of Charles' feelings—without overacting—lucidly, intensely and elegantly.

Variety was relatively positive about Williams:

> Though hemmed in by rather shallow script scrutiny of the character, Williams delivers an agitated, menacing, appropriately unstable portrayal of the crazy figure.

Variety's review was ultimately only half-negative: though it reduced the film to "an old-fashioned, pot-boiling, murder melodrama with new-fangled psychological overtones," it also concluded that

> [...] the wear and tear isn't as apt to disturb appreciably less particular consumers who, being less inclined to indulge in meticulous observation, will accept the picture as a standard piece of cinematic furniture in the psychological-suspense line. As such, the Warner Bros. release should prove a serviceable commodity [...].

Reviews of the film were generally lukewarm, mixing praise and criticism. *The New York Times*' Eugene Archer was particularly sarcastic in his tongue-in-cheek disdain.[372] Most of the reviewers' complaints were aimed at the film's collection of "murder-mystery clichés"[373] and at its lack of character development. Actually, the character of Charles Campbell *is* developed, but through explanation ("psycho-babble," which is a cliché in itself) and unimaginative dialogue.

Williams' performance is the best thing in the film, despite the trite material. His moments of rage and anguish are impressive, as is the young-man-next-door mask he wears when playing nice.

His best scene in the film, however, is the last. Disguised as a surgeon in a hospital room, scalpel in hand, Charles is about to finish off his psy-

---

372. Eugene Archer, "Four Other Films Also Have Premieres," *New York Times*, February 2, 1962.

373. Josephine O'Neill, "Show Business," *Sydney Sun-Herald*, June 21, 1964.

chiatrist Dr. Janz (Onslow Stevens), whom he did not succeed in killing in a previous scene taking place at a crowded stadium. The police arrive, accompanied by Charles's date Terry (the psychiatrist's secretary, played by Shirley Knight), just in time to witness Charles's realization that (through a double-exposure image) in his therapist he sees his dead abusive father (yawn). Brandishing his blade, Charles turns to face the police. Ordered to drop his weapon, he looks at Terry, and, in a mirror double-exposure image, sees her as his beloved sister Ruthie. Pure psychiatric cliché so far, albeit sweet.

Here something remarkable happens. As the music intones a childish music-box tune, and as Charles throws away his weapon, Williams takes us through a visual transformation of his character, via a series of facial expressions that are as logical as they are poetic. Charles smiles affectionately, then pouts childishly, then smiles again, this time mischievously. Then—as he crouches to a quasi-fetal position—he transforms his smile into a thing of innocence, and starts rocking in place, beaming sweetly as he looks at his "sister."

Unburdened by dialogue or cliché, Williams' visual transformation of Charles is revealing and dangerous, heartwarming and frightening, sexy and monstrous. Like some incredible time-lapse spectacle of nature, his metamorphosis fascinates and repels simultaneously. The moment is realistic, but skirts dangerously close to the borders of formal theater: like a stylized Japanese Noh performance or a moment of Brechtian estrangement, Williams' representation encapsulates the events of a human psyche in simple, mysterious cyphers. Not a mean feat for an actor.

Stardom or no stardom, Williams' acting is there for all to see, durably. Just how accomplished such acting is can be demonstrated, *ad absurdum*, by comparing Williams' final scene in the film with the same scene as described in Robert Bloch's novelization of his script.[374] In the reverse translation from screen to page, Bloch tries to render the finished film in terse, economical prose, with professional but mostly unexciting results (and with even more psychological explanations than in the film). Only some sociological musings about life in Los Angeles in the first chapter display true insight. But when Bloch tries to describe the protagonist's final scene, the outcome is disastrous: that final moment in the film is an

---

374. Robert Bloch, *The Couch*, Gold Medal Books, 1962.

An actor's moment: Grant Williams represents human feelings in fluid motion through facial change in his closing scene of *The Couch*. Frame captures.

actor's moment, a physical representation of human thoughts and feelings in fluid motion, and cannot be synthesized verbally without losing all its power.[375]

PT 109

It is true, as Leonard Maltin has written, that *PT 109* (1963) is "very much of its time" and an "action yarn."[376] The film, however, is skillfully written and benefits from expert character setups. Each person depicted in the story is given a taut, sharp introduction, and the characterizations are so lovingly chiseled that they amply compensate for what is stale or conventional in the film.

In addition, a few of the action sequences, especially those that do not relinquish their connection to the characters in the interest of action or plot, achieve a lilting, almost operatic poetry, both dramatically and visually. The night attack on PT 109 and the search for survivors in the dark waters of the South Pacific, as the pieces of the wreckage are ablaze all around the characters, is one such sequence. Aided by William Lava and David Buttolph's poignant music, the scene soars beautifully, far beyond the call of duty.

Lieutenant Alvin Cluster (Grant Williams) is not the protagonist of the film, but he is an important chaperone for the protagonist, Lieutenant J.F. Kennedy (Cliff Robertson). Williams is assigned some nice scenes, particularly in the first act: his introduction is funny and effective, with savvy physical actions (such as the business with a shoe while he is getting dressed) that are perfect to flesh out his characterization visually and subtly during dialogues.

The entire cast is game and does a beautiful job (even Ty Hardin, who looks like a parody of something Tom of Finland dreamed of,[377] does

---

375. *The New York Times* agreed. In its review of Bloch's novelization, it stated that "[t]he Hollywood 'original' clearly triumphs over Bloch's originality in his leaden rosary of clichés […]." Anthony Boucher, "Criminals at Large," *New York Times*, April 8, 1962.

376. Maltin (2009), op. cit.

377. Touko Valio Laaksonen, aka Tom of Finland (1920–1991), was a Finnish artist, famous especially for his finely-drawn homoerotic art with a fetishistic bent, where virile, muscular models engaged in various forms of homosexual contact

Character introductions: Lieutenant Alvin Cluster (Grant Williams) slumbers as J. F. Kennedy (Cliff Robertson) reports to his tent, in *PT 109* (1963). Frame capture.

Savvy characterization details: Grant Williams occupies himself with practical tasks—such as emptying the sand out of a shoe—to enliven an expository dialogue. Frame capture.

an outstanding job with his role), but it is the character actors who really shine, actors such as the wonderful James Gregory and Norman Fell. It all boils down to the interaction of good writing, good directing and good acting.

The film is particularly wise in adopting a lighthearted, ironic tone in the setup—for example during Williams' introduction, or during Gregory's inspection to the newly refurbished boat—and then turning the mood on its head in the dramatic moments. As effective as some of

---

in heavily male scenarios (the military, the Navy, trucking, construction, etc.). Laaksonen's work was hugely influential to twentieth-century gay culture. Hardin's likeness to Tom of Finland's military characters was also cheerfully noted by Jon Vater in his blog, *Poseidon's Underworld*.

the drama is, it is the lighter scenes that are most memorable, and Composers Lava and Buttolph seem to agree, writing witty tongue-in-cheek cues for the first act.

In its review, *Variety* liked both the humor and the action, and was pleased with the acting, lavishing special praise on Gregory. Ty Hardin, Robert Culp, and Grant Williams were lumped together with the comment, "[they] score in essentially surface characterizations of young naval officers."[378]

---

378. *Variety*, March 20, 1963.

12 *Hawaiian Eye, 1960–1963*

SAN FRANCISCO *HAOLE*[379]

Before *Magnum, P.I.* (1980–1988), before *Hawaii Five-O* (1968–1980, and reboot, 2010–), there was *Hawaiian Eye* (1959–1963). The Warner Bros. Hawaii-based television detective series might have been seen by Williams as a letdown from the point of view of his movie stardom, but it was in fact an amiable detective show and a good chance for him to showcase his talent on a weekly basis and become a household name. Williams joined the series in the second-season episode aired on December 21, 1960, and was incorporated into the filmed main-title sequence in October 1961.

In an August 1961 profile of Williams, Columnist Eve Starr was explicitly appreciative of Williams' talent, stating, boldly: "Williams is a talented man." She was also supportive of his joining the television series:

> In its ceaseless and not always successful search for young new faces, Warner Brothers has now come up with a third leading man for "Hawaiian Eye."
>
> Actually, Grant Williams is neither particularly young (he's 30) nor particularly new (14 pictures at Universal International, dozens of TV credits). [...]
>
> Williams' chief asset, however, is the fact that, compared to his two colleagues, he is an actor.[380]

---

379. In Hawaiian, a *Haole* is a foreigner or a Caucasian person.

380. Starr (1961), op. cit.

Candid Warner Bros. portrait of Grant Williams on the set of the
television series *Hawaiian Eye*, circa 1960.

Starr may appear excessively pointed towards Williams' co-stars in that
last statement, until one realizes that she is referring precisely to that discrepancy, or contradiction, that was so central in Williams' career: the
discrepancy between quality and success, or between acting and stardom.
Starr is not really saying that Williams' co-stars were not actors, but that,
compared to them, Williams was an actor's actor and not a television star.
She is saying that any comparison between Williams and his colleagues
would be a comparison between apples and oranges. Along similar lines,

Columnist Luke Feck, in an article discussing the casts of *Hawaiian Eye* and two other Warner Bros. television series, defined Williams as "probably the best actor among them [...]."[381]

The series rotated its investigators: each week's case was assigned to one, sometimes two of the detectives, Tracy Steele (the distinguished Anthony Eisley, replaced in season four by Troy Donahue's character Philip Barton) and Tom Lopaka (the muscular Robert Conrad);[382] Williams was not always the protagonist of the week, but neither were his colleagues. On the episodes where he was not showcased, Williams either was absent or made a cameo appearance.

Four secondary characters provided background color and comic relief, occasionally helping with the investigations: Kim the Taxi Driver (Poncie Ponce), Moke the Security Officer and control-desk Dispatcher (Doug Mossman), Cricket Blake the Photographer and night-club Singer (the adorable Connie Stevens, whose song numbers were an obligatory caesura in most episodes, alternating with Arthur Lyman's group and its "exotic" percussion sounds[383]), and Danny Quon the Police Lieutenant (Mel Prestidge).

On average, the series scripts were accomplished, if conventional. The dialogues had some wit to them, and each story usually contained equal shares of amiable repartee, suspense and action. Though Williams' participation in the show's lighthearted episodes was certainly charming, it was in the dramatic vein that he was particularly successful, as demonstrated by his entire tenure with the series and by one spectacular example (more about that later). Williams was the protagonist of thirty of his fifty episodes with the show.

Initially, Williams' character, handsome freelance Investigator Greg MacKenzie, is hired to help on a case. He is then offered a permanent job with the titular detective agency, and for the first six months or so commutes from San Francisco; soon, he decides to settle down in paradise and join the fold for good. According to a syndicated tidbit, there was a

---

381. Luke Feck, "Cute Shoulders," *Cincinnati Enquirer*, December 6, 1961.

382. According to Mulroney (KM), Conrad and Williams did not get along, at least when Williams was under the influence.

383. Arthur Lyman (1932-2002), American (Oahu-born) vibraphone and marimba Player, was famous for his "exotic" faux-Polynesian lounge sonorities. He recorded several popular LP records.

reason for this precarious presence of Williams' during the first season: "[the idea] is that this will make it easier to spring him from the show if another series Warner Brothers is concocting for him jells."[384] Another report gave a different explanation for Williams' precarious status, stating that "the producers took the precaution of adding another permanent member to the show because of Robert Conrad's continuing feud with the studio."[385]

Greg is a debonair *bon vivant* who, as befits the era, wears good suits, smokes a lot, drinks a lot, (but gracefully) and dates a lot. There is no deep humility to his character (except in one or two dramatic episodes); in fact, there is a touch of slick confidence to him, in line with the way detectives and policemen were depicted in the 1960s. When observed closely, however, Greg is revealed to be a friendly, compassionate man with a melancholy dignity to him, a trait that (together with the quality of Williams' acting) adds a certain nobility to the proceedings.

MacKenzie's first-season cameos are occasionally amusing. When they are used as comic relief, they are a chance for Williams to play relaxed, light-hearted comedy. These appearances are sometimes reduced to his walking into a scene with his packed bags and announcing he is off to San Francisco (once wearing a Tyrolean feathered hat, which elicits bemusement from his partners).

In the episode "The Humuhumunukunukuapaa Kid" (season 2, ep. 28) Williams shares investigative duties with Anthony Eisley, and his undercover scene playing a drunken blue-collar worker at a bar is a funny, vivacious showstopper.

Speaking of drunkenness, Williams gives a veritable acting lesson in "The Trouble with Murder" (season 2, ep. 25). In order to create a disruption and approach a man whose name he needs to learn (a man who is on a date with a potential murder victim), MacKenzie pretends to be drunk. This would be unremarkable, if it were not for the way Williams enacts the prank. Sitting quietly at the bar with his partner Tracy Steele, MacKenzie raises a warning finger at his partner, announcing solemnly: *"Regard the demonstration."* He then stands up, loosens his shirt collar and necktie, and runs his hands through his hair to ruffle it. His hair standing

384. "'Eye' on Grant," *Cincinnati Enquirer*, December 24, 1960.

385. *Orlando (FL) Sentinel*, December 21, 1960.

on end, he raises his voice an octave, fakes a Texas accent, and stumbles towards the couple's table, wreaking havoc with their peaceful dinner.

Williams' transformation into a drunk in five easy steps only appears to be external; in fact, it comes from within, having been prepared externally, and is a demonstration of both Method and non-Method acting techniques, joined harmoniously together.

Speaking of Method, a 1961 *Los Angeles Times* article written by Don Alpert and containing an extended interview with Williams dealt with the issue of Strasberg's technique, and of the offshoot of that technique that Williams called psycho-drama. Here is Williams commenting on its application in the realm of television:

> Stanislavsky invented a method of work, a piece of equipment, a technique with many exercises that go along with it. Psycho-drama deals mostly with the research work that goes along with playing the character. [...] Psycho-drama, with proper research, will give you automatic behavior.
>
> The method is used unconsciously by practically every actor except out and out egotists. What they're saying is 'Look at me, look at me.' This is true of most TV actors.
>
> Say I'm a killer in a western. I go to Dr. Leland Johnson and we study the script. We find reasons why the man likes to kill and when we learn his character then we know how he will react to other things.
>
> The schedule of TV prohibits the use of the method. The guy I play on 'Hawaiian Eye' isn't just me. I don't think just me would last more than two seasons. I use the best of me as far as I know and the only reason I know about that is because I go to an analyst personally.[386]

A Little Masterpiece

There are virtually no conventional clichés in the extraordinary season-three episode "Nightmare in Paradise" (airdate April 11, 1962), which stars Grant Williams in dazzling form.

---

386. Alpert (1961), op. cit.

The episode is endowed with an inspired teleplay by Richard H. Landau (1914–1993), who scripted five episodes for *Hawaiian Eye*. Landau's text, head and shoulders above most of the other scripts for the series (including his own), is an exercise in romantic *noir*, and a very good one, with sparkling, literate dialogues and a profound commitment to the characters, who are given a chance to express themselves in original yet truthful ways. The script is so special that one might suspect someone else lent a hand in writing it, perhaps even Williams himself: this splendid text is an actor's (as well as a writer's) paradise. In any event, it must have been with great enthusiasm that all the talents involved, writer, director (Charles R. Rondeau, 1917–1996), and cast, threw themselves into the realization of the episode.

At this juncture, the statements that Williams made to Eve Starr about his work on *Hawaiian Eye* might help us support the idea that Williams' contribution to the series was probably not a passive one, and that he was trying to leave his mark on the show. Williams believed in his work as an actor, and was probably ready to fight for it on occasion. Here are those statements (emphasis mine):

> We're going to lift 'Hawaiian Eye' out of its rut. We've got some good scripts coming up and some good directors to work with. *And I mean work with.*
>
> It's not enough just to have the handsome young detective go solve the crime. We're going to have more characterization, more adult dialogue, more interesting conflicts between people.[387]

Whether or not Williams actually wrote any dialogues for any of the episodes in which he starred (Starr pointed out that Williams had "written and sold a number of TV scripts"), one can feel from the above statements that, promotion of self and series aside, Williams wanted to add something of his own to the show.

Back to "Nightmare in Paradise." The story is a personal one for Greg MacKenzie. While driving on an isolated road with his date one night, MacKenzie is nearly hit by a swerving car; the offending vehicle crashes

---

387. Starr (1961), op. cit.

into a tree, and its driver turns out to be, not drunk but dead, apparently from his own shotgun. A suicide note next to him seems to confirm this conclusion, but MacKenzie is not convinced.

Greg's involvement in the case and his attraction to the dead man's young widow, Julie Gant (Abby Dalton), turn the investigation into a personal crusade for him. As it turns out, his suspicions were correct: there is more than meets the eye, and nothing is quite what it seems.

There is a vague resemblance between the story of "Nightmare in Paradise" and the story of The Third Man (1949). Like the protagonist of Carol Reed's film (Holly Martins, played by Joseph Cotten), Greg MacKenzie keeps investigating after the conclusion of the coroner's inquest because something does not sit right with him. Like Harry Lime (Orson Welles) in Reed's film, the dead man Greg is investigating turns out to have been smuggling dangerous counterfeit prescription drugs, and might not be dead at all. And Like Harry Lime's bereaved girlfriend Anna Schmidt (Alida Valli), Julie Gant the saddened widow tries to dissuade the infatuated protagonist from investigating.

In true film noir fashion, Greg sticks his neck out personally (he has not been hired by anyone), exposing himself to physical danger and to confrontations with unsavory characters in order to learn the truth. Like a true film noir investigator, Greg keeps going despite all the warnings, in the name of something deeply moral that just will not let him alone.

From the outset, the writing declares its intention to be original. The story is bookended by two graceful scenes depicting Greg's nighttime necking in his convertible with Anna (Eva Norde), his Danish date. It is clear from their first scene that she is interested in him, but has an even greater passion for food, and would rather talk about local delicacies—or go eat—than follow through with the lovemaking, much to MacKenzie's dismay. The two vignettes are humorous and delicate. Here is the first one, where Williams is able to avoid at least one cliché in his acting: where a lesser actor might have played the comedy, and colored McKenzie's moves with predatory self-assuredness, he underplays the dialogue with the boyish sheepishness of a young man who is on the brink of frustrated excitement and can barely speak, except haltingly.

(Greg, his arm around Anna's shoulder, is trying to kiss her and get to the next base.)

Greg: Ah. Smorgasbord. Delicious. But... what's Smorgasboad without a little akvavit?

Anna: Where's the mahi-mahi fingers you promised... and a skewed beef teriyaki?

Greg: Later.

Anna: And a Hukilai Punch.

Greg: Anna, can't we just skoal with akvavit?

Anna: I came all the way from Denmark to learn about your country. You haven't teach me anything.

Greg: Not—teach you anything? Why ... we are here exchanging culture. And—that never hurt any international relations. I was just trying to spread a little good will and—and bolster our foreign policy and—and organize my—one-man peace corps.

Anna: Later.

Greg: Anna, just one tiny more skoal—for a red-blooded All-American boy?

Anna: Later.

(Greg lets out a deep sigh, takes his arm away from around her shoulder, and sits straight in the driver's seat.)

Greg: All right. Mahi-mahi fingers and Hukilai Punch it is.

(Another sigh from Greg, but this time it comes out like a soft raspberry.)

Greg (cont'd): You know, now I understand why Hamlet was a melancholy Dane.

(He starts the car.)

After that gently comical opening, the story turns serious, starting with Greg's discovery of Paul Gant's body. Landau's work is nothing short of spectacular: he weaves verbal wit and poetic prose into an honest, insightful exploration of his characters. All the characters, even Kim and Cricket, are wiser than usual, and Cricket's nightclub song, a romantic blues, is a perfect *noir* number directed with finesse by Rondeau and ending with a sophisticated visual touch. Landau does all this and manages to avoid both triteness and flippancy. He never relinquishes his dramatic task throughout the story, expertly balancing the two elements: the words, and the character exploration. Even the scenes in which the story turns somber produce exciting lines for the actors, with sentiment but little sentimentality. In the world of sixties television, a literate, compassionate teleplay such as this counts as a little masterpiece.

Here is Greg's first confrontation with Fletcher (Jock Gaynor), the sophisticated thug who has been sent to intimidate him. The smartly-dressed man, a dark, slick, hulking figure, is at Greg's office (uninvited) when MacKenzie comes back from his question-asking errands, and is pouring drinks at Greg's bar. The following dialogue between them closes Act I:

> *Fletcher: Come in, old buddy. (Greg closes the door and approaches the bar.) Have a drink?*
> *Greg: Thank you.*
> *Fletcher: What'll you have?*
> *Greg: Oh, anything that's handy, I don't want to put you through a lot of trouble.*
> *Fletcher: No trouble at all.*
> *Greg: Well, maybe a little something to go on the rocks.*
> *Fletcher: Sure. (He pours both drinks. The two men raise their glasses.) Your health, old buddy. (Tasting the drink:) Hmm. Nice. Nice place you've got here.*
> *Greg: It's nice of you to approve.*
> *Fletcher: Nice pool, nice clean living. Everything nice and expensive.*
> *Greg: Well, it's nice to be nice.*
> *Fletcher: Funny fellow. Sense of humor too.*
> *Greg: Uh… question.*
> *Fletcher: Please do.*
> *Greg: Who's which?*
> *Fletcher: Now that's a good question. And I'm going to give you a choice. You can be you, or you. Alive, or dead.*
> *Greg: Oh. You got me right on the edge of my drink.*
> *Fletcher: You've been a busy busy boy, old buddy. Full of questions, questions, questions.*

Greg: How else can I get an education?

Fletcher: About a dead man, old buddy?

Greg: This grapevine you've got, do you own it? Or just rent?

Fletcher: You do ask a lot of questions.

Greg: Meaning what, old buddy?

Fletcher: Meaning don't.

Greg: There a law?

Fletcher: You might say.

Greg: Whose?

Fletcher: Let's have some secrets from each other, shall we?

Greg: You know, you make like the third one who's told me to forget about Paul Gant. Why?

Fletcher: Who mentioned any names?

Greg: I don't mind your quaint way of barging in here, or drinking my liquor or smoking my cigarettes, I don't even mind not liking you. But I do mind getting pushed; I do mind someone telling me what not to do.

Greg MacKenzie (Grant Williams) gets punched by Fletcher the gangster (Jock Gaynor) in "Nightmare in Paradise." Frame capture.

> *Fletcher: Tsk tsk tsk tsk tsk. Old buddy, you are a hard one to convince.*
>
> *(Pause. The two men are standing face to face now. Fletcher punches Greg in the stomach twice, hard. Greg slowly drops to the ground. Fletcher finishes his drink and starts walking towards the exit. Greg crawls painfully to the edge of the indoor pool, and loses consciousness. Fletcher leaves.)*

The dialogue, an affectionate nod to films like *The Big Sleep* (1946) and *Sweet Smell of Success* (1957), is a compound of many virtues: it adheres perfectly to the *film noir* conventions it homages while twisting them into a new original form that, ever so subtly and respectfully, transforms them into insights through verbal wit. Not bad for conventional weekly television fodder. The superiority of the writing does not merely concern the words, but also the drama: it allows the actors (especially Williams) to navigate swiftly from feeling to feeling and from moment to moment, and to deliver intelligent, complex portrayals. Greg MacKenzie was never more interesting than in this story.

Greg MacKenzie crawls to the edge of his indoor pool before losing consciousness, in "Nightmare in Paradise." Frame capture.

Williams is superb in the episode, inhabiting the terrific dialogues with agile technique and elegant measure but at the same time propelling the pace of both words and actions with the energy of a consummate theatrical actor.

Good writing and good acting go hand in hand, even in the most obligatory of transitional or expository scenes, such as the one in which Greg wakes up after his poolside knockout:

> (*Greg, lying on the sofa, regains consciousness. He opens his eyes and sees his associate Moke, but does not recognize him; reacting to the memory of his ordeal, he leaps for Moke as if to tackle him. Lieutenant Quon is standing some distance away, looking on.*)
>
> *Moke: Take it easy, Mr. MacKenzie, it's just me.*
>
> *Greg: Oh.*
>
> *Moke: You had me worried. I found you over by the pool.*
>
> *Greg: Yeah. O-oh, yeah. Oh. Hey, you think I could sell this stomach at a discount?*
>
> *Quon: It could've been worse. You might have rolled in and drowned.*
>
> *Greg: Oh, you positively fracture me with your drollery, Lieutenant. (to Moke:) Hey, get me a drink, huh?*
>
> *Moke: Sure thing, Mr. MacKenzie.*
>
> *Greg: Oh. Oh! (Painfully, he gets up and walks to the table, gets a cigarette which Quon lights for him. To Quon:) Where did you come from?*
>
> *Quon: With both your partners out of town, when Moke found you unconscious, he called me.*
>
> *Moke: I didn't know how to handle it, Mr. MacKenzie, so I thought it best to get hold of the Lieutenant.*
>
> *Greg: That's all right, Moke. That's what I pay taxes for.*
>
> *Moke: I'd better make my security rounds. Good night, Lieutenant.*
>
> (*Moke leaves. Greg walks painfully to an armchair to sit down.*)
>
> *Greg: Do you mind? I had a busy evening, and—that character had harpoons in his fists!*
>
> *Quon: Ever seen him before?*

Greg MacKenzie (Grant Williams) and Lieutenant Danny Quon (Mel Prestidge) discuss the aftermath of Greg's encounter with Fletcher, and there is no flat exposition in sight. Frame capture from "Nightmare in Paradise."

Greg: No. But I won't ever forget him. You know, it's funny. I start asking a few questions about a dead man, everybody starts screaming, "Shut up, hands off!" Why?

Quon: 'Cause you're walking on his grave.

Greg: Confuse me more.

Quon: You stub your toe on his tombstone, you might wind up in the same cemetery.

Greg: That's what I like about you, Danny. In just one short sentence you cleared everything up.

Quon: You didn't know Paul Gant. With the law he was pure white. But inside himself, dirt. All dirt.

Greg: What d'you call dirt?

Quon: All the dirt you can think of. Garbage. A human being was just a dollar sign, and the dreams he sold were nightmares. [...]

There is *some* exposition in the above scene, logically, but it is handled swiftly and imaginatively, while keeping the characters lively and interesting.

The dialogue-writing magic also extends to the tender exchanges between Greg and Julie, Mr. Gant's young widow. Dialogues that would normally be infested with clichés are instead little fountainheads of subtle insights, original phrasing, and dramatic color. Here are Greg and Julie in Greg's car, after their first date. On a lonely road (a leitmotif of this episode, it seems), Greg's car gets a flat tire. Greg slows down, then stops the car.

> Greg (laughing): I don't believe it!
> Julie: Lonely road, flat tire...
> Greg: I know. I know, it's the oldest established routine in the world. But somehow, I've never been out with a girl who could help me change one of them.
> (Greg gets out of the car. He goes to the trunk.)
> Julie: That's probably because you've never been out with a plain, simple country girl before.
> Greg: Oh? Are you a plain, simple country girl?
> Julie: M-hm.
> (Julie gets out of the car and joins Greg by the trunk.)
> Greg: What part of the farm?
> Julie: Wisconsin.
> Greg: Wisconsin! Gee, I've got an old buddy up in Madison. Maybe you know him! (He looks at Julie, who is staring at him.) Oh, no, you wouldn't know him.
> Julie: It's a big town.
> Greg: Yeah.
> (Greg starts gathering the tools for the operation.)
> Julie: And you?
> Greg: Me what?
> Julie: Are you a country boy or a city boy?
> (Greg crouches and starts setting up the wheel for the change.)
> Greg: Ah—city, I guess. But I've been everywhere. I kind of settled in San Francisco after Korea. That is, until Tracy and Tom asked me to join them about a year ago.
> (Julie goes back to her car seat. She turns on the car radio;

soft Hawaiian music is playing; she lights herself a cigarette.)

Julie: And now Honolulu.

Greg: Well, a partnership in Hawaiian Eye was a little hard to top.

(Julie comes back and stands next to Greg. He stands up.)

Greg (cont'd): See, there are so many fringe benefits. Like… well, like Waikiki, my favorite beach; mai tais, my favorite drink; the Trade Winds; and my favorite pastime, changing a flat tire on a lonely road with a beautiful woman.

Julie: Thank you.

Greg: Well. Let's get the operation under way here.

(He returns to the wheel and crouches.)

Greg (cont'd): Scalpel, nurse.

(Julie joins him by the wheel and hands him a tool.)

Julie: Scalpel, doctor.

Greg: Thank you.

(Greg exposes the tire damage.)

Greg (cont'd): Oh, nice clean incision. Clamp!

Julie (handing him a tool): Clamp, doctor. (pause) Cigarette, doctor?

Greg: Thanks.

(Julie puts her cigarette in his mouth while he works. Then she crosses her arms, looks up at the sky and lets out a sigh. Greg notices this and stands up to be next to her.)

Greg (cont'd): You know, there's no sky anywhere, and no stars, like this sky and these stars.

Julie: Star light, star bright, first star I've seen tonight…

Greg: I wish I may, I wish I might, have the wish I wish tonight.

(Greg and Julie look at each other. One would expect them to kiss; instead, they embrace lightly and begin a slow dance.)

Greg (cont'd): You know, flat tire, lonely road. There's a lot to be said for it.

Julie: Fringe benefits.

Greg: Uh-huh.

(They dance as the scene fades out.)

The tender, ironic writing of this scene could have been played at the extreme of flippancy or at the opposite extreme of sentimentality by a lesser team. Instead, Williams and Dalton strike just the right balance, mixing their breezy matter-of-fact delivery with a dollop of warm friendliness and a pinch of listfulness, and let the writing do the rest. Williams is especially skillful in his pacing: in his hands, the dialogue whizzes by as if it had no weight at all. It is only at certain key moments—where the mood becomes more meditative—that he uses the tone and pitch of his voice to color the words with a bit of poetry. (Wisely, neither he nor Dalton does this with the actual poetry of the nursery rhyme, which they deliver straight and without sentiment.)

A later scene at the beach finds Greg amorous, and Williams equally deft. Julie clings to her recent grief (or so Greg thinks), and harbors a secret she cannot share (her son is being held captive so she will not reveal the fact that her husband has faked his death). Greg does not understand her reluctance and tries to convince her to let go of the past. Here is the end of the little monologue that ends the lively scene and precedes their first kiss (Williams is masterful here, making the poetic prose believable through the pace and conviction of his acting and the innate musicality of his line readings):

> Greg: All right, he's dead! Are you going to be loyal to a memory for the rest of your life because once it was good? That kind of loyalty belongs in the grave with him! (Pause; Julie, who was facing away, turns to look at Greg) Oh, Julie, Julie. Can't you see tomorrow, and the day after? Come out of the cold and the dark. Let the sun put some light and warmth into your life.(Pause. They kiss.)

The denouement of the story, which obviously contains some obligatory convention to it, is topped by a beautiful moment of closure between Greg and Julie, who is finally free of her burden of threats and blackmail (Fletcher, who has indeed killed her husband, has been captured, and her son is safe). Greg says to her, *"Let's go get your boy,"* and that could be the close of the scene, but the writer and director let Julie have a liberatory cry; she starts sobbing, letting it "spill over," as Greg had advised her to do in an earlier scene; Greg holds her comfortingly, saying: *"Go on, bury it. They can't hurt you any more, Julie. It's all over."*

Greg MacKenzie (Grant Williams) and Julie Gant (Abby Dalton) are about to kiss in "Nightmare in Paradise." Frame capture.

The closing vignette in Greg's car with Anna the Danish gourmande finally allows Greg to score with her, but *he* is the reluctant party now: her excess of enthusiasm while she reminisces about the food she has eaten makes her ravenous in a rather predatory way. The episode ends thus:

> *Anna (all the while kissing Greg): Mahi-Mahi fingers delicious. But what is Mahi-Mahi fingers without Hukilai Punch?*
> *Greg: You—you said that before, Anna.*
> *Anna: And skewered beef Teriyaki.*
> *Greg: Ah—Anna!*
> *Anna: And golden fresh shrimp. Alialikai Punch washed down with Mai Tai.*
> *Greg: Anna! What is happened to you? You—what happened to culture?*
> *Anna: Skoal! You crazy mixed up hanai haole.[388] Skoal!*
> *(She kisses him aggresively)*

---

388. Here Ms. Norde's pronunciation is not clear; this is the closest I could guess without a written script.

Greg (sheepishly): Skoal. Skoal and Aloha to you!
(They kiss. The orchestra intones some solemn final chords.)

Mixed Bag

Another, less successful exercise in atmosphere can be found in the episode "Pursuit of a Lady" (airdate December 11, 1962), a gloomy, solemn, heartfelt *noir* which seems to be loosely based on another *noir* film, *Chicago Deadline* (1949). A celebrity tennis pro, Liz Downing (Diane McBain)—the woman to whom Greg MacKenzie has just proposed marriage—is killed, and the investigation of her murder turns into a re-evocation of her past, conducted through flashbacks and from multiple points of view. This could have been a powerful episode, and there are occasional glimmers of dramatic force, but the writing is maudlin and uninspired, and the result is hollow. Only the finale of the show really packs a punch:

> *(The whole unsavory truth about Liz Downing has been discovered; the culprit has confessed after being fatally wounded. Lieutenant Quon approaches Greg McKenzie, who is staring into space despondently in his office.)*
>
> *Quon: At least it's all over.*
>
> *Greg: Is it? I said I knew very little about Liz until after she was killed. Now I know a lot. But how do I forget? How do I forget?*
>
> *(Greg slowly walks, almost staggers, away from Quon, and exits the room. The orchestra intones some tragic chords. Fade out.)*

Here Williams, his voice pitched half an octave lower than usual, seems to be positively drowning in thick, inconsolable sorrow. His lines are spoken like a dirge to himself, or to life itself, and there is something wrenchingly tragic about the quiet, powerful scene.

Speaking of exercises in style, the episode "'V' for Victim" (airdate June 6, 1962) goes the Agatha-Christie/stormy-night/isolated-house route, and tries to be *And Then There Were None*. But the writing is flat and the episode feels like little more than a rehash of old clichés.

Diane McBain and Grant Williams in a Warner Bros. production still for the
episode "Pursuit of a Lady" (1962).

Farewells

The final episode of *Hawaiian Eye*, "Passport" (airdate April 2, 1963)
is a strange farewell in more ways than one.

Greg MacKenzie is the investigator and sole lead of the episode: his
partners are absent. The story, however, is not centered upon his character
(in fact, it tends to avoid looking at MacKenzie too closely) but on Roger
Alston (Roger Mohr), the man who is being investigated, and on his wife
Nan (Randy Stuart). Stuart gives a heartfelt dramatic performance, but,
curiously, has virtually no contact with Williams' character, with whom

she exchanges maybe two lines. It is as if the two characters were studiously avoiding each other; yet they skirt around each other throughout the story. The presence of Randy Stuart, of course, brings us back full circle to Williams' brightest moment as an actor six years earlier, the film *The Incredible Shrinking Man*, in which Stuart had played his wife.

Curiouser and curiouser: the episode does not take place in Hawaii but in Tokyo, where Alston's trafficking takes place. This change of location gives the episode a further sense of estrangement, as if both the series' iconic locale and its co-stars were being intentionally negated. By distancing itself from the series' setting *and* from Greg MacKenzie (who appears as nominal protagonist in this episode only to be isolated dramatically from the other characters), the episode becomes a symbolic triple farewell to Grant Williams, to his Warner Bros. contract, and to *Hawaiian Eye*.

The curmudgeonly television reviewer of the *Cincinnati Enquirer*, James Devane, was seldom happy about anything; he was absolutely contemptuous of *Hawaiian Eye*, and wrote a scathing piece about the series' cancellation in July 1963. Here is part of it:

> The other night while watching the soon-to-be disbanded firm of "Hawaiian Eye" bring yet another dastardly villain to justice, it came to me that there's more than one reason for closing the program.
>
> Ending the show and its pitiful scripts will be a boon to tired viewers who are always apt to dial in unwarily and then be caught lazily in an armchair with the TV knob just too far away.[389]

On a more tender note, AP Columnist Bob Thomas bade farewell to several canceled television series, including *Hawaiian Eye*.

> Alas, the time has come for our annual dirge for television's losers, the shows that won't make it back next season.
>
> It's a sad business, saying farewell to those series that started out with fond hopes of being another "Dr. Kildare" or a "Hazel" but never quite made it.

---

389. James Devane, "Those 'Hawaiian Eyes' Need A Rest," *Cincinnati Enquirer*, July 30, 1963.

It's even sadder to bid goodby to those successes that have lived their span and now must shuffle off to syndication. […] And so, so long to "The Untouchables"; too bad you ran out of ammunition. Goodby, "Hawaiian Eye," and toodle-oo, "G.E. True."

[…] Goodby, all of you. Sorry you have to move over for the bright new shows that will be taking your time slots this fall, most of which—alas—we'll be saying goodby to at this time next year.[390]

As Williams' tenure at Warner Bros. entered its second year, there was a subtle change in both the tone and the quantity of the studio's publicity for its star, and signs of strain appeared. The item that was printed by the *Los Angeles Times* in January 1962, for example, may have meant nothing both in terms of Williams' health and in terms of his relationship with Warner Bros. There is, however, something vaguely disquieting about it, and its tongue-in-cheek tone is far from reassuring given what we know of Williams' failing health in the two decades that followed:

All the Warner Bros. actresses volunteered for nursing duty when fellow actor Grant Williams became ill with a kidney infection. First to rush to the side of the ailing 'Hawaiian Eye' star was pretty Leslie Parrish.[391]

A February 1962 item may also have been innocent, or it may have hinted at signs of discontent in Williams' rapport with the studio:

Grant Williams is seeking permission from Warner Bros. to do a motion picture in Formosa titled "A Long Way from Home." Filming should be done when Williams completes this season's assignment on 'Hawaiian Eye.'[392]

---

390. Bob Thomas (AP), "TV Brings Down the Curtain On 'Dennis,' 'Dobie,' 'Ness,'" *Emporia (KS) Gazette*, April 23, 1963.

391. Joan Winchell, "In Rome, Turkey and Virginia Ham," *Los Angeles Times*, January 10, 1962.

392. "Hawaii Eye Star Eyes Another Island," *Los Angeles Times*, February 19, 1962.

The project was never to materialize. Williams' contract expired, and was not renewed. Nothing was written about it. After 1963, Williams' name all but disappeared from the press.

Nonetheless, according to Williams' former Secretary Nina Ingris, when *Bonanza* regular Pernell Roberts left the series in April–May 1965, Warner Bros. offered Williams a recurring role as a prodigal son of Ben Cartwright's returning to the Ponderosa fold. Williams apparently refused, outraged at being offered such a marginal part on the show. Yet another possible reason for his break with television in particular and with show business in general. Williams' refusal to become an unimportant regular on the series probably followed his role in the episode "Patchwork Man" on May 23, 1965.

New Freedoms

After the expiration of his contract with Warner Bros., Williams was no longer under any obligation to comply with the studio's choices (department stores, Girl Scout parades, restaurant beauty contests). So it may not be a coincidence that, free of the studio's influence, Williams chose to make his few public appearances at events that were actually interesting.

On January 4, 1967, we find Williams in Pasadena, attending a rather interesting social dinner given by dairy-industry magnate Aaron C. Marcus (President and Manager of the Dairymen's Association Ltd./ Beatrice Foods Co.) to honor British Actress Beatrice Lillie (1894-1989), who had just completed the film *Thoroughly Modern Millie*, slated to open in New York in March. Aside from Grant Williams, the guests included Playwright Franklin Lacey (1917-1988, co-author of *The Music Man*[393] with Meredith Willson), Actor Murray Matheson (1912-1985), Lillie's Manager John Phillips, and Marcus's brother and sister-in-law of Newport. After socializing with Ms. Lillie, the party attended the opening of a production of the Moss Hart/Kurt Weill musical *Lady in the Dark* at the Pasadena Playhouse, starring singer Marni Nixon (whom the *Los Angeles Times* termed "calamitous" in its otherwise positive review of

---

393. The musical ran on Broadway for 1,375 performances, from December 1957 to April 1961.

Warner Bros. *Hawaiian Eye* portrait, autographed by Williams.

the show[394]). The *Pasadena Independent* covered the event.[395]

An interesting actress/lady, a talented playwright, and affluent magnates in a comfortable, conservative business environment populated by enthusiastic patrons of the arts: now *that* sounds like an event fit for Grant Williams![396, 397]

---

394. Cecil Smith,"'Lady' Gets an 'A' for Effort," *Los Angeles Times*, January 6, 1967.

395. Lucie Lowery, "Bea Lillie on hand at Playhouse Show," *Pasadena (CA) Independent*, January 6, 1967.

396. Though Williams was definitely no longer a Warner Bros. player in 1967, he would guest-star in an episode of one of the studio's television series (*The FBI*) in 1968; it is remotely possible that relations were being patched up, and that the studio was somehow involved in this particular dinner.

397. "Gratefully" was a typical inscription for Williams when signing autographs. Conventional though this wording might have been, its frequency does indicate an inclination towards gratitude and a certain degree of gracious humility on Williams' part. This interpretation is consistent with what we know of Williams' character and disposition.

13

Music and Misnomers

A **PERSISTENT MISREPRESENTATION** has been making the rounds of the news mill in recent decades, involving sources that include IMDb and Wikipedia, as well as several online bloggers and biographers.[398] These sources state that Williams had a career as a professional operatic tenor. Wikipedia goes so far as to say that

> Williams originally was a singer and performed for five seasons with the New York City Opera. In 1959, he portrayed The Tenore Buffo in the world premiere of Hugo Weisgall's *Six Characters in Search of an Author*. Williams also sang with The Robert Shaw Chorale and played piano professionally. He then became interested in acting [...].[399]

This alleged dual career of Williams', perfectly in line with his indubitable versatility as well as with his proven love for music, presented some promising avenues for research involving the New York musical world of the 1950s. No hard data, however, were offered by those online sources, so I began to investigate, hoping to fill in the missing details.

I discovered that the name Grant Williams did indeed appear in the programs of dozens of interesting concerts, recitals, and operas in the fifties and sixties, with important companies such as the New York City Opera, the Robert Shaw Chorale, and the Martha Graham Dance Company,

---

398. For example alchetron.com, vipfaq.com and *Poseidon's Underworld*.

399. Wikipedia, "Grant Williams."

and at prestigious venues such as Carnegie Hall. I read reviews of these appearances—which included premieres of contemporary operas as well as performances of classic warhorses—in *The New York Times*. I even discovered a Robert Shaw Chorale recording of Stephen Foster (1826–1864) songs where Williams sang some lovely solos.

Gradually, however, my suspicion was aroused. I asked myself: was it possible for a working Hollywood actor to spread himself thin in such a way? Admirable as versatility is, was it likely that Williams, in the very midst of hitting the iron while it was hot during his painful almost-rise to Hollywood fame, would leave Los Angeles several times a year to sing professionally? When did he have time to train for this second, very muscular vocal career? Also, why did none of the reviews or programs in New York ever mention the singer's career as an actor in Hollywood, especially after his starring role in *The Incredible Shrinking Man*? Conversely, why did the Hollywood publicity machine, ever ready to latch onto the smallest of hype opportunities, not mention Williams' operatic career? In trying to answer these questions, I finally stumbled upon the truth.

The rumor of Grant Williams' operatic career is, in fact, false, and stems from a simple case of mistaken identity. There was indeed a tenor named Grant Williams who sang professionally in the fifties and sixties; but this Grant Williams was not the Grant Williams who starred in *The Incredible Shrinking Man*. The two artists were just homonyms. The operatic Williams had a long (and exclusively musical) career in New York and throughout the United States; he eventually formed his own Grant Williams Chorale in Detroit—which became the nucleus of the Detroit Symphony Chorus—before working as vocal coach and consultant for the Dallas Symphony Chorus until his death in 2004. A photograph of the New York City Opera production of Hugo Weisgall's opera *Six Characters in Search of an Author* (1959)[400] and a biography (with photograph) of Vocal Coach Williams in the Dallas Symphony Chorus website[401] cleared up the issue definitively.

400. In *New York City Opera Sings: Stories and Productions of the New York City Opera 1944–1979*, edited by Harold J. McKenna and the New York City Opera Guild Archives Committee, Richard Rosen Press, Inc., 1981, 322. The opera was based on Luigi Pirandello's iconic play by the same title (Luigi Pirandello, *Sei personaggi in cerca d'autore*, Bemporad, 1921; or, the English translation: Luigi Pirandello, *Six Characters in Search of an Author*, Methuen Drama, 1979).

401. www.dschorus.com/roster/bios.htm.

Photo of New York City Opera's production of Hugo Weisgall's opera *Six Characters in Search of an Author* (1959). Left to right: Beverly Sills, Grant Williams (the other one), and Ernest McChesnoy.

Despite this reality check, our Grant Williams was nonetheless a man of musical sensibility and talent; this sensibility and this talent are amply evident in his vocal delivery, in his sense of rhythm and movement, and in the memory of his piano playing in the people who knew him.

Nina Ingris, who was dating her future husband, Composer and Pianist Eduard Ingris, while doing secretary work for Williams, remembers the actor's love for music:

> Grant had an upright piano in his apartment, and he sometimes played it when I was at his place. He was very good.
>
> Grant took to my husband Eduard immediately, and the three of us continued to be friends for years, even after Eduard and I left Los Angeles. Whenever Eduard and I premiered an operetta in Los Angeles[402] (we did three of them, the first in

---

402. The operettas by Eduard Ingris performed in Los Angeles were the following: *The Mountain Rose*, Music Box Theatre, 6126 Hollywood Boulevard, April 28, 1963; *Marysa*, Wilshire Ebell Theater, 4401 West 8th Street, April 25, 1964; *By*

1963, plus a farewell revue), Grant would always be our "special guest"; he even brought dates and colleagues to the performances. Grant admired Edward, and was always interested in musical matters (NI).

Randy Stuart, Williams' co-star in *The Incredible Shrinking Man*, confirmed:

> I liked Grant immensely. He was much more talented than people were aware; did you know that he was an excellent classical musician? He played the piano beautifully, and he was a very well-read young man. [He was] just a very good kid. (TW, 308–309)

Williams' acting student Ken Mulroney also witnessed his teacher's musical prowess: "When Grant came to my house for Thanksgiving dinner, he played the piano for my family. He was wonderful at it." (KM) In an interview with Author Tom Weaver, Actress Anne Helm, who had a small part in the Williams vehicle *The Couch*, also remarked about Williams' gift for tickling the ivories:

> I knew Grant Williams and I *dated* Grant—he was a very gifted pianist, I remember *that*. He did concerts and things, and I often wondered why he'd gone into the acting profession, because he could have done a lot as a pianist.[403]

Williams' Warner Bros. biography that circulated in 1960 confirmed Williams' musicianship and added a few details about his interests: "Grant describes himself as a 'student concert pianist.' He maintains a bachelor apartment in Hollywood,[404] is an avid reader and student of religions."[405]

---

the *Mill Pond*, Sokol Hall, 500 N. Western Avenue, April 3 and 11, 1965; and *The Capricious Evening*, Blessed Sacrament Church hall, 6657 Sunset Boulevard, June 8, 1968.

403. Tom Weaver, *I Was a Monster Movie Maker*, McFarland & Company, Publishers, 2001, 82.

404. According to Ingris, a one-bedroom apartment.

405. *Dover (OH) Daily Reporter* (1960), op. cit.; the same source described him as a

And Eve Starr, in her profile of the actor, commented: "[Williams] plays a pretty good concert piano. At one time he intended to be a concert pianist but got sidetracked into acting. He still practices about two hours every day."[406]

In 1961, the *Los Angeles Times* amusingly reported musical shenanigans happening on the set of Williams' film *The Couch* (1962):

> There's lots of rhythm on the set of "The Couch" these days. Grant Williams and Shirley Knight provide it with their own private jam sessions between scenes. Grant studied to be a concert pianist while Miss Knight plays violin, xylophone and drums. Director Owen Crump listened attentively the other day, then turned and declared: "Maybe we should be making a musical instead of a thriller about a psychotic killer."[407]

Williams did make a few appearances at musical events in the Los Angeles area, though not as a musician. On Sunday, March 5, 1961, he participated as Speaker in an evening concert with the Hollywood Symphony Orchestra[408] conducted by Ernst Gebert.[409] The program consisted of Gustav Mahler's *The Song of the Earth* (*Das Lied von der Erde*, 1911) and was presented at Bancroft Auditorium, 929 N. Las Palmas Avenue, Hollywood.[410] In all likelihood, Williams read/narrated the English transla-

---

"handsome, dark-blond actor."

406. Starr (1961), op. cit.

407. John L. Scott, "Hollywood Calendar," *Los Angeles Times*, February 26, 1961.

408. The Hollywood Symphony Orchestra, not to be confused with its more famous sister, The Hollywood Bowl Symphony Orchestra, was created in 1958 (see "Hollywood Symphony Concert Set," *Covina (CA) Argus*, June 19, 1958) and, after some isolated concerts, made its official debut on January 28, 1961 (see "Music Events," *Los Angeles Times*, January 22, 1961). It was sponsored by the Hollywood Junior Chamber of Commerce and by the Hollywood Symphony Association. I could not find any mentions of this particular orchestra in the press after 1964.

409. Conductor Ernst Gebert was principal conductor of the Inglewood Symphony Orchestra in the 1950s, and guest-conducted several other orchestras. In November 1953 he conducted the world premiere of a new orchestral composition by his friend Erich Wolfgang Korngold, *Straussiana*.

410. *Los Angeles Times*, Calendar section, March 5, 1961.

tions of the six Chinese poems set to music by Mahler before the two singers (Mezzosoprano Margery MacKay and Tenor Richard Robinson) sang them in German accompanied by the orchestra.

Columnist Louella Parsons referred to Williams' appearance at the above March concert—and to other musical plans—in October 1961:

> Grant Williams, a star of "Hawaiian Eye," surprised a lot of people when he did the narration for the Hollywood Symphony last year. Grant will make a guest appearance at the keyboard next season as a classical pianist.[411]

I could not find any further reference to such keyboard performance; the plans probably fell through.

On April 29, 1962, Williams was present at another musical event, this time in Woodland Hills (a Los Angeles suburb in the San Fernando Valley). The *Los Angeles Times* announced the event in a shoddily written blurb:

> Financing new classrooms and an auditorium-gymnasium is the goal of the Louisville High School's Patron's Guild.
>
> To raise funds needed for the new constructions the guild is sponsoring a Musical Festival at the school, 2300 Mulholland Dr., today.
>
> The school's choir, under direction of Paul Salmunovich, will present a concert this afternoon. Two students, James Shadduck, pianist, and Marshall Rose, who plays with the Los Angeles Philharmonic Orchestra, will also be on the program.
>
> Members of the entertainment industry who are scheduled to appear during the event include Paul Picerni, Bob Eubanks, Timmy [Jon] Provost, Rip Masters [James Brown], Dick Dale, Grant Williams, Chatsworth Osborn [Osborne] Jr., Dobie Gillis [Dwayne Hickman], Jane Hyland and Reathia Sesma.[412]

411. Louella Parsons, *Philadelphia Inquirer*, October 4, 1961

412. "Music Festival to Aid School Fund," *Los Angeles Times*, April 29, 1962.

As late as 1964, Williams continued to be peripherally involved in musical matters. On November 15, the *Los Angeles Times* announced:

> Young Audiences of Greater Los Angeles, an organization devoted to giving narrated chamber music concerts for children, will hold a membership tea today at Rancho Park Country Club. Television actor Grant Williams will be guest speaker.[413]

Williams' love for music also embraced other correlated endeavors, such as songwriting. He referred to this in his July 1957 letter to L. Allan Smith:

> I am only too aware that this letter is long overdue, and can only ask your forgiveness. I have never been this tardy at answering mail and the reason very generally is that a constant flow of people from the East and a brand new interest—song writing—has kept me hopping. […]
>
> I am back studying the piano very seriously since meeting Herman Wasserman. He was George Gershwin's teacher and is sensational. He concertized in the thirties himself and knew my aunt—Mary Garden—the opera star years ago.
>
> I've also struck a friendship with Leonard Pennario, one of the nicest people I have ever known. This is where the song writing comes in. We've finished one (a Concert Song) entitled "Search." I've finished the lyrics for a pop ballad and have started another. Of course I do the lyrics and Leonard, the music.
>
> I was able to get a little vacation in with Leonard down at La Jolla for two weeks […] and am presently feeling pretty good and very anxious to go to work. (GW2, 1)

Leonard Pennario (1924–2008) was a celebrated pianist in his day. In the course of his career, he played under the best conductors, and formed a

---

413. "Membership Tea Set by Music Unit," *Los Angeles Times*, November 15, 1964. Young Audiences is a nationwide non-profit organization developed in the early 1950s from an idea by Violinist Yehudi Menuhin and officially incorporated by Mrs. Edgar M. Leventritt and Mrs. Lionello Perera in 1952.

Pianist Leonard Pennario in a 1961 press photo.

trio with Violinist Jascha Heifetz (1901–1987) and Cellist Gregor Piati-
gorsky (1903–1976). He also recorded more than sixty LPs with some
of the most important record labels, such as RCA Victor and Angel/
EMI.[414]

The three songs Williams wrote with Pennario were "Search," "Hazy
Dreams," and "Your Tomorrow." The Pennario estate has refused to grant
me permission to view the manuscripts or reproduce Williams' lyrics in
this book; the website pennario.org, at least, lists the songs as co-written
by "G. Williams," and corroborates with some historical perspective:

---

414. Sources: Wikipedia, and *The New York Times'* obituary: James Barron, "Leonard
Pennario, 83, Classical Pianist, Dies," June 28, 2008.

Leonard had many friends in the movie business, and he would often collaborate with some of them to write tunes, sometimes for a specific movie sometimes not. We were lucky enough to find about 20 of these original songs, many unpublished in Leonard's own hand, with words by various collaborators.

The *Los Angeles Times* made a passing reference to Williams and the Pennario family in their coverage of a musical event involving Leonard Pennario: the Hollywood Bowl's annual Family Night on August 3, 1957. The guest performers appearing with the Hollywood Bowl Pops Orchestra, conducted by Robert Armbruster, were: Dorothy Kirsten, soprano; Salvatore Baccaloni, bass; Lola Montes, dancer; Leonard Pennario, pianist; and Danny Kaye, actor and amateur conductor. On August 5, 1957, the *Los Angeles Times* wrote a long article about the evening, which included the following statement:

> The [...] Pennarios had come to see their son Leonard join performers at the piano. As guests they brought John McClean of Yonkers, N.Y., Grant Williams and Miss Lois Buchaneau.[415]

---

415. Albert Goldberg, "Danny Kaye Big Hit of Family Night," *Los Angeles Times*, August 5, 1957.

Grant Williams at home, with pet, circa 1956.

14 A Medicine for Melancholy

DISPOSITIONS

Many of those who knew Williams remember him as a gentle, melancholy man. Here is former acting student Ken Mulroney:

> In class, Grant was all business. Outside the class, he was very sociable. When I got married to my first wife, I invited him to my wedding and he came. He and my older brother, who was a movie buff, struck up a conversation; they went into the bar and spent the whole reception there talking about movies. A couple of years later, when Grant came over to my house for a Thanksgiving dinner, he engaged my dad, my mother, my brother, and my sister all evening. He was very easy to be with, socially. But, in a way, I believe he was *playing the role* of a sociable person: he was very private about his life, and it wasn't easy to guess what was really going on with him. (KM)

Shirley Knight, Williams' co-star in *The Couch*, confirms his disposition: "I only did the one film with Williams, but I remember him as a very kind man, and a good actor."[416]

And here is Williams' former Secretary Ingris, who knew him at the peak of his rise to fame, between *The Incredible Shrinking Man* and the end of his Warner Bros. tenure:

---

416. Shirley Knight, letter to the author, June 2016.

293

If I were to describe Grant, I wouldn't say he was what you would call "happy" or "cheerful," at least not in my presence. Perhaps you could say he was sweet. I can definitely say that he was calm: he was never choleric or particularly nervous. It is true, there was sadness in his eyes. He was generally not a very happy person. And I believe he was quite lonely. (NI)

One can take that "lonely" used by Ingris in the above quotation and place it against the words Williams himself writes in his April 1957 letter to Fan-Club President L. Allan Smith: "I'm not married as you know and have been quite alone most of my life. To live alone is sometimes pleasant, but to fight alone is terrifying." Considered side by side, those words, "lonely" and "alone," resonate against each other and reveal a character trait, or condition, of Williams'. Social and professional considerations aside, marital status aside, and stardom aside, it is Williams' sense of loneliness that transpires from those words. Company, someone might suggest, is the logical medicine for loneliness; but the problem singled out in passing by Williams ran deep, and could probably not be solved by physical proximity or social gregariousness. His confession that he had been "quite alone" most of his life seems to point to an existential condition, one that was probably exacerbated rather than cured by the social and/or sexual remedies readily available to a handsome Hollywood actor. Also, Williams' phrase "most of my life" seem to suggest an ancient, unresolved malaise stretching back in time, probably to his youth.

Williams might have thought that the problem had to do with his lack of a wife, and might have gone looking for a solution in romances of varying lengths. Unfortunately for him, the solution, the medicine, lay, not outside, but inside his inner world. The holy grail of happiness, of serenity, for someone as fractured as Williams, was not to be found in social gatherings or in the institution of marriage. Like many unhappy individuals, Williams evidently kept looking for outer solutions to his inner problems, and his frequentation of the bottle—as we will see later—only made matters worse.

Isabel Fisher, another acting student of his, confirms the presence of this disposition of Williams' during her acquaintance with him (1978–1979): "I think melancholy is a good word to describe him."[417] Melissa

---

417. Isabel Fisher, conversation with the author, March 2016. Further references to Fisher's conversation are cited in the text using the abbreviation IF.

Ward, who was his student in the same period, goes even further in her characterization of Williams:

> Grant was a really intense person, and by this I mean, he was a brilliant man, with a strong presence and a commanding personality. But he was fundamentally a tragic character. There was a great deal of sadness in there.[418]

Saying that Williams was "fundamentally a tragic character" is a bold statement on Ward's part, and should not be taken lightly. If one takes that definition seriously, one can sense that Williams' melancholy was not something born out of capriciousness or temperamental vanity. A dark, deep something lurked in Williams' breast, a ticking bomb that evidently only needed the spark of professional disappointment (and of alcohol) to go off. A hypothesis that is never mentioned is that this something could have been a post-traumatic stress disorder stemming from his experiences in the Korean War.

From the point of view of both personal disposition and acting style, Ward's remark that Williams "was a really intense person [...] with a strong presence and a commanding personality" points to a trait that only appears to contradict Williams' melancholy inclination. If one looks at his best performances, at least in his "golden" period, one can see that even in the saddest, most meditative moments, Williams seldom lets the emotional energy of his characters lag. Sadness and melancholy never become an excuse to become languid, or passive. There is always an alertness to Williams, a lively inner rhythm that keeps his performances buoyant. Intensity and melancholy may occasionally clash, but from that clash arises an electricity—a subtle fight between opposite polarities: Williams did not express resignation to that melancholy, at least not until 1967.

June Moncur, Williams' Barter Theatre audition co-winner, elaborates on Williams' personality:

> Grant was a nice person—talented, handsome, dependable, and gracious. As I look back on those months in 1953, I remember him as a sensitive person, and a bit of a loner, too.

---

418. Melissa Ward, conversation with the author, March 2016. Further references to Ward's interview are cited in the text using the abbreviation MW.

I had the impression that there was something unresolved about him. Grant was such a fine-looking and friendly young man, one would think he would have had lots of friends; but it doesn't always work out that way, does it. (JMW)

The sentence that Williams told Don Alpert of the *Los Angeles Times* (in their cited 1961 interview) is all the proof one needs of the fact that all was not well with the actor, and that his disposition was not a cheerful one: "I have a private life that I think is horrible."[419] In a world of face-saving reticence and fabricated publicity hype, that sentence was the equivalent of a desperate cry for help.

Czech-born Nina Ingris, who worked with Williams for some eight years and became an American citizen while living in Los Angeles, stayed in touch with the actor for some time after leaving her job with him; she too did not have the complete picture, but can add a few pieces to the puzzle with some degree of authority. In the following passage, she describes Williams' kindness and elegance.

Grant was a kind man, polite and friendly. He was a quiet, warm man. He never balked at giving personal advice—he didn't keep things strictly business-like when I worked for him, but became a true friend. He was the man who persuaded me to go back to my natural blond hair color when I was dying my hair dark.

He was also a man of some class: he valued elegance, and always wore nice suits. These he often used while working on films or television, so he had to have a wide range of them: actors always had to wear new suits. I remember those high-quality suits.

Soon after my mother and I had become American citizens, we flew back to Czechoslovakia for a visit, and Grant gave me several of his suits to take with me for my cousin, who was slender like Grant and of similar height. We had a very large suitcase filled with them, and our luggage was packed with many other items one could not get in the old country at that time, such as, believe it or not, toilet paper. At the Czechoslo-

---

419. Alpert (1961), op. cit.

vakian border—where I asked my mother not to speak while I pretended not to know the old language well—the guard who inspected our car trunk almost got to the suitcase, but did not open it. Had he done so, it would have been hard to pretend those suits were our own. (NI)

Williams' attention to dress codes was confirmed by the U-I pressbook for *The Monolith Monsters,* where Williams was introduced with these paragraphs:

> Discovered, the new-generation Hollywood celebrity who never effects a uniform of sweat shirts, skin-tight levis and sneakers.
> Grant Williams, film star, is also "conservative" in another way. He doesn't mumble his lines, nor does he strike attitudes in front of the camera.[420]

Parenthetically, U-I's above remarks about Williams are interesting, for—in the oblique manner of the publicity of the times—they reveal an artistic truth. The fact that Williams did not "mumble his lines" or "strike attitudes in front of the camera" points both to a personal inclination and to a way of acting.

The mumbling of lines is a mannerism associated—often simplistically and incorrectly—with a Stanislavskian approach to acting, or with Method actors. Countless parodies of actors like Marlon Brando or James Dean have focused on such mannerism to ridicule the Actors-Studio style. To paraphrase Actress Uta Hagen, a teacher of the Method that Williams often quoted in his master classes, actors can be divided into two main style categories: "representational" and "presentational."[421]

To this day, there is some controversy as to the exact difference between the two terms; simply put, presentational style is the manner most associated with the Actors Studio, while representational style is associated with more formal, traditional (for example British or Italian) actors. In presentational style, the actor and the character merge as a result of an inner investigation, and the truthful discoveries the actor makes *within*

---

420. Universal-International pressbook for *The Monolith Monsters,* 1957.

421. See: Uta Hagen, *Respect for Acting,* Macmillan, 1973.

himself, about himself and the character, are "presented" outwardly. In representational style, the actor "represents" ("acts") the character externally via his technique. Soul and truth on the one hand, technical schooling and critical sensibility on the other.

There are plenty of exceptions to this rule, and plenty of actors who mix the two techniques seamlessly; but the fact remains that the pure Method tends to yield a result that is, so to speak, devoid of "style," or of "formality." Traditionally, for example, diction, voice projection, social poise, class division, and formal movement techniques are not primary concerns for Method actors. Hence their mumbling of lines, and their being more adept at modern realistic drama than at period or stylized comedy.

Grant Williams was a Method actor, but his diction and enunciation of American English were controlled and precise; he obviously valued truthfulness in his performances, and went to great lengths to investigate the connections between himself and his characters, yet his use of body and voice had a formal, old-school elegance to it. Williams' acting style was firmly anchored in conservative tradition.

Williams' conservativeness in clothing was showcased by the *Los Angeles Times* in 1961 when it chose Williams as the subject of its main photograph accompanying an article by Jack Hyde entitled "Hollywood Likes British Atmosphere in Clothing." The photo showed Williams striking a relaxed, masculine pose and wearing a dark blazer and a light-colored ascot. The caption was: "Debonaire—Grant Williams' ascot typifies British sophistication in informal attire. It contrasts with open-collared shirt, single-breasted blazer."[422]

Still another confirmation of Williams' poise and taste in clothes came from Eve Starr's cited profile of the actor, where the columnist, in discussing his recent starring role on *Hawaiian Eye*, stated:

> As the third detective, he dresses as a refugee from the Ivy League (he will not under any circumstances wear a Hawaiian sport shirt), avoids physical combat and passes himself off as a writer rather than a detective.[423]

---

422. Jack Hyde, "Hollywood Likes British Atmosphere in Clothing," *Los Angeles Times*, November 12, 1961

423. Starr (1961), op. cit.

One can reasonably extend this minor inclination (preference for formal elegance) to other aspects of Williams' worldview and entertain the suspicion that he was indeed a conservative.[424] He was certainly a Republican: in November 1966, the *Los Angeles Times* printed a full-page ad containing a petition by industry supporters of Ronald Reagan, the Republican candidate for Governor in the upcoming elections on November 8. The list, distributed over six columns, included some 175 Hollywood names, big and small. Grant Williams was among them.[425] Reagan won the election.

Williams' generous disposition and propensity towards altruism, described by Ingris in her travel anecdote, was occasionally featured in the American press. Here is a Hollywood-written blurb (probably originating from Warner Bros.) that appeared in December 1960:

> Grant Williams, starred in "Hawaiian Eye," was a talent agent before turning to an acting career. He still is one at heart.
>
> Whenever he sees new talent of promise, he arranges an interview with studio "brass" for a possible screen test. Grant does this in token of appreciation for those who helped him climb the ladder of stardom.[426]

Most eyewitnesses agree that Williams was polite, friendly, and gracious—if melancholy. Eve Starr adds another color to the picture, an element that seemingly contradicts the character traits described so far but is actually a natural extension, or development, of the conservatism we have detected:

> [Williams] takes his work very seriously. He also tends to take himself rather seriously, but that's par for the course in Hollywood. An actor without ego is no actor at all.[427]

---

424. One can also include his desire to set "kids who have gone wrong" straight, see Chapter 8.

425. "The People Who Work with Ronald Reagan Say..." (full-page ad, *Los Angeles Times*, November 3, 1966). The ad also appeared in other newspapers, such as the *San Bernardino (CA) Daily Sun*, between November 3 and 5.

426. "Williams Offers Helping Hands," *Bloomington (IL) Daily Pantagraph*, December 31, 1960.

427. Starr (1961), op. cit.

This trait is perfectly in tune with Williams' conservative inclination, with his conflicted introversion, with his attention to poise, and with his ambition as an actor—an ambition that he had not abandoned yet when Starr's article was written.

On the frivolous side, Mulroney adds a detail about Williams' leisure activities:

> Grant enjoyed gourmet food. He once gave me a recipe for garlic mashed potatoes; I made them, and they were the best mashed potatoes ever. I don't know how much he cooked, but he certainly knew a lot about cooking and a lot about food. (KM)[428]

Williams could also astonish on occasion, and reveal a contrasting aspect of his personality. On June 15, 1959, *The Philadelphia Inquirer* compiled a full-page anthology of "*ipse-dixit*" quotations from stage and screen personalities previously reported by an assortment of famous columnists. The spread was divided into two sections: "Best of Hollywood" and "Best of Broadway." Among the columnists, there were names like Armand Archerd, Mike Connolly, Leonard Lyons, George E. Phair, Sidney Skolsky, Jimmy Starr, Herb Stein, and Walter Winchell.

The central section, listing quotations termed the "cream of the crop," contained an unexpected quote from Grant Williams, reported by Mike Connolly. Here it is:

> Grant Williams: "The only thing that ever cheated a dame out of the last word was an echo." (Mike Connolly)[429]

This aphorism seems to contrast with Williams' personality as we know it. Granted, there is no specific reason to suppose that Williams did not have a sense of humor, and a rather biting one at that, but the above quote is still rather shocking in my view. Male chauvinism and cynicism notwithstanding, I wish we could see more of that particular Grant Williams.

---

428. The 1961 edition of the magazine *Who's Who in Hollywood* lists Williams' hobbies as "reading and swimming."

429. *Philadelphia Inquirer*, June 15, 1959

Hollywood Temblors

As the early sixties gave way to the mid-sixties, one can clearly see Williams' name wane from the nation's press. After 1963–1964, there were no more juicy press releases about Williams' past, no witty plugs, no in-depth behind-the-scenes articles about his shoots; only an occasional mention of his remote successes in the film or television listings. Grant Williams no longer existed as an object of Hollywood curiosity or gossip.

One item stands out, and it is a disheartening one. It appeared in September 1965. The topic: American actors having careers in foreign (mostly European) film industries or returning to the United States, and the changes taking place in Hollywood. The reporter: Williams' old "friend," Lorraine Gauguin.

> Another young man, Richard Harrison, longs to come back but he is also a top star over there. Grant Williams, who used to star in "Hawaiian Eye," ran into Harrison in the bar at the Castellana Hilton in Madrid. "Do you think I could get a job in Hollywood?" Harrison asked. Williams was out of work himself and told him to stay put.[430]

American Actor Richard Harrison (born 1936) had a modest start in Hollywood in the late 1950s (at Twentieth Century Fox and American International Pictures), then moved to Italy and became one of the top stars in Italian genre cinema: he made more than fifty films there, some of them quite good. His Italian career virtually covered the entire genre spectrum and lasted from 1961 to about 1982. Williams' case was antithetical to Harrison's, and his being out of a job stemmed from complex personal reasons; but the phenomenon denounced with mixed feelings in Gauguin's series of six weekly articles (August 21–September 24, 1965) on the state of Hollywood art was real for both men, and for many others besides them.

With the gradual crumbling of the old studio system and the advent of television, Hollywood was in the throes of a new kind of growing pain, one connected with a change of status, and with a reversal. The change of

---

430. Lorraine Gauguin, "It's 'Home Sweet Home' for the Movies," *Waukesha (WI) Freeman*, "Saturday Review," September 11, 1965.

Richard Harrison on the balcony of his home in the then-exclusive neighborhood of Vigna Clara, Rome, circa 1967, during the peak of his fame as an Italian genre-film star; Harrison would end up starring in some fifty films in Italy, and staying on until about 1985. Courtesy of Richard Harrison's private collection.

status had to do with—among other things—the movie industry having to compete with television and with rising costs; the reversal, with American talent either fleeing or returning to America.

If there was a Hollywood renaissance of sorts (and Gauguin was convinced there was), it involved accepting that the film industry would never be the same. The golden years were gone, and Hollywood would have to come to terms with a new state of things, one that was not going away.

A complex change in styles of management, in ownerships, in production methods, in marketing, and in audience tastes was under way, but this crisis had actually started more than a decade earlier: the 1950s had been the real watershed. The explosion of new techniques such as VistaVision, Cinerama, 3D, CinemaScope, and Todd-AO had been a reaction to such crisis, and a palliative one. In the 1960s, it became clear just how futile the battle had been. The studios were in trouble, and the rise of professional guilds and unions delivered a final blow. Corporate takeovers followed, and the industry was now in the hands of a new class of managers and businessmen. Already in 1957, for example, Universal-International had gone through a reorganization: Vice-President Muhl had found his decisional power diminished, and several Producers, such as Albert Zugsmith (Producer of *The Incredible Shrinking Man*) and William Alland, had fled the studio. (DMR, 110) Hollywood did somehow find a new lease on life, but the creature emerging from its own ashes in the sixties was significantly different from the one that had burned so brightly in previous decades.[431]

This crisis, or painful renaissance, involved changes for actors too. If the new business regime was to include television, this meant a doubling of competition on the one hand and a diminution of prestige on the other. Without the old studio contract system to bear the costs, more and more actors would be left to fend for themselves—in the sink or swim manner—in a sea of new minor opportunities. Those actors who were already

---

431. In his autobiography, Actor Basil Rathbone was even more catastrophic about the origin of such changes. In recounting his abandonment of Hollywood for the New York stage in 1946, he stated: "We certainly had no idea how lucky we were to be getting out at this time, for in the next two years motion pictures were to take one of the biggest nose dives in their history" (Basil Rathbone, *In and Out of Character*, Doubleday & Company, Inc., 1962, 189).

stars struggled to keep their status; those who were not would probably never be, at least not in the old sense.

Like any actor without a steady long-term contract, and probably more so given his sensitive nature and tormented personality, Grant Williams must have felt a deep insecurity after the expiration of his Warner Bros. contract in 1963.

Rumors and Maladjustments

There has been some speculation as to the reasons for Williams' uneven—one might even say ruinous—personal and professional life. The most popular unsubstantiated rumor is the one concerning Williams' supposed homosexuality and battle against Hollywood homophobia, which Williams denied strenuously. (RL, 293) As far as I could ascertain, corroboration for such rumor consists of exactly one Internet-blog post, by an anonymous person claiming to have known Williams in the late sixties. Here is what that person writes:

> I knew Grant in the late 60's. We lived in the same highrise apartment building on Doheny Drive and became friends. He had many problems. He was unable to come to terms with his homosexuality and he was also psychotic.[432] He self-medicated with copious amounts of alcohol. It made his psychosis worse. It was sad, but not surprising when he died. I assumed it was due to AIDS.[433]

While the hypothesis of Williams' homosexuality might have its allure and even a degree of plausibility, many of those who knew the actor dis-

---

432. Lamparski stated that Williams kept "several loaded guns in his apartment" (RL, 293).

433. *Poseidon's Underworld* blog, "The Incredible Shrinking Career"; entry posted January 27, 2015. The statement that Williams was actually "psychotic" (as early as the late 1960s) sounds extreme, even though psychosis is often a symptom of alcoholism, and finds no corroboration from any of the witnesses I have queried. "Tormented" might be a more compassionate term. As for the "highrise apartment building on Doheny Drive" mentioned by the post, it is not compatible with Lamparski's 1982 mention of Williams as living in the "Miracle Mile" area of Los Angeles. It is therefore reasonable to assume that Williams moved at least twice after his North Hayworth Avenue address in the 1950s.

agree with it. Still, if one looks hard enough for coincidences to fit a theory, there may be coincidences to be found. Consider the following:

(a) Williams was a lifelong bachelor; (b) Williams was, briefly, managed by notorious gay Agent Henry Willson; (c) both Edward Muhl, Head of Production at Universal Pictures when Williams signed his contract there, and William T. Orr, Vice-President for Television Production at Warner Brothers during Williams' *Hawaiian Eye* tenure, were well acquainted with Henry Willson; Orr had even been Willson's client/protégé during his early acting days, and in both cases there were rumors of homosexual dalliances (RH, 235–238); (d) Williams was friends with George Nader,[434] who, with his lifelong partner Mark Miller, was probably Rock Hudson's best friend (Nader was the sole heir of Rock Hudson's estate, and Miller was Hudson's Secretary for several years, according to *Variety*);[435] (e) Williams was also friends with Lilyan Miller, President of the George Nader Fan Club and co-founder of the Grant Williams Fan Club, and with William F. Singer, who gravitated around many a fan club and allegedly had a long-term romantic relationship with a man (NI); (f) according to Hofler, in 1972 Henry Willson took a one-bedroom apartment in the same West Hollywood building where Williams had lived, at 1314 N. Hayworth Avenue (RH, 408); and (g) the decline of Willson's career in the 1960s coincided with the decline of the careers of many of his clients, such as Rock Hudson, Tab Hunter, and Troy Donahue (RH, 385–406).

These coincidences, however, are meaningless. All they really prove is that Hollywood in the fifties and sixties was a small world after all. Henry Willson's menagerie, for example, included plenty of heterosexual actors, and, though there have been reports claiming that many of those actors were willing to experiment sexually, in the interest of their careers or of pleasure,[436] there is ultimately no proof that their association with Willson was a reflection on their own orientations.

---

434. Wilson (1956), op. cit.

435. Army Archerd, "Nader's death another sad finale to a glamorous H'w'd life," *Variety*, February 4, 2002.

436. See RH. See also: Scotty Bowers with Lionel Friedberg, *Full Service: My Adventures in Hollywood and the Secret Sex Lives of the Stars*, Grove Press, 2012; William J. Mann, *Behind the Screen*, Viking, 2001; David Ehrenstein, *Open Secret*, William Morrow and Company, Inc., 1998.

William T. Orr in a publicity still for the Warner Bros. film *Navy Blues*, 1941. Before being Vice-President for Television Production at Warner Bros., young Orr tried his hand at acting under the aegis of Agent Henry Willson.

At any rate, Willson was not Williams' agent for long. In fact, nobody was. In the course of his film and television career, Williams changed agents, and agencies, quite often. The *Academy Players Directory* reveals that even a partial list (from 1955 to 1967) would have to include the following: MCA Artists, Ltd. (1955 and 1958); Universal-International (1955–1958); the Goldstone-Tobias Agency (1958); the William Morris Agency (1960); Warner Bros. (1961–1963); the Kumin-Olenick Agency, with Agents Fred Spektor and Fred Amsel, and personal management by Richard Heckenkamp (1964); the Louis Scherr Agency (1964); the Salkow-Kennard Agency (1965); the Stephen Draper Agency, New York (1965); the Henry Willson Agency (1965); Arthur Kennard Associates; Bernice Cronin, Associate (1966); the William Schuller Agency (TV commercials, 1966–1967); General Artists Corp. (1967); the Robert Raison Agency (1967); and the Robert Longenecker Agency (TV commercials, 1967).[437]

---

437. *Academy Players Directory*, Margaret Herrick Library, Academy of Motion

The above list—especially when cross-referenced with Williams' 1982 statement to Richard Lamparski that he had been "poorly managed" (RL, 293)—confirms the suspicion that Williams was afflicted with an ineradicable restlessness that extended to many areas of his personal and professional life. That list is not so much a symbol of the inefficiencies and fickle affections of agents, as a symbol of Williams himself. Williams' inability to stay with any one agency for a significant amount of time was akin to his inability to form long-lasting relationships, with film studios and people alike.

Regarding the issue of Williams' sexual orientation, former acting student Melissa Ward does not believe that Williams was gay, but adds:

> I am not saying that he couldn't have had a thing for men, but I think that, especially when it comes to persons with issues like Grant, you can't really divide people into categories and put easy labels on them such as gay, straight, etc. It's much more complex, and there are all sorts of gray areas.
>
> I also know from speaking with a number of men who were in the military that there is a lot of bonding going on when you're away from home and living with men during a war. Under those circumstances, sometimes men develop emotional relationships with other men, relationships that might become physical; and yet during peacetime those same men might never have acted on those impulses. (MW)

Ingris, more conservative in her thinking, believes Williams was actually in search of a steady female mate, and saw him on several traditional dates, though in her opinion Williams was the target of young women who used him as a means to gain access to the film industry, and was invariably disappointed in his earnest pursuit of a relationship. As possible (or partial) corroboration of this view, Lamparski writes about Williams: "He never dates women who are actresses." (RL, 293) Former acting student Mulroney is also sure of Williams' heterosexuality, and witnessed Williams living with a young woman. Given these contradictory opin-

Picture Arts and Sciences, Beverly Hills.

ions, the only hypothesis that one can prudently make (if one so wishes) is that Williams might have been bisexual, or that, as Ward puts it, his sexuality belonged in one of those mixed "gray areas."

Those gray areas, when it comes to people with issues like Grant Williams, do not merely concern sexual orientation; they concern sex per se, as well as feelings in general, and any number of deep personal preoccupations. Williams was a conflicted person, regardless of the specific personal issue at hand. Assuming that Williams was gay because of his conflicted nature—as many have done in the past and continue to do today with a certain glibness—is a speculative (and stereotyped) leap. Though sensitivity, melancholia, and loneliness might seem to be necessary conditions for unresolved, and sometimes resolved, gay men, they are certainly not sufficient conditions.

If speculate one must, one should do so based on concomitant clues. If Williams had written reams and reams of personal letters expounding on personal as well as universal issues, and if one could read those letters, such clues might be available. As it is, one can only rely on what little direct testimony the actor left behind, and on the opinions of others. Williams' letter dated July 31, 1957, cited earlier, is the closest thing we currently have to a personal statement. It is in some ways a business letter, dealing as it does with fan-club matters; but it is filled with personal details. That letter (and its April 1957 sister), straddled between the two registers of business communication and personal expression, may be as far as Williams ever went in confessing his innermost thoughts on paper.

Williams mentions that Ellie Evers was his guest in Los Angeles for three weeks. To describe her, he uses the term "my galfriend," which seems to imply the absence of sexuality; he also groups her with other guests, Father Carey and Father Thomas of New York's Blackfriars Theatre. He expresses affection for his guests ("I love these people"), but his affection does not sound intimate, merely friendly. (GW2, 1)Model Ellie Evers was a minor figure artistically, and she might have been a minor presence in Williams' life. She is, however, the *only surviving mention* of a female companion of any sort coming directly from Williams and not from the press of the time or from second-hand hearsay.

Based on the facts at our disposal, the idea that Williams had many friendships—some of them perhaps quite warm—but few, if any, truly intimate or long-lasting relationships might be a reasonable speculation. Personally speaking, I must confess that I find the activity of labeling people sexually uninteresting.

Williams' letter reveals another fact: all the people that Williams mentions, he mentions to corroborate some fact of his career. One way or another, those "friends" are all confirmations of his own professional talent and ambition; they are pianists, composers, theater producers, film studio executives, famous portrait photographers, and models with acting ambitions. Perhaps, at least in 1957, Williams was "all business," even in his personal expressions; which may be what Nina Ingris means when she states, a propos of his marital status, that, "Maybe he was married… to his career […]."

Another factor should be considered: despite Williams' occasional protestations to the contrary, one gets the impression from his statements, from his lifestyle, and from his tastes that he was something of a "square." Conservative in his attire and in his politics, Williams was a solitary, melancholic person with an interest in religion, in acting, in the arts, and in his veteran's past.

The press never even suggested any sexual problems when writing about Williams. Only in one instance did a columnist offer a tiny veiled

Model for the game show *The Big Payoff* (1951–1959): Ellie Evers in themed costume to celebrate the 49th and 50th states, Alaska and Hawaii, with Uncle Sam. Undated, but probably June 1959. Photo by CBS via Getty Images.

hint. The columnist was Lee Mortimer, and the topic was Williams' free time during the filming of *The Couch* (1962); Williams' date was the customary May Heatherly, apparently a constant companion of his in that period. Here is the item: "DON'T BLAME ME (I only work here): Grant Williams is spending his weekends away from Warner's "The Couch" with May Heatherly, the beautiful Irish gay bull fighter...."[438]

Here, Mortimer's qualification of Heatherly as "gay" seems cryptically, and maliciously, pointed; but whatever point Mortimer thought he was making by pointing a slanderous finger at Heatherly and then hiding it behind his back, he ended up not making it.

When former acting student Mulroney talks about Williams outside the acting class, he describes a talented, engaging person who may have been "playing the role of a sociable person." There was, in other words, something inscrutable, or insincere, about him. Some kind of maladjustment (not necessarily sexual) motivated Williams to act—even in real life: perhaps to hide some secret, perhaps simply because he did not know how to let his guard down and be natural. One need not imagine any grave pathology in this respect, only a rather common psychosocial awkwardness that many "normal" people share with Williams—shy, sensitive or introverted people in particular. Fame, success, and ambition only amplified that awkwardness.

This amplification took the form of a pressure for Williams, a pressure to which he did not respond positively. Whatever the secret was that he felt he had to hide, Williams was probably a person who did not feel completely comfortable with others, and who needed to compensate for such discomfort. According to his acting students, this compensation took the form of alcohol consumption, which in all likelihood became one of the causes of Williams' personal and professional downfall. Apparently, his attitude under the influence could be quite belligerent, and he would fly into rages on the sets; his misbehavior allegedly got him suspended from the TV series *Hawaiian Eye*.[439]

It would appear that Williams came from an unhappy family situation, and that, throughout his life, he was never able to receive the love he felt he

---

438. Lee Mortimer, "New York Confidential," *The Terre Haute (IN) Tribune-Star*, March 19, 1961.

439. In his conversation with Lamparski (RL, 293), Williams claimed he had never been suspended. His acting students remember differently.

deserved, or desperately needed, from his mother: Helen Tewes Williams had always preferred Grant's brother Robert to him. In a stronger man, this would probably have created a tougher skin, or a defensive hard shell; in Williams, a sensitive man inclined towards brooding, it created a vulnerability and, evidently, an obsession. The cherry on top of this particular cake is the anecdote (told by Williams himself to a friend, who in turn relayed it to Mulroney) wherein Williams flew to New York to be at his mother's side as she was dying; asked if she had ever loved him, she replied, "I hate you." (KM)This yearning for love, this sense of loss and abandonment on Williams' part, might certainly shed some light on that feeling of tormented sadness the actor was able to tap into during his best performances—for example, in *The Incredible Shrinking Man* (1957) or in his scene in *Allen in Movieland* (1955). It might also explain how, through his Method training, Williams was able to turn this feeling inside out and expose its bitter flip side—tinting it with a perverse humor, as in his show-stealing turn as killer Chet Swann in *Red Sundown* (1956), or with psychotic rage, as in *Outside the Law* (1956) and *The Couch* (1962). We are still in the realm of speculation, but this fact about the actor's life does help us make an educated guess about his person. One could also say that the oedipal unease, the sexual conflict, and the alcohol abuse (together with Williams' religious bent) are not mutually exclusive: the coexistence of the three factors is not illogical.

Speaking of *The Couch* and of Williams' preparation work for it, his psychiatric investigation of his character and of himself via his sessions with Psychologist Dr. Leland Johnson might only have been a convenient ploy devised by Warner Bros. to promote their film and its main gimmick, psychiatry. It was, however, a unique tie-in, and one uniquely appropriate to the film's melancholy, restless star. If ever an actor needed such sessions, Williams did. In fact, Williams' readiness to talk about that investigation during interviews (with the excuse of Method techniques) reveals more than he might have intended. If this interpretation is true, and if Williams the person did feel an urgent need to explore his own psyche, then the actor's need to explore his character's psyche was a perfect excuse for that personal exploration.

From a financial point of view, Williams' decision to choose Hollywood over Broadway in 1955 had been perfectly logical. From a human point of view, and seen from the safety of hindsight, it had been a miscalculation. The dog-eat-dog film industry was probably the worst environment for a sensitive, melancholy artist like Grant Williams.

Lost Weekends

Former acting student Melissa Ward recalls her brushes with Williams' alcohol problem:

> When I asked him, very innocently (I was only twenty-two at the time, and hadn't been around Hollywood long enough to know better), whether he was still acting and making movies, Grant told me that he had said the wrong thing to the wrong person on the set of *Hawaiian Eye* while drunk. He had great regret that this had ever happened, but there was nothing he could do after the fact. So he got blacklisted from ever working again, and the only alternative he had was teaching.[440] He said he put everything into his teaching, because he was no longer allowed to work as an actor.
>
> One night later on, after I had been in his master class for a number of months, he called our house; everybody was gone except me, and he was drunk. He told me he was in love with me and wanted to marry me. It really frightened me: I didn't know what to say. He was beside himself. He told me he couldn't stop thinking about me, he was obsessed. Afterwards, I didn't mention the incident, and neither did he. (MW)

Williams never mentioned his addiction officially, though he talked about it with a few of his students, and probably with his truly intimate friends, assuming he had any. His official explanation to Lamparski for the failing of his career was that "he was poorly managed. He [denied] rumors that he had bitter quarrels with his studios, stating that he never refused a role and was never suspended [and added that] the only strong disagreement he ever had was with Jack Webb during a *Dragnet* show. [...]" (RL, 293)

Ingris remembers Williams as a health enthusiast during her frequentation of him, post-*Shrinking Man* (1958–1965), but she reluctantly admits that he drank:

---

440. Williams might have had trouble on *Hawaiian Eye*, but the fact that the entire series closed down in April 1963 and that Williams was the showcased protagonist of its last two episodes makes Lamparski's explanation of Williams' blacklisting, from a later incident on *Dragnet 1967*, more likely. (RL, 293)

During the first period of my work as Grant's secretary, I kept wondering what all those bottles filled with pills were in his kitchen. I discovered they were not drugs, but vitamins, and dietary supplements. I followed his example and started taking them too, especially a few years later when I was touring the country with my husband Eduard [Ingris] for lectures and film showings, in all kinds of weather and for all kinds of distances.

Yes, Grant smoked a lot, and drank. Mostly whisky, I think. I rarely saw him without either a cigarette in his hand, or a drink, or both. But, speaking of movies, that was really the model that was presented by Hollywood at the time. Smoking and drinking.

I don't believe his drinking could be called a problem during the time I knew him in California. I never even saw him tipsy! I do remember telling him that drinking was not good for his liver, especially since he had contracted malaria while in Korea. Of course, after I left California I was not around Grant, and I don't know how serious his drinking might have got in later years. (NI)

Ingris's amiability in seeing the Williams glass half full might be justifiable given the period of her frequentation of him. By the late seventies, however, there could no longer be any doubt that Williams had a problem. Isabel Fisher, who studied acting with Williams in 1978, states that Williams had the reputation of being an alcoholic.

I don't recall ever smelling alcohol on his breath or anything like that, certainly not while he was teaching. When he was teaching he was always present, he was all there. He took his teaching very seriously. But he had a reputation as an alcoholic, and *looked* like an alcoholic. He had that look, skin and all. He also looked much older than his age. When I think of the man I knew in 1978, in my mind's eye I picture a man of sixty-five. He was in fact forty-seven. (IF)

As Williams' career regressed and stalled in the mid-1960s, one can see a numbness creeping into his performances, performances that became prudent and unimaginative (though in all fairness the scripts and roles did not help); one can guess that he was gradually giving up.

Mysteries and Endings

One thing is clear: Williams' professional difficulties and his personal difficulties were inextricably meshed, and one can surmise that the latter were more likely to have been the cause of the former than vice versa. To paraphrase the short story by Ray Bradbury that gives the title to this chapter, the name of Grant Williams' ailment was Grant Williams.[441]

Nina Ingris proposes an additional contrasting factor to explain Williams' lack of success:

> Grant told me he was always discriminated and derided for being a devout Catholic.[442] Whether this derision stemmed from a clash with the predominantly Jewish film industry community or not, I do not know. But there was definitely a clash. (NI)

Williams' feeling that he was the victim of religious discrimination sounds positively medieval, but it may be true. It may also hide the fear of any number of different discriminations. At a minimum, the secrecy with which the actor shrouded much of his life seems to point to his need to protect himself; from what exactly, we may never know. Whatever he felt he was under attack for, *his feeling that he was under attack* was his vulnerable spot, whether other people realized it or not.[443] In this respect at least, through his reserve Williams succeeded in muddying the waters to such an extent that his true personal life was ultimately

---

441. Ray Bradbury. "A Medicine for Melancholy," in *A Medicine for Melancholy*, Doubleday & Company. Inc., 1959

442. In this respect, the *Daily Reporter* 1960 promotional article (op. cit.), which stated that Williams was "an avid reader and student of religions," might be interpreted as a veiled reference to a touch of fanaticism on the actor's part. At any rate, it indicates a sincere interest in an interesting field of study.

443. This might be the "psychosis" to which that anonymous witness referred in his *Poseidon's Underworld* blog post.

concealed from public view almost completely. He became invisible—a tactical move that clearly backfired, both in terms of his profession and in terms of his inner peace.

The same mystery and idle speculation that surround much of Grant Williams' life also shroud his death (July 28, 1985). Reports mention one of two causes: toxemia[444] (or blood poisoning)[445] and peritonitis.[446] In both cases, we are dealing with a poisoning of the blood. Those who favor the sexual line of inquiry interpret these reports as a cover-up for an AIDS-related death; those who see alcoholism as the cause view them as a metonymy for cirrhosis of the liver.

The fact, reported by Mulroney, that Williams' mother had died a short time earlier could support the latter theory, for it is not difficult to imagine Williams spiraling into a bout of suicidal drinking following that personal loss.

Ingris offers a third, less conflictual, interpretation of the official reports:

> After contracting malaria in Korea, Grant was plagued by liver problems for the rest of his life. Blood poisoning, or toxemia (for which he was treated at the Veterans' Hospital), is not inconsistent with that state of things. (NI)

Williams might have sensed that something was going to happen to him, as Ingris recalls:

> Once I received a call from Grant where he asked if he could name me as executor in his last will and testament. I laughed it off, and told him, of course he could, but I did not want to believe that he was serious about it; why would he think of death when he was so young? We were the same age and I certainly was not thinking about a will yet.
>
> Grant never sent me any papers, never called about it again, and it was all forgotten, until Bill Singer, a former Fan-

---

444. *Los Angeles Times* obituary, August 1, 1985.

445. "Deaths Elsewhere," *Philadelphia Inquirer*, August 2, 1985.

446. Wikipedia, "Grant Williams."

Club member, informed me that Grant had died, and that Grant's brother had taken his remains to New York. I later called the National Cemetery in Los Angeles; they confirmed that his cremated remains were indeed buried under his Los Angeles grave spot, and that he was buried with his real birth name, John Joseph Williams (even though the tombstone displays his stage name). Obviously, the report that Grant's brother had transported his remains to New York was false. I never found out if Grant had written a will and named me in it or not. (NI)

On August 2, 1985, a short UPI article reported that funeral services had been held for Williams:

> Funeral services were held for actor Grant Williams, who gained a considerable cult following as "The Incredible Shrinking Man" in the 1950s, officials said Thursday [August 1].
> Williams, 54 [sic], died Sunday at the Veteran's Administration Hospital in West Los Angeles. He was being treated for toxemia, a condition that spreads toxic substances through the body, a hospital spokesman said.

Grant Williams and Coleen Gray in one of their hormonal scenes from *The Leech Woman* (1960). Frame capture.

A small funeral service was held Wednesday evening in the chapel at Pierce Bros. Moeller-Murphy Funeral Home of Santa Monica, a spokeswoman said. A private burial was planned for the Los Angeles National Cemetery on an undisclosed date.[447]

447. "Services Held for Actor Grant Williams," *Alexandria (LA) Daily Town Talk*, August 2, 1985.

15   Swan Songs

FOR ALL THEIR BEAUTY, swans have an ungainly voice, and their songs are graceless laments. The final entries in Williams' body of work are graceless indeed.

The FBI

After more than two years of inactivity, Grant Williams received a handout from Warner Bros. Television. The attempt must have proven unsuccessful, for not only was Williams' part an infelicitous one; it also led to no developments.

In the episode "Breakthrough" (airdate November 17, 1968) of the television series *The FBI* (1965–1974), Williams played SAC Kirby Greene, a useless third wheel to Inspector Lewis Erskine (Efrem Zimbalist Jr.) and Special Agent Tom Kolby (William Reynolds).

Williams is not listed as a "special guest star" in the main titles, only as a guest star in the end titles. Williams' character appears to serve no dramatic purpose except giving exposition and carrying out practical tasks ("*Give this to the lab*"), and Williams is visibly uncomfortable. He spends the episode being inexpressive, with his hands clasped in front of him as if he were holding on in order not to fall down, or with his arms folded defensively. It is not a pretty sight.

Dragnet 1967

The main gimmick of the short-lived (1967–1970) TV series *Dragnet 1967* was Jack Webb's reprisal of his role as LAPD officer Joe Friday from the original series *Dragnet* (1951–1959), but in NBC living color. The other gimmicks were realism and a hagiography of the dedicated LAPD officers who man the desks of the various police departments.

The episode "B.O.D.: DR-27" (aired January 23, 1969) is fundamentally a paratactic series of vignettes depicting the various customers and situations of a day in the Business Office Department. Grant Williams guest-stars as Father Barnes, a priest who spends the day with the Office to observe and help.

There is something stale about the show, and about Williams' performance. While the quiet deadpan of Joe Friday and of his LAPD colleagues may be pleasant, the reverence towards the police and the moralistic bent of the values represented through relentless expository passages make the show insufferably Manichaean, endowing its main characters with a sickly goodness that is as fake as it is commendable.

Williams looks mummified in the episode. His performance is truthful enough, and professional; but it is as if even his liveliest moments (and they are not very lively) were nothing but an attempt to fight a deep boredom. This is the episode where, according to Lamparski, Williams had a "bitter disagreement" with Webb that led to his being blacklisted in Hollywood. (RL, 293) According to Ward and Mulroney, a similar episode on the set of *Hawaiian Eye* had been the cause of Williams' banishment, in which case this appearance could be seen as a late charitable offering to him on the part of the industry.

The Outcasts

The press was silent about Grant Williams' participation in the episode "The Candidates" of the short-lived (1968–1969) western series *The Outcasts*. And when I say it was silent I mean that Williams' name was never mentioned in the plot summaries that appeared in American newspapers on the episode's airdate (January 27, 1969). Here is one such plot summary:

> Madeline Sherwood, Mother Superior on "The Flying Nun," displays her considerable talents on THE OUTCASTS, playing the

part of a slightly addled lady. She is the wife of a candidate for mayor whom the bounty hunters suspect as a possible embezzler. Complicating matters further is the man's daughter, a long lost love of Corey's, who sparks the old flame and provides star Don Murray with a chance to show his romantic potentials.[448]

My Friend Tony

Producer Sheldon Leonard's 1969 series *My Friend Tony* was over almost before it began: it lasted all of sixteen episodes. Its main reason for existing seemed to be the presence of fresh-faced discovery Enzo Cerusico (1937–1991), a young import from Italy who co-starred with protagonist James Whitmore.

The newspapers of 1969 were crowded with plugs for the series' unusual casting choice. On the day the episode in question was aired (February 2, 1969), Grant Williams' name was not mentioned at all.

Doomsday Machine

Brain of Blood was released in 1971, and therefore technically precedes *Doomsday Machine* (1972) by one year; but significant parts of the latter Z-movie were filmed in 1967, and I like to consider it a film of the sixties. Compared to *Brain of Blood*, *Doomsday Machine* looks and feels more like a sixties movie.

Doomsday Machine has a bad reputation, and one cannot honestly make a convincing argument in its favor. However, if one looks closely, it is not significantly worse than any number of television serials (including—blasphemy—*Star Trek*, which was an uneven serial with many middling episodes). Nor is it significantly worse than many European B-movies of the sixties and seventies; even Mario Bava's *Terrore nello spazio* (*Planet of the Vampires*, 1965), for all its designer aliens (which actually influenced one design in Ridley Scott's *Alien*, 1979) and inspired pulp cinematography, is a tedious and static affair from the point of view of plot and dialogue. Nor, in truth, is *Doomsday Machine* worse than Williams' *Brain of Blood*.

---

448. *Pittsburgh (PA) Press*, January 27, 1969.

Doomsday Machine is not a good film; but some of the lighting is pretty, Williams looks dignified enough, and the film certainly has camp value after the fact. Its greatest sin, one for which the filmmakers cannot be easily forgiven, is its wasteful misuse of serviceable actors such as Grant Williams and Bobby Van. In just over ten years, Grant Williams had gone from *The Incredible Shrinking Man* to *Doomsday Machine*. In less than fifteen years, Bobby Van had gone from *Kiss Me, Kate!* (1953) to *Doomsday Machine*. Those are two great falls. Both actors died before reaching the age of fifty-five. *Doomsday Machine* died on impact.

Brain of Blood

As mentioned earlier, *Brain of Blood* (1971) looks like a seventies movie; both it and *Doomsday Machine* end up being grubby, trashy films, but the difference is that *Brain of Blood* seems to *want* to be a grubby, trashy film, whereas *Doomsday Machine* aspires to some kind of weird psychedelic slickness. It fails, but there is some kind of aspiration. There appears to be no such aspiration in *Brain of Blood*.

I suppose the need to do something, anything, by way of work must have weighed heavily on Grant Williams' decision to participate in this horror film, for from the outset its poverty of ideas and of means is painfully evident. Maybe Williams thought he was signing up for a Hammer-type movie; but there is no Terence Fisher at the helm here, no Christopher Lee to balance Williams' quasi Peter Cushing. Above all, there is no elegance in the writing and no visual sumptuousness: there is none of the European dash with color and lighting that makes even the dullest of Hammer movies a dignified show. There are no Victorian sets, no stained-glass windows, no Damascus curtains. Everything is plain, flat, and poor.

Judging from the video copies currently in circulation, the film is also poorly composed and photographed. Cropped down to 1.33:1 video from a 1.85:1 print (not a significant loss), the film seems bent on viewing everything close up, possibly so as not to reveal the absence of production values, and looks awkward and stifling in its imagery: even its close-ups are awkward. In terms of storytelling, the plot it stretches out to fill its eighty-seven-minute running time is so slim and derivative that the result feels sluggish, repetitive, and lifeless.

Grant Williams makes no attempt at camp or at stylistic exaggeration, and this is a pity, for his understated theatrical honesty, which would have been (and had been) perfectly honorable in more professional products, achieves here the opposite effect, making him seem even more of a fish out of water and flattening his performance out completely. If the script were wittier, or at least livelier, the writing might carry some of the weight and permit underplaying; as it is, Williams' subtlety appears like timidity, or embarrassment. In terms of screen time, his part is big, but in all other ways, it is stillborn.

This pair of films (*Doomsday Machine* and *Brain of Blood*) is one reason why Williams' career appears so disjointed in hindsight, despite his many positive accomplishments: it symbolizes a downward spiraling movement, a deterioration that leaves a bitter aftertaste in one's mouth. Synecdochically, and unfairly, these products come to represent the whole of the actor's output. Had Williams quit his career early, Garbo style, he might at least have been spared this particular indignity.

How's Your Love Life?

The film *How's Your Love Life?* was shot in 1971 and released in the United States in October 1977. Here is how the website Temple of Schlock introduces the film's plot:

> Jack Romanti runs a peculiar theatre club in Hollywood where he gives scholarships to youngers seeking to get ahead in the entertainment industry and who pays for this through admissions to the public performances and also contributions from sponsors. But it is the behind-the-scenes entertainment which intrigues the "participating" sponsors, both men and women, for they have free access to the students, via appointment, to satisfy their sexual whims.

And here is Grant Williams' own comment, as quoted by Richard Lamparski in 1982: "One of my last pictures was edited into a near-porno film. The ads for it suggested that I was playing a character who was gay." (RL, 293)In Lamparski's paraphrase, Williams then goes on to say he "would never play a homosexual," which, suspiciously, seems to put a stress on the sexual issue where a stress was not needed. One could spin circles around this quotation trying to psychoanalyze it, and some have tried (the blog *Poseidon's Underworld*, for one), but that would be twisting the knife in the wound (for there was obviously a wound of some kind there) as a fruitless, sadistic exercise.

Since its release, the film has disappeared with hardly a trace. From the point of view of historical research, we should lament this disappearance; in all other respects, we should probably count our blessings.

Family Feud

The ungraceful song of the dying swan rose to a hysterical screeching pitch when Grant Williams, aged fifty-one but looking at least ten years older, made his last two television appearances, as himself, on the game show *Family Feud*. The dates were April 15 and May 11, 1983. Together with his *Hawaiian Eye* co-stars (Connie Stevens, Troy Donahue, Anthony

A prematurely aged Grant Williams is a celebrity contestant on *Family Feud*,
April 15, 1983. Frame capture.

Eisley, and Poncie Ponce), he played against the resurrected stars of *Gilligan's Island* (April 15) and *Lost in Space* (May 11). Williams deported himself with dignity and charm on both occasions, but the whole affair was a sad, sad anticlimax to his career.

In what was possibly an unintentional piece of tragic irony, the first question Williams had to answer on April 15 was: "Name something that people substitute for sex." His answer was: "Unfortunately, I think it's liquor." The answer was correct. Williams died two years later.

16

A Voice in Their Head

THE *POSEIDON'S UNDERWORLD* BLOG, in its affectionate—but heavily colored by the idea of failure—profile of Grant Williams, speaks of the actor's "retreating to a more private existence as an acting teacher." Richard Lamparski, in his 1982 portrait of Williams as a "has-been," quoted Williams as saying that he had "outgrown" acting. These views of Williams' activity as an acting teacher imply not only a defeat (those who can't do, teach) but also a disenchantment with the craft on Williams' part. Between the lines, the two profiles reduce the motive for Williams' decision to teach his master classes to the lowest common denominator of survival.

Money and survival must have played a part, of course. It seems to me, however, that Williams' decision to teach was also a clear expression of his love for acting, and of his desire to keep exploring the craft in some form—from the other side of the fence.

According to his students, Williams was a brilliant, generous teacher. His prices were reasonable and his commitment to the courses enormous. He taught long hours (as former student Ken Mulroney puts it, "We got done when we got done.") and shared his knowledge of acting with his students in an unselfish, enthusiastic manner. Teaching was also a way for Williams to demonstrate his command of the craft, and to indulge in acting himself from time to time (by way of demonstration). His renderings of Shakespearean monologues in class were reportedly quite inspired. He never drank before or during his classes, and was stalwart in his helpfulness towards the occasional student who suffered the effects of that same problem. In his teachings, he was a stickler for punctuality and professionalism, and he encouraged his students to uphold a golden standard in their forays in the industry and in their craft. This does not sound like a retreat, nor like a defeat. Show business and the film-going public, however, have traditionally been obsessed with fame and success; it is in this respect, and only in this respect, that one can view teaching as a failure.

Former acting student Melissa Ward recalls Williams' course as an invitation-only class:

> You couldn't just show up and pay some money to gain access. Grant had to choose you. Traditionally, a candidate would be invited through another student, audit a class as an observer, meet Grant and talk with him. I was friends with Isabel Fisher, who was taking his class at the time, so that is what I did. I met Grant and he immediately wanted me to join the class. (MW)

Former student Isabel Fisher remembers the structure of the course thus:

> Grant was a practitioner of the Stanislavsky Method acting. He was definitely a Method actor. He used a system; if I recall correctly, it was a two-year system designed to get you to that inner place as an actor. I have always regretted not sticking around beyond the first year: I only got half-way through the system. I was very young, and had other distractions in my life. (IF)

Ward remembers that the course required students to be quite committed, and to do a lot of hard work, both in class and at home:

> We met for classes twice a week, at a studio on Robertson, just off Santa Monica Boulevard; each session lasted at least four hours; usually longer. But the hardest, and most time-consuming work, was the homework we had to do outside the classroom. We were assigned a part in a scene, with a partner, and there was a lot of preparation work involved.
>
> Grant picked great material for us to work on: the best of the classic scenes from notable playwrights of his era, mostly

the fifties and sixties: among them were Edward Albee, Michael Gazzo, Leonard Melfi, and Jean-Paul Sartre. The finest classic material.

First, we had to learn our lines. The way Grant would have us learn them was to write them down continuously on sheets of paper, without stopping, like a stream of consciousness. We had to get that part out of the way, in order to have access to the words without having to think about them. If you memorize your lines that way, they will just be in there, available when needed. Like something you keep in your back pocket without thinking about it; when you need it, you just grab it.

Then we would have to do a complete breakdown of the character: we had to analyze the character, learn their motivations, their fears, their hopes, etc. All this work was just the foundation for a lot of rehearsing we had to do with our partner, on our own, outside the classroom. It was like a full-time job. (MW)

Mulroney, who stayed with Williams' course for over four years, adds detail to the process:

When you're learning your lines, you write them down without any punctuation or expression marks. Without any emotion. Then, when you go through them you try to get a feel for what is really going on in the scene, beyond the descriptions the author might write in it; the author might write "laughing" or "crying," but you may find that there is a different emotion for your character at that moment, which you have to find for yourself. This process usually lets you avoid a conventional reading. (KM)

Mulroney also elaborates on the course description, and confirms that, when it came to the craft of acting and the task of teaching, Williams was dead serious:

We started at 7 o'clock at night, on Tuesdays and Fridays, and we got done when we got done. Some nights I was there until two in the morning. Grant only charged seventy-five dollars a month, which was a bargain, because you were getting premium instruction. Grant would never accept more than ten students per course, and he only took students that were serious; if he felt you wouldn't be able to make a commitment, he wouldn't let you in.

Tuesday nights were exercise nights and Friday nights were performance nights. He would have students scheduled on Tuesday night to learn different exercises. On Friday he would have people lined up to do scenes. He would have two scenes scheduled plus one backup scene in case one of the groups didn't show. We would perform the scene, which typically was between ten and twenty minutes long, then Grant would critique it and let all the other students give comments too. Grant ran the course pretty much the way Lee Strasberg had run the Actors Studio in New York.

The animal exercise was interesting. You studied an animal and learned everything you could about it through observation (why does it move, what causes tension, why does it do what it does?), then you went home and re-enacted what you had seen that day. You tried to figure out how the animal thought. Then you brought what you had learned to the human stage: you took the mindset of the animal and projected it onto your character using the characteristic of the animal. I used a tiger for my characterization of a serial killer. You can use a mouse to portray a fearful character, or a gorilla when you want to portray confidence or roughness etc. If you can't do it yourself—if it's hard for you to be rough—you use the animal characterization to help. (KM)

Ward mentions another exercise and elaborates further on the preparation work:

The class included exercises, of various types. Grant would have us imagine a situation ("You're sitting at your desk in the office, and this man comes in waving a gun....") and see what we would do with it. He used to talk about being in the Korean

War, and once he brought a reel-to-reel tape recording of battle noises he had recorded when he was over there, and he had us crawling on our bellies as if under barbed wire, trying to escape from the enemy, to the accompaniment of those sounds.

After a few weeks, we would have our first trial run of the scene, in class. When we were done, Grant would give us notes; more than that: he would actually write his notes—copious notes—directly in our workbooks, so that we would have his notes side by side with our own. He was relentless in pointing out failings in our continuity, in our truthfulness and in our logic. Everything had to be seamless, airtight, genuine, and authentic. Grant had very high standards. (MW)

According to Ward, there was also room for socialization in the process. Mulroney never participated in these social outings with Williams—which typically took place very late at night—because he had a day job, but Ward recalls these occasions with fondness:

One night we would finally do our final version of our scene, the polished version, after we had fixed it with Grant's observations, and after class we would go out with him to a place he liked to hang out at, called Ollie Hammond's Steakhouse.[449] Ollie Hammond's was on La Cienega; it was a nice, old-fashioned 24-hour restaurant with stained glass windows and carved woodwork; they had a private dining room in the basement. You knew when you went with him to Ollie Hammond's that he was a regular at that place: that was his drinking spot. We used to go down to that private room in the basement and drink. You felt special, because you could hang out with Grant. (MW)

Isabel Fisher confirms her admiration for both the teacher and the process:

---

449. Three Ollie Hammond steakhouses existed: the first opened in 1934 on Wilshire Boulevard; the second in 1940 on North La Cienega; the third in 1942 at Third and Fairfax Streets. The restaurants were open 24 hours a day, seven days a week. They closed in 1979.

Grant was very strong-minded, very strict in his approach. I was impressed with his cadre of students: he had some superb actors in his group, and he got some brilliant things out of them. I saw some of those students do scenes that definitely showed how the step-by-step process had been successful. Some of these were folks who had been there close to the two years, or in some cases beyond the two years of the class. I believed in Grant's vision of the acting process. He really transformed people; he brought depth out of people. He was talented and

Portrait of Grant Williams as a cowboy, probably for his appearance on Disney's series *Texas John Slaughter* (1959).

dedicated; acting was his passion, you could see that every step of the way. And his students were as committed to the process as they were devoted to him: they looked to him as a master of his craft, and I don't think they were wrong. (IF)

Ward concurs, and adds a curious side effect:

> Above all, Grant wanted you to abandon your safe place and your own little world; get rid of your own little thoughts. Grant made a very big impression on me and many of the things that he said or taught have stayed with me to this day. That is a sign of an excellent teacher, when their voice is still in your head many years later. (MW)

In other words, there was something haunting about Grant Williams. For those of us who did not know him in person, his performances are ample proof of this.

Afterword

ONE OF THE LIMITATIONS of the biographer is the dearth of reliable first-hand accounts about the subject of the biography.

In the case of Grant Williams, there is another problem, one that may apply to many other film stars as well: Williams was a man with secrets. Whether the attempt to hide these secrets—whatever they might have been—produced actual lies or merely a semi-fictional self-portrait the actor painted in interviews, and what the extent of that fiction was, we cannot know conclusively.

In the early years of his career, this portrait was probably sketched for Williams by the publicity departments at the studios where he worked; in later years, it was his own creation. Either way, that portrait was a screen to shield Williams from deeper scrutiny. There are no indications that what was being hidden from public view was anything particularly embarrassing: there appear to have been no great scandals and no unspeakable truths when it came to Grant Williams. Nonetheless, the portrait that was presented to the public was a sketch, and not a detailed rendering. Only his relationship with the acting craft was painted in any detail.

Thus, the true character of this guarded loner continues to remain something of a mystery, and a considerable amount of speculation is necessary. The puzzle is incomplete: one can guess the picture from the pieces that are available, but not see it completed. Investigating Grant Williams is like trying to take a clear photograph of a ghost.

Even in the presence of first-hand sources, however, conclusiveness in the drafting of a person's life story is a utopian goal, and the truthfulness of such story is far from guaranteed. The issue is a complex one; some points at least can be broached here.

In the case of the depiction that the American press of the fifties and sixties made of Grant Williams (and of many other celebrities, large and small), there is a gaping hole where his person should be. That press was no innocent bystander, and should be assigned at least some of the blame for such "vanishing." In discussing some of the articles written about Williams in his heyday, I have called them "simultaneously coy and boastful." They were coy because they teased the public with hints rather than truths, providing tidbits that made one *guess* about the celebrity they were describing; reticently, they refused to tell the stories that were relevant from a human standpoint, except when they corroborated the celebrity's value as a "business asset" and as an audience pleaser. They were boastful because they filled the readers with irrelevant detail that either glorified the celebrity's past or made promises about his future, but only insofar as these related to industry propaganda; they gave false information about the celebrity, and fabricated a fantasy life for him instead of focusing on the life that he actually had.

Humanly speaking, most of what passed for information about Grant Williams was no information at all, but entertainment. From a journalistic point of view, for example, it is incredible that a sentence such as the one spoken by Williams in his 1961 interview to the *Los Angeles Times*[450] did not elicit some kind of investigation from the journalist hearing it. Williams' statement ("I have a private life that I think is horrible,") was a wrenching break precisely from that coyness and that boastfulness that the press embodied. It might have been an intentional provocation or an accidental slip; either way, it fell upon deaf ears.

What kind of person was Grant Williams? What did he believe in? Whom did he love, whom did he hate? What were his regrets? What were his thoughts and feelings? Who were the people that had changed his life, for better or for worse? Why did he drink? Why did he love acting? What exactly did he love about music, and who were his favorite composers? These questions the press might have asked; these questions the press avoided. Grateful as one is to learn the myriad factoids and factlets the press churned out about Grant Williams, actor and studio commodity, af-

---

450. Alpert (1961), op. cit.

ter reading them one is left with a yearning for something more intimate, more authentic, about Grant Williams the person. One is left with the desire to get to know the person, warts and all.

One would think that eyewitnesses, at least, could offer a more reliable, more definitive truth about the subject. That is not the case. As Playwright and Novelist Luigi Pirandello stated obsessively in his *oeuvre*, the truth about a person is a slippery, evanescent thing, one that is refracted through the prism of subjective opinion, memory, and prejudice. Each person remembers differently, thinks differently, and judges differently. Physical and temporal proximity, even intimacy, offer few guarantees that what is known or remembered about a person is the truth. Pirandello's concept was radical: even the person under investigation might not know himself, or might furnish the world with a version of his own story that is the version the world wants to hear.

Pirandello's insightful—and entertaining—novel *Uno, nessuno e centomila* (*One, None, and a Hundred Thousand*), for example, begins with its protagonist learning from his wife that his nose leans slightly to the right; startled by this casual but unexpected revelation, he begins an investigation to ascertain how his friends and acquaintances see him, physically at first. From each of them he learns a different physical "flaw" that is not his nose. He then asks them about his person, and realizes that for each individual around him (including his wife, who claims she knows him well) he is a different man, with a different personality, different ideas, different feelings, and different tastes. The solidity of his concept of himself is undermined from every direction: he then realizes he does not really know who he is *for himself*.

The identity that we imagine for ourselves may be as false as the identity that others imagine for us; thus, our entire network of human relationships may be based on a Gordian knot of reciprocal misconceptions. This idea, which in Western culture is indelibly associated with Pirandello's work (and with other authors after him, such as Samuel Beckett and Harold Pinter), was embodied in Japan by Akira Kurosawa's *Rashomon* (1950). In Kurosawa's film, four separate eyewitnesses tell contrasting versions of an event, each version casting irreparable doubt on the preceding accounts. When it comes to human beings and their relationships, Kurosawa seems to be saying, the truth is unattainable.

Other elements may stand in the way of truthfulness in the case of eyewitnesses, such as, for example, discretion or moralism. An eyewitness may have received information in confidence, and may be reluctant (even after the subject's death) to expose an embarrassing fact. Or, the eyewitness's own sensibility may be an obstacle to forming a certain hypothesis about the subject; a friend, for example, may feel compelled only to think and say nice things about the subject, and may not want to risk sullying the subject's reputation by proposing a more complex interpretation of certain facts. Those facts, or that interpretation, might clash with the eyewitness's morality, and might be conveniently forgotten.

Lastly, many facts about the subject's life are not known by anyone simply because the subject did not wish them to be known. The subject may have harbored secrets. In the case of a fervent Catholic like Grant Williams, his own moral ideology might have been an obstacle to some truths about himself.

For all these reasons, I am sometimes skeptical of biographies (whether authorized or not) that appear too perfect or too "definitive." That narrative perfection seems to me a veneer of fiction that must hide an infinite number of doubts in order for the author to appear authoritative. The author has to make continuous assumptions about the subject, and correlate the known "facts" at an infinite number of bifurcations. Correlating these "facts" of the subject's life means drawing conclusions about them in place of the subject: it means interpreting and guessing. Even when a living subject is telling the story (whether in an authorized biography or in an autobiography), all we can really establish definitively is that the story the subject is telling represents a point of view. The writing of personal history through exterior events does not guarantee that the truth about the deep reasons for those events will be revealed.

Any autobiography, for instance, may be more interesting for the worldview that transpires between the lines of the subject's telling the story of his life than for the story itself. What the subject feels he or she has to hide (or not investigate) may be more fascinating than what he or she reveals readily. In other words, what the subject wants the world to know is not the whole story, even when the story is true.

The above process of gathering and correlating facts, of drawing conclusions or hypotheses, of interpreting and of guessing, which is often buried under the narration in traditional biographies, has been brought

One of Universal Pictures' early studio portraits of Grant Williams,
enthusiastically inscribed by him to an undetermined publicist. © 1956,
Universal Pictures Company, Inc.

to the surface in this one, by clearly separating the "facts" from the interpretations. I claim no definitive answers in my biography of Grant Williams. I only profess a positive, respectful search for the truth and a reluctance to draw conclusions, in the belief that the combination of these
two processes leads to the healthiest way of examining any human being,
dead or alive.

A note about Grant Williams the actor: that Williams was an actor
dedicated to his craft and to emotional truthfulness is evident from his
performances. What is also evident is his lack of narcissism: his performances were not star-like. Williams employed a minimalist, almost invis-

ible style that might be perceived as a lack of style. Virtually everything in his playing was outwardly subtle, including his use of the body. There are many moments in his performances when all of Williams' craft seems concentrated in his eyes and in his voice. His was not a very physical approach, and this distinguished him significantly from some of his more famous Actors Studio peers. Williams' bodily restraint made his playing extremely measured—and possibly less noticeable.

With his deadpan (not the deadpan of an Alan Ladd or of a Robert Taylor, but the deeper deadpan of a John Garfield), Williams was what one could call an unspectacular actor; so unspectacular, in fact, that even his public, his critics, and his producers and directors were often not seduced. Williams made no effort to ingratiate himself to his audience: he did not play cute and he did not play big. He refused to pander to the pleasures of the spectator, and remained rigorously anchored to the feelings he discovered in the character—and in himself. If the expression did not risk sounding backhanded, one could say that he refused to be a star.[451]

This refusal led to another kind of "invisibility": Williams became unclassifiable in the eyes of many—of the many who had to make decisions about him and his career. No easy label was at hand to pigeonhole him or typecast him: Williams was not a "type." The film that made him almost famous, the film that everyone remembers him by, was itself a felicitous accident that eluded the standard labels by which it was normally indicated—and still is to this day: *The Incredible Shrinking Man* is not really a science-fiction film, just as it is not really a horror film. If it is anything, it is a character piece, a melancholy allegorical drama about life. Williams was perfect for that piece because it was an opportunity for him to do what he did best: act without labels and without easy glamour or pandering. Significantly, the film did not make him a star; it proved him an actor. Peter O'Toole's character in the film *My Favorite Year* (1982), Alan Swann the fading alcoholic movie star, says about himself defensively: "*I'm not an actor, I'm a movie star!*" Williams' outcry, if one could imagine him protesting drunkenly on one of his sets, was likely to be the opposite: "I'm not a movie star, I'm an actor!"

---

451. One reviewer hit the nail on the head when he defined (positively) Williams' acting in *The Monolith Monsters* (1957) as "the muted acting of Grant Williams [...]." (Marion Porter, "Stony Film Monsters Are 'Uneasily Realistic'," *Louisville (KY) Courier-Journal.* December 13, 1957.

To make the most of such "lack of style," an actor like Williams needed the proper texts; he needed sharp, intelligent screenplays that concentrated on the human core of the characters; he needed texts where the
word took care of itself, sparkled by itself, while weaving in and out of an
earnest exploration of the character. Aside from *The Incredible Shrinking
Man*, few texts provided Williams with the chance to do such authentic
acting; among them, the most spectacular were the episode "Nightmare
in Paradise" of the series *Hawaiian Eye*, *The Millionaire*'s "Millionaire Gilbert Burton," and the film *Lone Texan*.

Like a comet from outer space, Grant Williams streaked across life
on this earth; he was not a creature fit for the strife of terrestrial existence,
which he ill endured, or for permanence. He obviously had an interest in
the arts, and an uncommon sensitivity for the observation of people and
characters: the melancholy feelings that he transmitted were authentic,
as were his portrayals of human beings. Life itself, however, was not for
him; after observing what he could, restlessly, he abandoned it. His was
an attempt at life, and not a particularly successful one (in terms of inner
peace).

Notwithstanding his maladjustment and sadness, however, there was
always a lightness of touch to him, a weightless quality in his acting and in
his presence; not in the comedic sense, or in the sense that there was no
depth to him, but rather in the sense that, physically, Williams was barely
here: he was barely incarnated on this planet. As befits a comet passing
through, he did not really belong here on earth. In this sense at least, Williams was—briefly—a true star

Appendix: Film and Television Credits (1954–1983)

The Mask (TV Series)

"Fingers of Fear" (March 21, 1954)

Gary Merrill (Walter Guilfoyle), William Prince (Peter Guilfoyle), Mary Linn Beller, Grant Williams.

Story: Philip MacDonald.

ABC.

Kraft Television Theatre (TV Drama)

"Alice in Wonderland" (May 5, 1954)

Carl White (Tweedledee), Iggie Wolfington (Tweedledum), Grant Williams (Knave of Hearts), Fredd Wayne (March Hare), Joe E. Marks (Dormouse), Arnold Moss (Red Knight), Chandler Cowles (Caterpillar), Una O'Connor (Cook), Cliff Hall (Duchess), Joey Walsh [Joseph Walsh] (White Rabbit), Blanche Yurka (Queen of Hearts), Ernest Truex (White Knight), Arthur Treacher (Cheshire Cat), Robin Morgan (Alice), Art Carney (Mad Hatter), Bobby Clark (King of Hearts), James Barton (Mock Turtle), Ed Herlihy (Announcer–voice).

Music: Ernest Watson.

Teleplay: Jack Riche, based on the novel by Lewis Carroll.

Directed by: Maury Holland (uncredited).

J. Walter Thompson Agency/NBC.

Kraft Television Theatre (TV Drama)

"Deliver Me from Evil" (June 17, 1954)

Claudia Morgan, Anthony Ross, Grant Williams.

Executive Producer: George Lowther.

J. Walter Thompson Agency/NBC.

Studio One (TV Drama)

"Sail with the Tide" (January 17, 1955)

Claude Dauphin, Mai Zeterling, Betty Furness, Grant Williams, Meg Mundy.

Teleplay: Michael Dyne, based on a short story by Honoré de Balzac.

Directed by: Paul Nickell.

CBS.

Soldiers of Fortune (TV Series)

"The Lady of Rajmahal" (February 9, 1955)

John Russell (Tim Kelly), Chick Chandler (Toubo Smith), Lisa Daniels (Lady Diane), Ian Keith (The Rajah), Grant Williams (Kingsley Miller).

Story: Joseph Leal Henderson, Jack Leonard; Teleplay: Lawrence Kimble.

Directed by: John English.

Revue Productions/Studios USA Television.

Lux Video Theatre (TV Drama)

"Shadow of a Doubt" (March 24, 1955)

Ken Carpenter (Himself–Announcer), George Chandler (Joe), Byron Foulger (Herby Hawkins), Frank Lovejoy (Uncle Charlie), Charles Meredith (Reverend), Helena Nash (Mrs. Potter), Barbara Rush (Charlotte), Sarah Selby (Emmy), Grant Williams (Jack Graham).

Art Direction: William Craig Smith; Musical Director: Rudy Schrager.

Produced by: Cal Kuhl; Teleplay: Ben Simcoe, based on a screenplay by Sally Benson, Alma Reville, Thornton Wilder.

Directed by: Richard Goode.

J. Walter Thompson Agency/NBC.

Allen in Movieland (TV Movie, July 2, 1955)

Steve Allen, Keith Andes, Jeff Chandler, Buck Clayton, Mara Corday, Dani Crayne, Pat Crowley, Tony Curtis, Danny Dayton, Dante Di Paolo, Douglass Dumbrille, Stan Getz, Clint Eastwood, Benny Goodman, Urbie Green, Gretchen Houser, Jane Howard, Lou Grugman, Gene Krupa, Muriel Landers, Piper Laurie, Jean Mahoney, Audie Murphy, Tommy Rall, Rex Reason, Dan Riss, Betty Scott, Grant Williams, Teddy Wilson.

Written by: Don McGuire

Directed by: Dick McDonough.

Oldsmobile/NBC.

Lux Video Theatre (TV Drama)

"The Amazing Mrs. Holliday" (October 6, 1955)

Claud Allister [Claude Allister] (Henderson), Robert Burton (Ferguson), Herb Butterfield [Herbert Butterfield], Ken Carpenter (Himself–Announcer), Gerald Charlebois [Michael Forest], Virginia Gibson, Dorothy Gish, Craig Hill, Frieda Inescort (Louise), Otto Kruger (Himself–Host), Betsy Paul (Karen), Lydia Reed (Elisabeth), Barbara Rush (Ruth), Joseph Sweeney (Timothy), Grant Williams (Tom), Will Wright (Commodore).

Art Direction: William Craig Smith; Musical Director: Rudy Schrager; Story Editor: Richard McDonagh [Richard P. McDonagh]; Technical Director: Joe Strauss.

Produced by: Cal Kuhl; Executive Producer: Stanley Quinn; Story: Sonya Levien; Screenplay: John Jacoby, Frank Ryan; TV Adaptation: S.H. Barnett.

Directed by: Richard Goode.

J. Walter Thompson Agency/NBC.

Matinee Theater (TV Drama)

"Arrowsmith" (December 5, 1955)

John Conte (Himself–Host), Gregory Gaye, Maudie Prickett, Reba Tassell [Rebecca Welles], Grant Williams (Dr. Martin Arrowsmith).

Teleplay: Robert Howard Lindsay, Kathleen Lindsey, based on the novel by Sinclair Lewis.

Directed by: Boris Sagal.

NBC.

Red Sundown (March 1956)

Rory Calhoun (Alec Longmire), Martha Hyer (Caroline Murphy), Dean Jagger (Sheriff Jade Murphy), Robert Middleton (Rufus Henshaw), Grant Williams (Chet Swann), Lita Baron (Maria), James Millican (Bud Purvis), Trevor Bardette (Sam Baldwin), Leo Gordon (Rod Zellman), David Kasday (Hughie Clore), Terry Gilkyson (Title song vocalist–Voice).

Ray Bennett (uncredited), Gail Bonney (Mrs. Clore, uncredited), Lane Bradford (Mike Zellman, uncredited), Chet Brandenburg (Townsman, uncredited), Helen Brown (Mrs. Baldwin, uncredited), Steve Darrell (Bert Flynn, uncredited), Franklyn Farnum (Hotel Clerk, uncredited), Scott Morrow (Chet, uncredited), Eddie Parker (Slim, uncredited), Dick Rich (Harry Felcher, uncredited), Stephen Wooton (Chuck, uncredited).

Director of Photography: William Snyder [William E. Snyder]; Editing: Edward Curtiss; Art Direction: Alexander Golitzen, Eric Orbom; Set Decoration: John P. Austin, Russell A. Gausman; Costume Design: Jay A. Morley, jr.; Makeup: Bud Westmore; Hair Styling: Joan St. Egger; Assistant Directors: William Holland, James Welch; Music: Hans J. Salter, Heinz Roemheld (uncredited); Music Supervision: Joseph Gershenson.

Produced by: Albert Zugsmith; Screenplay: Martin Berkeley, based on the novel by Lewis B. Patten.

Directed by: Jack Arnold.

Universal-International Pictures/Universal Pictures.

Outside the Law (June 1956)

Ray Danton (John Conrad, aka Johnny Salvo), Leigh Snowden (Maria Craven), Grant Williams (Don Kastner), Onslow Stevens (Chief Agent Alec Conrad), Raymond Bailey (Philip Bormann), Judson Pratt (Agent Maury Saxton), Jack Kruschen (Agent Phil Schwartz), Floyd Simmons (Agent Harris), Mel Welles (Milo), Alexander Campbell (Warden Lewis), Kaaren Verne (Mrs. Pulenski), Maurice Doner (Mr. Pulenski), Jess Kirpatrick (Bill MacReady, Customs Official), Arthur Hanson (Agent Parker), Richard H. Cutting (Agent Pomery), Amapola Del Vando (Mama Gomez), Vernon Rich (Redding), Dan Sturkie (Clinton).

Director of Photography: Irving Glassberg; Editing: Irving Birnbaum; Art Direction: Alexander Golitzen, Eric Orbom; Set Decoration: Oliver Emert, Rusell A. Gausman; Costume Design: Rosemary Odell; Makeup: Bud Westmore; Hair Styling: Joan St. Egger; Assistant Director: Ronald R. Rondell [Ronnie Rondell]; Special Effects Photography: Clifford Stine; Music: Henry Mancini (uncredited), Hans J. Salter (uncredited), Frank Skinner (uncredited), Herman Stein (uncredited), Stanley Wilson (uncredited); Music Supervision: Milton Rosen.

Produced by: Albert J. Cohen; Screenplay: Danny Arnold; Story: Peter R. Brooke.

Directed by: Jack Arnold.

Universal-International Pictures/Universal Pictures.

Away All Boats (June 16, 1956)

Jeff Chandler (Captain Jebediah S. Hawks), George Nader (Lieutenant Dave MacDougall), Lex Barker (Commander Quigley), Julie Adams (Nadine MacDougall), Keith Andes (Doctor Bell), Richard Boone (Lieutenant Fraser), William Reynolds (Ensign Kruger), Charles McGraw (Lieutenant Mike O'Bannion), Jock Mahoney (Alvick), John McIntire (Old Man/Film intro voice-over), Frank Faylen (Chief Phillip P. 'Pappy' Moran), James Westerfield ('Boats' Torgeson), Don Keefer (Ensign Twitchell), Kendall Clark (Lieutenant Jackson), George Dunn (Hubert), Charles Horvath (Boski), Jarl Victor ('Sacktime' Riley), Arthur Space (Doctor Flynn), Parley Baer (Doctor Gates), Hal Baylor (Chaplain Hughes), Sam Gilman (Lieutenant Jim Randall), Grant Williams (Lieutenant Steve Sherwood, uncredited).

Director of Photography: William Daniels [William H. Daniels]; Editing: Ted J. Kent; Art Direction: Alexander Golitzen, Richard H. Riedel; Set Decoration: Oliver Emert, Russell A. Gausman; Assistant Directors: Marshall Green, Terence Nelson (uncredited), James Welch (uncredited); Special Photography: Clifford Stine; Music: Frank Skinner; Music Supervision: Joseph Gershenson; Additional music: Heinz Roemheld (uncredited).

Produced by: Howard Christie; Screenplay: Ted Sherdeman, from the novel by Kenneth M. Dodson.

Directed by: Joseph Pevney.

Universal-International Pictures/Universal Pictures.

Walk the Proud Land (September 1956)

Audie Murphy (John Philip Clum), Anne Bancroft (Tianay), Pat Crowley (Mary Dennison), Charles Drake (Tom Sweeny), Tommy Rall (Taglito), Robert Warwick (Chief Eskiminzin), Jay Silverheels (Geronimo), Eugene Mazzola (Tono), Anthony Caruso (Disalin), Victor Millan (Santos), Ainslie Pryor (Captain Larsen), Eugene Iglesias (Chato), Morris Ankrum (General Wade), Addison Richards (Governor Safford), Maurice Jara (Alchise), Frank Chase (Stone), Ed Hinton (Naylor); Grant Williams (Woodworth Clum, Narrator; voice only, uncredited).

Director of Photography: Harold Lipstein; Editing: Sherman Todd; Art Direction: Alexander Golitzen, Bill Newberry; Set Decoration: Russell A. Gausman, Ray Jeffers; Costume Design: Bill Thomas; Assistant Directors: Phil Bowles, Ray DeCamp (uncredited), James Welch (uncredited); Special Photography: Clifford Stine; Music: William Lava (uncredited), Hans J. Salter (uncredited), Henry Mancini (uncredited), Herman Stein (uncredited); Music Supervision: Joseph Gershenson.

Produced by: Aaron Rosenberg; Screenplay: Gil Doud, Jack Sher, based on the biography by Woodworth Clum.

Directed by: Jesse Hibbs.

Universal-International Pictures/Universal Pictures.

Showdown at Abilene (October 1956)

Jock Mahoney (Jim Trask), Martha Hyer (Peggy Bigelow), Lyle Bettger (Dave Mosely), David Janssen (Verne Ward), Grant Williams (Chip Tomlin), Ted de Corsia (Dan Claudius), Harry Harvey Sr. [Harry Harvey] (Ross Bigelow), Dayton Lummis (Jack Bedford), Richard H. Cutting (Nelson), Robert G. Anderson [Robert Anderson] (Sprague), John Maxwell (Frank Scovie).

Director of Photography: Irving Glassberg; Editing: Ray Snyder; Art Direction: Alexander Golitzen, Richard H. Riedel; Set Decoration: Russell A. Gausman, Ruby R. Levitt; Costume Design: Rosemary Odell; Music: Henry Mancini (uncredited), Hans J. Salter (uncredited), Frank Skinner (uncredited), Herman Stein (uncredited); Music Supervision: Joseph Gershenson.

Produced by: Howard Christie; Story: Clarence Upson Young; Screenplay: Berne Giler.

Directed by: Charles Haas [Charles F. Haas].

Universal-International Pictures/Universal Pictures.

Kraft Television Theatre (TV Drama)

"I Am Fifteen and I Don't Want to Die" (October 17, 1956)

Bennye Gatteys (Christine Arnothy), Grant Williams (Pista), Richard Morse (Gabriel), Russell Collins (Mr. Posanyi), Nehemiah Persoff (Mr. Arnothy), Paul Tripp (Radnai), Nan McFarland, Mary Leigh-Hare, Peter Brandon, Undine Forrest.

J. Walter Thompson Agency/NBC.

Written on the Wind (December 1956)

Rock Hudson (Mitch Wayne), Lauren Bacall (Lucy Moore Hadley), Robert Stack (Kyle Hadley), Dorothy Malone (Marylee Hadley), Robert Keith (Jasper Hadley), Grant Williams (Biff Miley), Robert J. Wilke (Dan Willis), Edward C. Platt [Edward Platt] (Dr. Paul Cochrane), Harry Shannon (Hoak Wayne), John Larch (Roy Carter), Joseph Gramby (R.J. Courtney), Roy Glenn (Sam), Maidie Norman (Bertha), William Schallert (Reporter).

Director of Photography: Russell Metty; Editing: Russell F. Schoengarth; Art Direction: Robert Clatworth, Alexander Golitzen; Set Decoration: Russell A. Gausman, Julia Heron; Costume Design: Bill Thomas, Jay A. Morley, Jr. (uncredited); Special Photography: Clifford Stine; Music: Frank Skinner; Music Supervision: Joseph Gershenson.

Produced by: Albert Zugsmith; Screenplay: George Zuckerman, based on the novel by Robert Wilder.

Directed by: Douglas Sirk.

Universal-International Pictures/Universal Pictures.

Four Girls in Town [4 Girls in Town] (January 16, 1957)

George Nader (Mike Snowden), Julie Adams (Kathy Conway), Sydney Chaplin (Johnny Pryor), Marianne Cook [Marianne Koch] (Ina Schiller), Elsa Martinelli (Maria Antonelli), Grant Williams (Spencer Farrington Jr.), Gia Scala (Vicky Dauray), John Gavin (Tom Grant), Herbert Anderson (Ted Larabee), Hy Averback (Bob Trapp), Ainslie Pryor (James Manning), James Bell (Walter Conway), Mabel Albertson (Mrs. Conway), Dave Barry (Vince), Maurice Marsac (Henri), Helene Stanton (Rita Holloway), Irene Corlett (Mildred Purdy), Eugene Mazzola (Paul).

Director of Photography (CinemaScope, color): Irving Glassberg; Editing: Fredrick Y. Smith; Art Direction: Alexander Golitzen, Ted Haworth; Set Decoration: Russell A. Gausman, Julia Heron; Costume Design: Rosemary Odell; Assistant Director: Dick Mayberry [Richard Mayberry]; Special Photography: Clifford Stine; Music: Alex North, Irving Gertz (uncredited), Frederick Herbert (uncredited), Milton Rosen (uncredited), Frank Skinner (uncredited), André Previn (trumpet, uncredited), Ray Linn (piano, uncredited); Music Supervision: Joseph Gershenson.

Produced by: Aaron Rosenberg; Screenplay: Jack Sher.

Directed by: Jack Sher.

Universal-International Pictures/Universal Pictures.

The Incredible Shrinking Man (February–March 1957)

Grant Williams (Robert Scott Carey), Randy Stuart (Louise Carey), April Kent (Clarice Bruce), Paul Langton (Charlie Carey), Raymond Bailey (Dr. Thomas Silver), William Schallert (Dr. Arthur Bramson), Frank Scannell [Frank J. Scannell] (Barker), Helene Marshall (Nurse), Diana Darrin (Nurse), Billy Curtis (Midget), John Hiestand (KIRL TV Newscaster, uncredited), Joe La Barba (Joe–Milkman, uncredited).

Director of Photography: Ellis W. Carter; Editing: Al Joseph [Albrecht Joseph]; Art Direction: Robert Clatworthy, Alexander Golitzen; Set Decoration: Russell A. Gausman, Ruby R. Levitt; Costume Design: Jay A. Morley, Jr., Martha Bunch (uncredited), Rydo Loshak (uncredited); Make-Up: Joan St. Oegger (hair stylist), Bud Westmore (make-up), Virginia Jones (hairdresser, uncredited), Jack Kevan (make-up, uncredited); Production Management: Bob Larson (uncredited), Lew Leary (uncredited); Art Department: Floyd Farrington (props, uncredited), Ed Keyes (prop master, uncredited), Whitey McMahon (prop maker, uncredited), Roy Neel (assistant prop master, uncredited); Sound Department: Leslie I. Carey, Robert Pritchard, Donald Cunliffe (recordist, uncredited), Bob Hirsch (sound editor, uncredited), Henry Janssen (cable man, uncredited), Roger A. Parish (mike man, uncredited); Special Effects: Cleo E. Baker (uncredited), Fred Knoth (uncredited); Visual Effects: Everett H. Broussard (optical effects), Roswell A. Hoffman [Roswell A. Hoffmann] (optical effects); Special Photography: Clifford Stine; Still Photographer: Richard Walling (uncredited); Music Supervision: Joseph Gershenson, Harris Ashburn (uncredited); Music: Irving Gertz (uncredited), Earl E. Lawrence (uncredited), Hans J. Salter (uncredited), Herman Stein (uncredited); Ray Anthony (trumpet soloist).

Produced by: Albert Zugsmith; Screenplay: Richard Alan Simmons (uncredited), Richard Matheson, based on his novel.

Directed by: Jack Arnold.

Universal-International Pictures/Universal Pictures.

Matinee Theater (TV Drama)

"The Flashing Stream" (April 12, 1957)

John Conte (Himself–Host), David Frankham, Grant Williams, Patrick O'Neal.

Teleplay: Charles Morgan, based on his play.

NBC.

Lux Video Theatre (TV Drama)

"Paris Calling" (May 30, 1957)

Jan Arvan (Waiter), Jacques Aubuchon (Captain Schwabe), Edgar Barrier (Andrew Benois), Ken Carpenter (Himself-Announcer), Joanne Dru (Marianne), Jason Johnson (Mouche), Gordon MacRae (Himself–Host), Tony Millard [Maurice Millard] (Plane Commander), Werner Reichow (Nazi Soldier), William Roerick (Lieutenant Lautz), Anne Seymour (Madame), Abraham Sofaer (Professor), Chet Stratton (British Officer), Michael Vallon (Resistance Leader), Grant Williams (Nick).

Art Direction: William Craig Smith; Costume Design: Olaja; Makeup: Paul Stanhope; Audio: Howard Cooley; Lighting Director: Del Jack; Musical Director: Rudy Schrager.

Produced by: Earl Eby; Executive Producer: Stanley Quinn; Screenplay: Benjamin Glazer, Charles Kaufman; TV Adaptation/Teleplay: S.H. Barnett.

Directed by: Norman Morgan.

J. Walter Thompson Agency/NBC.

"Barren Harvest" (August 8, 1957)

Mabel Albertson (Mrs. Chester), Florenz Ames (Bayard), Jack Arthur (Mitchell), Ken Carpenter (Himself–Announcer), Audrey Dalton (Barbara), Byron Foulger (Renton), Mitchell Garth (Tait), Craig Stevens (Himself–Guest Host), Vaughn Taylor (Partridge), Grant Williams (David).

Art Direction: Gerry Decker; Costume Design: Dina Joseph; Makeup: Paul Stanhope; Audio: Howard Cooley; Musical Director: Rudy Schrager.

Produced by: Earl Eby; Executive Producer: Stanley Quinn; Teleplay: Henry F. Greenberg, based on the play and novel by C. M. Nelson.

Directed by: James P. Yarbrough.

J. Walter Thompson Agency/NBC.

The Monolith Monsters (December 1957)

Grant Williams (Dave Miller), Lola Albright (Cathy Barrett), Les Tremayne (Martin Cochrane), Trevor Bardette (Prof. Arthur Flanders), Phil Harvey (Ben Gilbert), William Flaherty (Police Chief Dan Corey), Harry Jackson (Dr. Steve Hendricks), Richard Cutting [Richard H. Cutting] (Dr. E.J. Reynolds), Linda Scheley (Ginny Simpson), Dean Cromer (Highway Patrolman), Steve Darrell (Joe Higgins), William Schallert (Weatherman), Troy Donahue (Hank Jackson, uncredited), Paul Frees (Narrator, uncredited), Carol Morris (Nurse, uncredited), Paul Petersen (Bobby-Paperboy, uncredited), Ezelle Poule (Ethel-Telephone Operator, uncredited).

Director of Photography: Ellis W. Carter; Editing: Patrick McCormack; Art Direction: Alexander Golitzen, Robert E. Smith [Robert Emmett Smith]; Set Decoration: Russell A. Gausman, William Tapp [William P. Tapp]; Costume Design: Marilyn Sotto; Sound: Leslie I. Carey, Frank Wilkinson [Frank H. Wilkinson]; Special Photography: Clifford Stine; Special Effects: Frank Brendel (uncredited); Music: Irving Gertz (uncredited), Henry Mancini (uncredited), Herman Stein (uncredited); Music Supervision: Joseph Gershenson.

Produced by: Howard Christie; Story: Jack Arnold, Robert M. Fresco; Screenplay: Norman Jolley, Robert M. Fresco.

Directed by: John Sherwood.

Universal-International Pictures/Universal Pictures.

Jane Wyman Presents The Fireside Theatre (TV Drama)

"Tunnel Eight" (February 20, 1958)

Jane Wyman (Herself–Hostess), Preston Foster (Colonel Dan Mc-Gann), Grant Williams (Lieutenant Larry Dunham), Tom Brown (Roy Evans), Jack Elam (Quirt Avery), Roy Roberts (Boomer Doyle), Karl Swenson (Pat Casey), Dori Simmons (Candy), Joseph Crehan (General Ulysses S. Grant), Francis De Sales (Dr. Howard).

Director of Photography: John L. Russell; Editing: Marston Fay; Art Direction: George Patrick; Makeup: Jack Barron, Florence Bush; Sound: William H. Lynch; Costume Supervisor: Vincent Dee.

Teleplay: George Waggner.

Directed by: George WaGGner [George Waggner].

Lewman Productions/NBC.

Matinee Theater (TV Drama)

"The End of a Season" (June 3, 1958)

John Conte (Himself–Host), Grant Williams, Mark Roberts, Julie Bennett, Nancy Hadley.

Teleplay: S.S. Schweitzer, based on a play by Bernard Schubert.

NBC.

Shirley Temple's Storybook (TV Series)

"The Wild Swans" (September 12, 1958)

Shirley Temple (Herself–Narrator), Bob Banas [Robert Banas] (Brother), Bob Chapman (Brother), Melville Cooper (Binky), Olive Deering (Queen Flavia), Lisa Golm, Phyllis Love (Elisa), Buzz Martin

(Brother), Anne O'Neal, Alfred Ryder (First Minister), Grant Williams (King Julio), Joseph Wiseman (Sorcerer).

Director of Photography: Gert Andersen; Editing: Henry Batista; Casting: Edith Hamlin.

Produced by: Alvin Cooperman; Teleplay: Jean Holloway, based on a story by Hans Christian Andersen.

Directed by: Richard Morris.

Henry Jaffe Enterprises, Inc./NBC.

Man with a Camera (TV Series)

"Another Barrier" (November 28, 1958)

Charles Bronson (Mike Kovac), Norma Crane (Liz Howell), Grant Williams (Major Sandy Dickson), Peter Walker (Captain Lyle), Morgan Jones (Captain Shaler), Jess Kirkpatrick (Sgt. Joe Garr), David Whorf (Ernie), Ann Morrison (Mrs. Burns).

Director of Photography: Robert B. Hauser; Editing: J.R. Whittredge; Casting: Harvey Clermont; Art Direction: Ralph Berger, Duncan Cramer; Set Decoration: William L. Stevens [William Stevens]; Makeup: George Lane.

Associate Producer: Jason H. Bernie; Producer: A.E. Houghton Jr. [Buck Houghton]; Teleplay: Stanley Niss.

Directed by: Gerald Mayer.

MWC/ABC.

Walt Disney Presents (TV Series)

"The Peter Tchaikovsky Story" (January 30, 1959)

Grant Williams (Peter Tchaikovsky the Man), Rex Hill (Peter Tchaikovsky the Boy), Leon Askin (Anton Rubinstein), Lilyan Chauvin (Fanny Durbach), Narda Onyx (Desiree Artot), Gregory Gay [Gregory Gaye] (Major Mashovsky), John Banner (Office Supervisor), Edith Evanson (Mother Tchaikovsky), Alex Gerry (Father Tchaikovsky), Galina Ulanova (Odette in 'Swan Lake').

Director of Photography: Walter H. Castle [Walter Castle]; Editing: George Gale; Art Direction: Marvin Aubrey Davis; Set Decoration: Hal Gausman, Emile Kuri; Costume Design: Chuck Keehne; Make-up: Pat McNalley; Assistant Director: Vincent McEveety; Special Art Work: Dick Anthony; Sound: Robert O. Cook; Music: George Bruns.

Produced by: Clyde Geronimi; Teleplay: Otto Englander, Joe Rinaldi.

Directed by: Charles Barton.

Walt Disney Productions/ABC.

Gunsmoke (TV Series)

"The Bear" (February 28, 1959)

James Arness (Matt Dillon), Dennis Weaver (Chester), Milbrun Stone (Doc), Amanda Blake (Kitty), Grant Williams (Joe Plummer), Norma Crane (Tilda), Denver Pyle (Mike Blocker), Russell Johnson (Harry Webb), Guy Wilkerson (Pete Wilkins).

Casting by: Lynn Stalmaster. Produced by: Norman MacDinnell; Teleplay: John Meston, based on the radio series created by Norman MacDonnell, John Meston; Developed for television by: Charles Marquis Warren (uncredited).

Directed by: Jesse Hibbs.

CBS.

Lone Texan (March 1, 1959)

Willard Parker (Clint Banister), Grant Williams (Greg Banister), Audrey Dalton (Susan Harvey), Douglas Kennedy (Maj. Phillip Harvey), June Blair (Florrie Stuart), Dabbs Greer (Doc Jansen), Barbara Heller (Amy Todd), Rayford Barnes (Finch), Tyler McVey (Henry Biggs), Lee Farr (Riff), Jim Murphy [Jimmy Murphy] (Rio), Dick Monaghan [Richard Monahan] (Jesse), Robert Dix (Carpetbagger), Gregg Barton (Ben Hollis), I. Stanford Jolley (Trader), Sid Melton (Gus Pringle), Shirle Haven [Shirley Haven] (Nancy).

Director of Photography: Walter Strenge; Editing: Robert Fritch (uncredited); Art Direction: Edward Shiells; Set Decoration: Harry Reif;

Makeup: Harry Littlefield, Lillian Shore; Assistant Director: Lou Perlof; Costume Supervisor: Clark Ross; Music: Paul Dunlap.

Produced by: Kack Leewood, Richard E. Lyons (uncredited); Screenplay: James Landis, Jack Thomas [Jack W. Thomas] (uncredited), based on the novel by James Landis.

Directed by: Paul Landres.

Regal Pictures/20th Century Fox Film Corporation.

Yancy Derringer (TV Series)

"Longhair" (March 5, 1959)

Jock Mahoney (Yancy Derringer), Kevin Hagen (John Colton), X Brands (Pahoo-Ke-Ta-Wah), Grant Williams (George Armstrong Custer), Frances Bergen (Madame Francine), Kelly Thordsen (Colorado Charlie), Robert McCord III [Robert McCord] (Captain Fry), Roy Jensen [Roy Jenson] (Captain MacBain), Charlene James (Pearl Girl), Woodrow Chambliss [Woody Chambliss] (Captain Tom), Gene Collins (Willy Quill).

Director of Photography: Robert B. Hauser; Editing: Sherman A. Rose; Casting: Harvey Clermont; Art Direction: Ralph Berger, Duncan Cramer; Set Decoration: William L. Stevens [William Stevens]; Makeup: George Lane, Louise Miehle.

Produced by: Mary Loos, Richard Sale; Executive Producers: Warren Lewis, Don W. Sharpe [Don Sharpe]; Series Created by: Mary Loos, Richard Sale; Story: Kellam De Forest [Kellam de Forest], Marjorie Helper; Teleplay: Coles Trapnell.

Directed by: William F. Claxton.

Derringer Productions, Sharpe Lewis/CBS.

Walt Disney Presents: Texas John Slaughter (TV Series)

"The Man from Bitter Creek" (March 6, 1959)

Tom Tryon (Texas John Slaughter), Stephen McNally (Bill Galagher), Norma Moore (Adeline Harris), Sidney Blackmer (Sam Underwood), Bill Williams (Paul Forbes), John Larch (Frank Boyd), Grant Williams

(Mike Forbes), H.M. Wynant (Yancy), Don Kelly (Jed), Walt Disney (Himself–Host).

Director of Photography: William Snyder, A.S.C.; Editing: Robert Stafford; Art Direction: Marvin Aubrey Davis; Music: Franklyn N. Marks;

Produced by: James Pratt; Teleplay: David P. Harmon.

Directed by: Harry Keller.

Walt Disney Productions/ABC.

"The Slaughter Trail" (March 20, 1959)

Tom Tryon (Texas John Slaughter), Harold J. Stone (John Chisholm), Sidney Blackmer (Sam Underwood), Norma Moore (Adeline Slaughter), Bill Williams (Paul Forbes), John Larch (Frank Boyd), Grant Williams (Mike Forbes), H.M. Wynant (Yancy), Don Kelly (Jed), Slim Pickens (Buck), Herbert Rudley (Judge), Walt Disney (Himself–Host).

Music: Franklyn N. Marks; Director of Photography: William Snyder, A.S.C.; Editing: Robert Stafford; Art Direction: Marvin Aubrey Davis.

Produced by: James Pratt; Teleplay: David P. Harmon.

Directed by: Harry Keller.

Walt Disney Productions/ABC.

The Millionaire (TV Series)

"Millionaire Gilbert Burton" (April 29, 1959)

Marvin Miller (Michael Anthony), Carleton Carpenter (Gilbert Burton), Paul Frees (John Beresford Tipton–voice), Sid Clute [Sidney Clute] (Max), Dolores Donlon (Maggie 'Margo' Carter), Grant Williams (Mike 'Maurice' Carter).

Director of Photography: George T. Clemens; Editing: Charles Van Enger; Set Decoration: Sandy Grace; Makeup: Charles Blackman; Sound: Glen Glenn.

Produced by: Don Fedderson; Executive Producer: Fred Henry; Teleplay: Jack Roche.

Directed by: James Sheldon.

CBS.

Alcoa Presents: One Step Beyond (TV Series)

"Dead Ringer" (December 1, 1959)

John Newland (Himself–Host), Norma Crane (Esther Quentin/Emily Harkness), Grant Williams (Bill Quentin), Ed Prentiss (Doctor Parks), Olive Blakeney (Mrs. Harney), Dort Clark (Chief Wilson), Kathleen Mulqueen (Sister Agatha).

Cinematography: Dale Deverman; Editing: Henry Berman; Art Direction: George W. Davis, Field Gray [Field M. Gray]; Set Decoration: Henry Grace, Jack Mills; Assistant Director: Tom McCrory; Music: Harry Lubin.

Produced by: Collier Young; Associate Producer: Merwin Gerard; Series Created by: Merwin Gerard; Writer: Catherine Turney; Executive Writer: Larry Marcus [Lawrence B. Marcus].

Directed by: John Newland.

Joseph M. Schenck Enterprises/ABC.

The Iron Horseman (Unaired TV Pilot, 1960)

Barry Kelley, Grant Williams, Rush Williams.

Produced by. Louis F. Edelman; Associate Producer: Richard V. Heermance; Executive Producer: Walter Mirisch; Teleplay: Richard Alan Simmons, Leslie Stevens.

Directed by: Lesley Selander.

Mirisch Television/NBC.

Bonanza (TV Series)

"Escape to Ponderosa" (March 5, 1960)

Lorne Greene (Ben Cartwright), Pernell Roberts (Adam Cartwright), Dan Blocker (Eric 'Hoss' Cartwright), Michael Landon (Joseph 'Little Joe' Cartwright), Joe Maross (Jimmy Sutton), Gloria Talbott (Nedda),

Grant Williams (Lieutenant Paul Tyler), Chris Alcade (Capt. James Bolton), Dayton Lummis (Col. Metcalfe), James Parnell (Pvt. Harry Mertz), Sherwood Price (Corporal).

Director of Photography: Lester Shorr; Editing: Marvin Coil; Art Direction: Earl Hedrick [A. Earl Hedrick], Hal Pereira; Set Decoration: Sam Corner, Grace Gregory; Makeup Supervisor: Wally Westmore; Music: David Rose; Theme Music: Ray Evans.

Produced by: David Dortort; Story: Bill Barrett, Malcolm Stuart Boylan; Teleplay: Robert E. Thompson.

Directed by: Charles F. Haas.

NBC.

13 Fighting Men (April 1960)

Grant Williams (Captain John Forrest), Brad Dexter (Major Simon Boyd), Carole Mathews (Carole Prescott), Robert Dix (Lt. Wilcox), Richard Garland (Capt. John Prescott), Richard Crane (Loomis), Rayford Barnes (Sgt. Yates), Rex Holman (Root), John Erwin (Cpl. McLean), Bob Palmer Boyd Holister] (Pvt. Jensen), Mauritz Hugo (Walter Ives), Dick Monahan [Richard Monahan], Ted Knight (Samuel), Fred Kohler [Fred Kohler Jr.] (Corey), Stephen Ferry (Sgt. Wade), I. Stanford Jolley (Pvt. Ebb), Walter Reed (Col. Jeffers), John Merrick [John Frederick] (Lee), Mark Hickman (Sgt. Mason), Ford Dunhill (Pvt. Harper), Brad Harris (Pvt. Fowler).

Director of Photography: Walter Strenge; Editing: Harry Gerstad [Harry W. Gerstad]; Art Direction: Ned Shiells; Set Decoration: Harry Reif; Makeup: Bob Littlefield [Robert Littlefield]; Special Effects: Pat Dinga; Music: Irving Gertz.

Produced by: Jack Leewood; Screenplay: Robert Hamner, Jack W. Thomas.

Directed by: Harry Gerstad [Harry W. Gerstad].

Associated Producers Incorporated/20th Century Fox Film Corporation.

The Leech Woman (May 1960)

Coleen Gray (June Talbot), Grant Williams (Neil Foster), Phillip Terry (Dr. Paul Talbot), Gloria Talbott (Sally), John Van Dreelen (Bertram Garvay), Estelle Hemsley (Old Malla), Kim Hamilton (Young Malla), Arthur Batanides (Jerry), Murray Alper (Drunk, uncredited), Harold Goodwin (Detective Joe, uncredited), Charles Keene (Chief Detective, uncredited).

Director of Photography: Ellis W. Carter; Editing: Milton Carruth; Art Direction: Robert Clatworthy, Alexander Golitzen; Set Decoration: Russell A. Gausman, Clarence Steensen; Costume Design: Bill Thomas; Makeup: Bud Westmore, Larry Germain; Music: Irving Gertz, Hans J. Salter (uncredited), Henry Vars (uncredited), Frank Skinner (uncredited); Music Supervision: Milton Rosen.

Produced by: Joseph Gershenson; Story: Ben Pivar, Francis Rosenwald; Screenplay: David Duncan.

Directed by: Edward Dein.

Universal-International Pictures/Universal Pictures

Mr. Lucky (TV Series)

"Stacked Deck" (May 28, 1960)

John Vivyan (Mr. Lucky), Ross Martin (Andamo), Grant Williams (Conrad), Yvette Mimieux (Margot), Fay McKenzie (Sheila Wells), Tom Brown (Lieutenant Rovacs).

Director of Photography: Philip Lathrop [Philip H. Lathrop]; Editing: Russell Schoengrath [Russell F. Schoengrath]; Art Direction: Phil Barber [Philip Barber], George W. Davis; Set Decoration: H. Web. Arrowsmith [H. Web Arrowsmith], Henry Grace; Assistant Director: James Welch; Theme Music: Henry Mancini (uncredited); Music: Henry Mancini.

Produced by: Jack Arnold; Associate Producer: Jack McEdward; Executive Producer: Gordon Oliver; Series Created by: Blake Edwards (uncredited); Story: Milton Holmes; Teleplay: Jameson Brewer.

Directed by: Jack Arnold.

CBS Television Network, Spartan Productions/CBS.

SurfSide 6 (TV Series)

"Par-a-kee" (November 7, 1960)

Lee Patterson (Dave Thorne), Van Williams (Ken Madison), Troy Donahue (Sandy Winfield II), Diane McBain (Daphne Dutton), Margarita Sierra (Cha Cha O'Brien), Mousie Garner [Paul 'Mousie' Garner] (Mousie), Grant Williams (Keith Minter), Raymond Bailey (Reginald Dutton), Donald Barry [Don 'Red' Barry] (Lt. Snedigar), Lyle Talbot (Alan Crandell), Michael Harris (Eddie Geer), J. Edward McKinley (Manders), Ben Welden (Joe Bundy), Mike Ragan (Monk).

Director of Photography: Ray Fernstrom; Editing: Robert Watts; Art Direction: Howard Campbell; Set Decoration: William L. Kuehl; Makeup: Gordon Bau; Sound: Samuel F. Goode; Theme Music: Mack David; Music Supervisors: Paul Sawtell, Bert Shefter; Music Editor: Sam E. Levin.

Produced by: Mack David; Executive Producer: William T. Orr; Story: Mack David; Teleplay: William L. Stuart.

Directed by: William J. Hole Jr.

Warner Bros. Television/ABC.

The Roaring 20's (TV Series)

"Brother's Keeper" (November 19, 1960)

Donald May (Pat Garrison), Dorothy Provine (Pinky Pinkham), Whit Bissell (Judge Seward), Wally Brown (Chauncey Kowalski), John Dehner (Duke Williams), Andrew Duggan (David Lawrence), James Flavin (Robert Howard), Dianne Foster (Zena Lawrence), Louise Glenn (Gladys), Carolyn Komant (Dixie), Sue Randall (Kathy Potter), Rex Reason (Scott Norris), Mike Road (Lt. Joe Switolski), Herman Rudin (Rossi), Gary Vinson (Chris Higbee), Linda Watkins (Claire Seward), Grant Williams (George Lawrence).

Makeup Supervisor: Gordon Bau; Theme Music: Mack David, Jerry Livingston.

Produced by: William T. Orr.

Directed by: Robert Altman.

Warner Bros. Television/ABC.

Hawaiian Eye (TV Series)

Regular Players: Anthony Eisley (Tracy Steele), Robert Conrad (Tom Lopaka), Connie Stevens (Cricket Blake), Poncie Ponce (Kim), Leslie Parrish (Marcella), Mel Prestidge (Lt. Danny Quon), Bartlett Robinson (Ellis P. Adams), S. John Launer (Frank Carter Bell), Michael Pate (Joe Gordon), Anita Sands (Bonnie), Judy Dan (Kelly Chou), Doug Mossman [Douglass Mossman] (Moke), Grant Williams (Greg MacKenzie, after December 21, 1960), Troy Donahue (Philip Barton, after October 2, 1962).

Executive Producer: Wm. T. Orr [William T. Orr]; Supervising Producer: Howie Horwitz; Producers: Charles Hoffman, Stanley Niss, Ed Jurist, Joel Rogosin, Jerry Davis, Tom McKnight.

Main Writers: Robert C. Dennis (5 episodes), Gloria Elmore (8 episodes), Gibson Fox (10 episodes), Lester Fuller (6 episodes), Robert Hamner (8 episodes), W. Hermanos (6 episodes), Ed Jurist (6 episodes), Richard H. Landau (6 episodes), Erna Lazarus (3 episodes), Lee Loeb (7 episodes), Silvia Richards (6 episodes), Sam Ross (7 episodes), Philip Saltzman (8 episodes), Robert J. Shaw (19 episodes), Charles B. Smith (6 episodes), Robert Tallman (6 episodes).

Main Directors: Robert Altman (1 episode), Richard Benedict (5 episodes), André de Toth (4 episodes), Edward Dein (14 episodes), Alvin Ganzer (6 episodes), Charles F. Haas (4 episodes), Howard W. Koch (2 episodes), Paul Landres (6 episodes), Irving J. Moore (14 episodes), Charles R. Rondeau (12 episodes), Robert Sparr (12 episodes), Robert Totten (4 episodes).

Warner Bros. Television/ABC.

Episodes co-starring Grant Williams with their respective airdates (the episodes marked with an asterisk are those in which Williams was the protagonist or co-protagonist of the story):

"Services Rendered" (December 21, 1960)*
"Baker's Half Dozen" (December 28, 1960)
"Made in Japan" (January 4, 1961)*
"A Touch of Velvet" (January 11, 1961)

"Talk and You're Dead" (January 18, 1961)
"Robinson Koyoto" (January 25, 1961)
"The Manabi Figurine" (February 1, 1961)*
"Caves of Pele" (February 8, 1961)
"Man in a Rage" (February 15, 1961)
"The Stanhope Brand" (February 22, 1961)*
"The Trouble with Murder" (March 1, 1961)*
"The Man from Manila" (March 8, 1961)
"Her Father's House" (March 15, 1961)*
"The Humuhumunukunukuapuaa Kid" (March 22, 1961)*
"Maid in America" (May 24, 1961)
"Satan City" (September 27, 1961)*
"The Kupua of Coconut Bay" (October 4, 1961)
"The Moon from Mindanao" (October 11, 1961)
"The Doctor's Lady" (October 18, 1961)*
"Pill in the Box" (November 1, 1961)*
"Kill a Gray Fox" (November 18, 1961)*
"The Queen from Kern County" (November 22, 1961)
"The Final Score" (November 29, 1961)*
"Two for the Money" (December 6, 1961)*
"Concert in Hawaii" (December 27, 1961)*
"Little Miss Rich Witch" (January 10, 1962)
"Big Fever" (January 17, 1962)*
"Four-Cornered Triangle" (February 14, 1962)*
"Blackmail in Satin" (February 28, 1962)*
"The Meeting on Molokai" (March 21, 1962)*
"Nightmare in Paradise" (April 11, 1962)*
"Rx Cricket" (May 2, 1962)
"Location Shooting" (May 9, 1962)*
"Across the River Lethe" (May 16, 1962)*
"Among the Living" (May 30, 1962)
"'V' for Victim" (June 6, 1962)*
"Koko Kate" (June 13, 1962)
"Lalama Lady" (June 20, 1962)
"The Broken Thread" (October 23, 1962)*
"Lament for a Saturday Warrior" (October 30, 1962)*
"The Sign-Off" (November 20, 1962)

"A Night with Nora Stewart" (November 27, 1962)*
"Pursuit of a Lady" (December 11, 1962)*
"Kupikio Kid" (January 8, 1963)
"Maybe Menehunes" (January 15, 1963)*
"Pretty Pigeon" (January 22, 1963)
"Two Too Many" (January 29, 1963)
"Two Million Too Much" (February 26, 1963)*
"The Sisters" (March 26, 1963)*
"Passport" (April 2, 1963)*

Surfside 6 (TV Series)

"Bride and Seek" (December 26, 1960)

Lee Patterson (Dave Thorne), Troy Donahue (Sandy Winfield), Van Williams (Ken Madison), Diane McBain (Daphne Dutton), Margarita Sierra (Cha Cha O'Brien), Grant Williams (Frank Anders), Warren Stevens (Arnie Helmen), Kaye Elhardt (Lois Culver), Linda Bennett (Nancy Clayborne), Louise Lorimer (Mrs. Clayborne III), Paul Carr (Stan Ritchie), Donald Barry [Don 'Red' Barry] (Lt. Snedigar).

Director of Photography: Robert Hoffman; Editing: Victor C. Lewis Jr. [Victor Lewis]; Art Direction: Howard Campbell; Set Decoration: Hoyle Barrett; Makeup: Gordon Bau; Assistant Director: James T. Vaughn; Sound: M.A. Merrick; Theme Music: Mack David, Jerry Livingston; Music Editor: Erma E. Levin; Music Supervisors: Paul Sawtell, Bert Shefter.

Produced by: Jerome L. Davis [Jerry Davis]; Executive Producer: William T. Orr; Story: Steve Goodman; Teleplay: Anne Howard Bailey.

Directed by: Charles Haas [Charles F. Haas].

Warner Bros. Television/ABC.

Here's Hollywood (TV Series–Interview Show)

Season 1, episode 220 (August 11, 1961)

Dean Miller (Himself–Host), Denise Darcel (Herself–Guest), Grant Williams (Himself–Guest).

Executive Producer: Peer Oppenheimer; Associate Producer: Esme Chandlee.

Desilu Productions/NBC.

Meet the Star (TV Series–Interview Panel Show)

"Grant Williams" (October 8, 1961)

Bill Bradley (Himself–Host), Grant Williams (Himself–Guest).

Susan Slade (November 8, 1961)

Troy Donahue (Hoyt Brecker), Connie Stevens (Susan Slade), Dorothy McGuire (Leah Slade), Lloyd Nolan (Roger Slade), Brian Aherne (Stanton Corbett), Grant Williams (Conn White), Natalie Schafer (Marion Corbett), Kent Smith (Dr. Fane), Bert Convy (Wells Corbett), Guy Wilkerson (Slim), Everett Glass (Mr. White, uncredited).

Director of Photography: Lucien Ballard; Editing: William Ziegler [William H. Ziegler], Art Direction: Leo K. Kuter; Set Decoration: William L. Kuehl; Makeup Supervisor: Gordon Bau; Assistant Director: Russell Llewellyn; Dialogue Supervisor: Bert Steiner; Music: Max Steiner.

Produced by: Delmer Daves; Screenplay: Delmer Daves, based on the novel by Doris Hume.

Directed by: Delmer Daves.

Warner Bros./Warner Bros.

The Couch (February 21, 1962)

Grant Williams (Charles Campbell), Shirley Knight (Terry Ames), Onslow Stevens (Dr. Janz), William Leslie (Dr. David Lindsey), Anne Helm (Jean Quimby), Simon Scott (Lt. Kritzman), Michael Bachus (Sgt. Bonner), John Alvin (Sloan), Harry Holcombe (District Attorney), Hope Summers (Mrs. Quimby)

Director of Photography: Harold E. Stine; Editing: Leo H. Shreve; Art Direction: Jack Poplin; Set Decoration: William L. Kuehl; Makeup: Gordon Bau; Music. Frank Perkins.

Produced by: Owen Crump; Story: Blake Edwards, Owen Crump; Screenplay: Robert Bloch.

Directed by: Owen Crump.

Warner Bros./Warner Bros.

Stump the Stars (TV Series–Game Show)

"PT Boat Cast" (May 20, 1963)

Mike Stokey (Himself–Host), James Gregory (Himself–Guest Panelist), Grant Williams (Himself–Guest Panelist), Ty Hardin (Himself–Guest Panelist), Robert Culp (Himself–Guest Panelist), Sebastian Cabot (Himself–Regular Panelist), Hans Conried (Himself–Regular Panelist), Beverly Garland (Herself–Regular Panelist), Ross Martin (Himself–Regular Panelist).

Mike Stokey Productions, Columbia Broadcasting System/CBS.

PT 109 (June 19, 1963)

Cliff Robertson (Lt. John F. Kennedy), Ty Hardin (Ensign Leonard J. Thom), James Gregory (Commander C.R. Ritchie), Robert Culp (Ensign George 'Barney' Ross), Grant Williams (Lt. Alvin Cluster), Lew Gallo (Yeoman Rogers), Errol John (Benjamin Kevu), Michael Pate (Lt. Reginald Evans), Robert Blake (Gunner's Mate Charles 'Bucky' Harris), William Douglas (Gerard Zinser), Biff Elliott [Biff Elliot] (Seaman Edgar E. Mauer), Norman Fell (Machinist Edmund Drewitch), Sam Gilman (Raymond Starkey), Clyde Howdy (Machinist Leon Drawdy), Buzz Martin (Gunner's Mate Maurice Kowal), James McCallion (Patrick 'Pappy' McMahon), Evan McCord [Joseph Gallison] (Harold Marney), Sammy Reese [Sam Reese] (Torpedoman Andrew Kirksey), Glenn Sipes (William Johnson), John Ward (Radioman John Maguire), David M. Whorf [David Whorf] (Seaman Raymond Albert).

Director of Photography: Robert L. Surtees [Robert Surtees]; Edited by: Folmar Blangsted; Art Direction: Leo K. Kuter; Set Decoration: John P. Austin; Makeup Supervisor: Gordon Bau; Music: David Buttolph, William Lava.

Produced under the personal supervision of: Jack L. Warner; Produced by: Bryan Foy; Adaptation: Howard Sheehan, Vincent X. Flaherty; Screenplay: Richard L. Breen, based on the novel by: Robert J. Donovan.

Directed by: Leslie H. Martinson.

Warner Bros./Warner Bros.

Stump the Stars (TV Series–Game Show)

"PT Boat Cast Encore" (August 12, 1963)

Mike Stokey (Himself–Host), James Gregory (Himself–Guest Panelist), Grant Williams (Himself–Guest Panelist), Ty Hardin (Himself–Guest Panelist), Roddy McDowall (Himself–Guest Panelist), Sebastian Cabot (Himself–Regular Panelist), Dorothy Hart (Herself–Regular Panelist), Beverly Garland (Herself–Regular Panelist), Ross Martin (Himself–Regular Panelist).

Mike Stokey Productions, Columbia Broadcasting System/CBS.

The Munsters (TV Series)

"The Sleeping Cutie" (December 10, 1964)

Yvonne De Carlo (Lily Munster), Al Lewis (Grandpa), Beverley Owen (Marilyn Munster), Butch Patrick (Eddie Munster), Fred Gwynne (Herman Munster), Grant Williams (Dick Prince), Gavin MacLeod (Paul Newmar), John Hoyt (George Spelvin), Walter Woolf King (Mr. Hadley).

Director of Photography: Fred Mandl; Editing: Bud S. Isaacs; Art Direction: Howard E. Johnson; Set Decoration: Robert C. Bradfield, John McKarthy [John McKarthy Jr.]; Costume Supervisor: Vincent Dee; Music: Jack Marshall.

Produced by: Joe Connelly, Bob Mosher; Production Executive: Irving Paley; Developed by: Norm Liebmann, Ed Haas; Teleplay: James B. Allardice, Tom Adair.

Directed by: Norman Abbott.

Kayro-Vue Productions/CBS.

Perry Mason (TV Series)

"The Case of the Ruinous Road" (December 31, 1964)

Raymond Burr (Perry Mason), Barbara Hale (Della Street), William Hopper (Paul Drake), William Talman (Hamilton Burger), Ray Collins (Lt. Tragg), Wesley Lau (Lt. Anderson), Grant Williams (Quincy Davis), Barton MacLane (Archer Osmond), Joan Blackman (Hilary Gray), Allen Case (Adam Conrad), John Howard (Harley Leonard), Meg Wyllie (Marguerite Keith), Les Tremayne (Ed Pierce), Bert Freed (Joe Marshall), Willis Bouchey (Judge).

Director of Photography: John M. Nickolaus Jr.; Editing: Richard Cahoon; Art Direction: Lewis Creber [Lewis H. Creber]; Set Decoration: Carl Biddiscombe; Music: Richard Shores; Theme Music: Fred Steiner.

Produced by: Arthur Marks, Art Seid; Executive Producer: Gail Patrick Jackson [Gail Patrick]; Associate Producer: Jackson Gillis; Story: Samuel Newman; Teleplay: Bob Mitchell, Esther Mitchell.

Directed by: Jesse Hibbs.

Paisano Productions/CBS.

The Outer Limits (TV Series)

"The Brain of Colonel Barham" (January 2, 1965)

Grant Williams (Maj. Douglas McKinnon), Elizabeth Perry (Jennifer Barham), Anthony Eisley (Col. Alex Barham), Douglas Kennedy (Gen. Daniel Pettit), Paul Lukather (Ed Nichols), Martin Kosleck (Dr. Leo Hausner), Wesley Addy (Dr. Rahm), Peter Hansen (Maj. Locke), Robert Chadwick (Guard).

Director of Photography: Kenneth Peach; Editing: Tony Di Marco [Anthony DiMarco]; Art Direction: Jack Poplin; Set Decoration: Chester Bayhi; Makeup Supervision: Fred B. Phillips; Music: Harry Lubin.

Produced by: Ben Brady; Associate Producer: Sam White; Executive Producer: Leslie Stevens; Story: Sidney Ellis; Teleplay: Robert C. Dennis.

Directed by: Charles Haas [Charles F. Haas].

Villa Di Stefano, Daystar Productions, United Artists Television/ABC.

Bonanza (TV Series)

"Patchwork Man" (May 23, 1965)

Lorne Greene (Ben Cartwright), Pernell Roberts (Adam Cartwright), Dan Blocker (Eric 'Hoss' Cartwright), Michael Landon (Joseph 'Little Joe' Cartwright), Grant Williams (Albert 'Patch' Saunders), Bruce Gordon (Dan Bronson), Sue Randall (Ann Fleming), Ray Teal (Sheriff Roy Coffee), Lane Bradford (Stimson), Grandon Rhodes (Doctor), Mike Ragan (Charlie).

Director of Photography: Lester Shorr; Editing: Marvin Coil; Art Direction: Earl Hedrick [A. Earl Hedrick], Hal Pereira; Set Decoration: Sam Corner, Grace Gregory; Makeup Supervisor: Wally Westmore; Music: David Rose; Theme Music: Ray Evans.

Produced by: David Dortort; Teleplay: Don Tait, William Koenig.

Directed by: Ralph E. Black.

NBC.

Perry Mason (TV Series)

"The Case of the Baffling Bug" (December 12, 1965)

Raymond Burr (Perry Mason), Barbara Hale (Della Street), William Hopper (Paul Drake), William Talman (Hamilton Burger), Richard Anderson (Lt. Steve Drumm), Grant Williams (Dr. Todd Meade), Dee Hartford (Rhonda Coleridge), Ben Cooper (Lowell Rupert), Alizia Gur [Aliza Gur] (Dr. Nina Revelli), Gilbert Green (Dr. Malcolm Scranton), Byron O'Byrne [Bryan O'Byrne] (Horace Lehigh), Teru Shimada (Dr. Maseo Tachikawa), S. John Launer (Judge), Mary Treen (Bess), Robert Okazaki [Bob Okazaki] (Manager).

Director of Photography: John M. Nickolaus Jr.; Editing: Richard W. Farrell; Art Direction: Lewis Creber [Lewis H. Creber]; Set Decoration: Carl Biddiscombe; Music: Richard Shores; Theme Music: Fred Steiner.

Produced by: Arthur Marks, Art Seid; Executive Producer: Gail Patrick Jackson [Gail Patrick]; Teleplay: Orville H. Hampton.

Directed by: Vincent McEveety.

Paisano Productions/CBS.

The FBI (TV Series)

"Breakthrough" (November 17, 1968)

Efrem Zimbalist Jr. (Inspector Lewis Erskine), Philip Abbott (Arthur Ward), William Reynolds (Special Agent Tom Colby), Peter Mark Richman (Vincent Preston Gray), Edward Andrews (Victor Russell), Dorothy Provine (Irene Minnock), Grant Williams (SAC Kirby Greene), Bill Zuckert (Joe Darwin), John P. Ryan (Ernie Flood), Jeff Davis (Bobby Pollack), Joe Perry [Joseph V. Perry] (Stan Jason), Rose Hobart (Maid).

Director of Photography: William W. Spencer; Editing: Jerry Young; Art Direction: Richard Y. Haman; Set Decoration: Hoyle Barrett; Music: John Elizalde.

Produced by: Charles Larson; Executive Producer: Quinn Martin; Supervising Producer: Adrian Samish; Associate Producer: Mark Weingart; Story: James Byrnes [Jim Byrnes]; Teleplay: Frank Crow.

Directed by: Robert Day.

Quinn Martin Productions, Warner Bros./Seven Arts Television/ABC.

Dragnet 1967 (TV Series)

"B.O.D.: DR-27" (January 23, 1969)

Jack Webb (Sergeant Joe Friday), Harry Morgan (Officer Bill Gannon), Grant Williams (Father Barnes), Len Wayland (Capt. Stanley), Vic Perrin (John Franklin), Nydia Westman (Mrs. Morrison), David Bond (Henry), Roy Glenn (Mr. Farrell), Tim Donnelly (Mr. Morris), Robert Carricart (Mr. Diedrich), Robert Carricart Jr. [Bob Carricart] (Ray Diedrich), Ed Deemer (Sgt. Jim Slagle), Judd Laurance (Male Hippie), Pamela McMyler (Female Hippie), Susan Seaforth [Susan Seaforth Hayes] (Policewoman Olson), Rhoda Williams (Mrs. Maynard), Charles Brewer (Officer Iddings), Pilar Del Rey (Mrs. Alvarez), Marco Lopez (Mr. Alvarez, uncredited).

Director of Photography: Alric Edens; Editing: Richard M. Sprague; Art Direction: John E. Chilberg II; Set Decoration: John McCarthy [John McCarthy Jr.], John Sturtevant; Makeup: Bud Westmore; Music: Frank Comstock.

Produced by: Jack Webb; Associate Producer: Wm. Stark [William Stark]; Teleplay: James Doherty.

Directed by: Jack Webb.

Mark VII Ltd., Dragnet Productions, Universal Television/NBC.

The Outcasts (TV Series)

"The Candidates" (January 27, 1969)

Don Murray (Earl Corey), Otis Young (Jemal David), Edward Faulkner (Willis), Susan Howard (Julie Mason), Art Metrano (Sheriff Calloway), Madeleine Sherwood (Suellen), Bill Walker (Samuel), Grant Williams (John Mason).

Director of Photography: Harold E. Stine; Editing: Norman Colbert; Art Direction: Ross Bellah, Robert Peterson; Set Decoration: Alfred E. Spencer; Makeup Supervisor: Ben Lane; Music: Hugo Montenegro.

Produced by: Jon Epstein; Executive Producer: Hugh Benson; Associate Producers: Louis H. Goldstein, Sheldon Schrager; Teleplay: Ben Brady, Don Brinkley.

Directed by: Leslie H. Martinson.

Screen Gems Television/ABC.

My Friend Tony (TV Series)

"The Lost Hours" (February 2, 1969)

James Whitmore (Prof. John Woodruff), Enzo Cerusico (Tony Novello), Don Dubbins, Eduard Franz, Willi Coopman, Marcia Rodd, Grant Williams, Lana Wood.

Music: Earle Hagen.

Series Created by: Ivan Goff, Ben Roberts; Teleplay: Jackson Gillis.

Directed by: Arthur Marks.

Sheldon Leonard Productions/NBC.

Brain of Blood (August 1971)

Grant Williams (Bob), Kent Taylor (Dr. Trenton), John Bloom (Gor), Regina Carrol (Tracy), Vicki Volante (Katherine), Angelo Rossitto (Dorro), Reed Hadley (Amir), Zandor Vorkov (Mohammed), Richard Smedley (Angel), Gus Peters (Charlie), Margo Hope (Pale Girl), Bruce Kimball (Jim).

Director of Photography: Louis Horvath; Editing: J.P. Spohn; Set Decoration: Mike McClosky [Mike McCloskey]; Makeup: Lee James.

Produced by: Al Adamson, Samuel M. Sherman; Executive Producer: Kane W. Lynn; Associate Producer: J.P. Spohn; Story: Samuel M. Sherman; Screenplay: Joe Van Rodgers.

Directed by: Al Adamson.

Independent-International Pictures, Phil-Am Enterprises Ltd./Hemisphere Pictures.

Doomsday Machine (1972)

Bobby Van (Danny), Ruta Lee (Dr. Marion Turner), Mala Powers (Maj. Georgianna Bronski), James Craig (Dr. Haines), Grant Williams (Maj. Kurt Mason), Henry Wilcoxon (Dr. Christopher Perry), Chia Essie Lin (Girl Spy), Casey Casem (Mission Control Officer), Lorri Scott (Lt. Katie Carlson), Scott Miller [Denny Miller] (Col. Don Price), Mike Farrell (1st Reporter).

Director of Photography: Stanley Cortez; Art Direction: James E. Schwarm; Director of Special Effects Photography: William C. Davies.

Produced by: Harr Hope; Executive Producer: Oscar L. Nichols [Oscar Nichols]; Story and Screenplay: Stuart J. Byrne.

Directed by: Harry Hope, Lee Sholem, Herbert J. Leder (uncredited).

First Leisure/Cine-Find.

How's Your Love Life? (October 1977)

John Agar (Police Lt. Rafferty), Leslie Brooks (Dr. Maureen John), Grant Williams (Paul Miller), Mary Beth Hughes (Linda Roberts), Russel Vincent (Jack Romanti), Rick Cooper (Rick Stewart), William

Hudson (Mr. Dunn), Vera Allen (Adagio Dancer), John Armond (Mr. Rivero), Babette (Ann Dunn), Alicio Balsa (Adagio Dancer), Doris Barton (Rita Rivero), Mel Blanc (Blackie), Eve Brent (Mrs. Ryan), Joe Castagna (Jim Hunter), Regina Champlin (Showgirl), Sean Kenney (Steve Roberts).

Director of Photography: Robert Caramico; Editing: Lee Osborne; Music: Robert 'Bumps' Blackwell.

Produced by: Russ Vincent [Russel Vincent]; Executive Producer: William J. McCarthy; Screenplay: Russ Vincent [Russel Vincent].

Directed by: Russ Vincent [Russel Vincent].

Sportsfilms Inc./Cal-Tex Distributing.

Family Feud (TV Series–Game Show)

"Gilligan's Island vs. Hawaiian Eye" (April 15, 1983)

Richard Dawson (Himself–Host), Jim Backus (Himself–Panelist), Natalie Schafer (Herself–Panelist), Alan Hale Jr. (Himself–Panelist), Russell Johnson (Himself–Panelist), Dawn Wells (Herself–Panelist), Connie Stevens (Herself–Panelist), Troy Donahue (Himself–Panelist), Anthony Eisley (Himself–Panelist), Poncie Ponce (Himself–Panelist), Grant Williams (Himself–Panelist).

Mark Goodson Television Productions, The Family Company/ABC.

"Lost in Space vs. Hawaiian Eye" (May 11, 1983)

Richard Dawson (Himself–Host), Guy Williams (Himself–Panelist), Angela Cartwright (Herself–Panelist), June Lockhart (Herself–Panelist), Bob May (Himself–Panelist), Marta Kristen (Herself–Panelist), Connie Stevens (Herself–Panelist), Troy Donahue (Himself–Panelist), Anthony Eisley (Himself–Panelist), Poncie Ponce (Himself–Panelist), Grant Williams (Himself–Panelist).

Mark Goodson Television Productions, The Family Company/ABC

Select Bibliography

BOOKS

Alighieri, Dante. *The Divine Comedy*. Oxford Paperbacks, 1998.

Anouilh, Jean. *Pièces noires*. Editions Balzac, 1942.

Bach, Richard. *Illusions: The Adventures of a Reluctant Messiah*. Delacorte Press, 1977.

Baxter, John. *Science Fiction in the Cinema: 1895-1970*. A.S. Barnes, 1970.

Blum, Daniel, ed. *Theatre World, Season 1953-54*. Greenberg: Publisher, 1954.

———. *Theatre World, Season 1954-55*. Greenberg: Publisher, 1955.

Bond, Tony. *Il Mondo: One Man's World*. AuthorHouse, 2012.

Bowers, Scotty and Friedberg, Lionel. *Full Service: My Adventures in Hollywood and the Secret Sex Lives of the Stars*. Grove Press, 2012.

Bradbury, Ray. *A Medicine for Melancholy*. Doubleday & Company, Inc., 1959

Bradley, Matthew R. *Richard Matheson on Screen*. McFarland & Company, Inc., Publishers, 2010.

Butler, Ivan. *Horror in the Cinema*. A. Zwemmer Limited/A.S. Barnes, 1970.

Calvino, Italo. *Il visconte dimezzato*. Einaudi, 1952.

—— ——. *Il cavaliere inesistente*. Einaudi, 1959.

Calvino, Italo. *The Nonexistent Knight, The Cloven Viscount*. Houghton Mifflin Harcourt, 1977.

Campbell, Joseph. *The Hero with a Thousand Faces*. New World Library, 2008.

Carroll, Lewis. *Alice's Adventures in Wonderland*. Macmillan & Co., 1866.

Clarens, Carlos. *An Illustrated History of the Horror Film*. G.P. Putnam's Sons, 1967.

Coffee, Lenore and Cowen, William Joyce. *Family Portrait*. Samuel French, 1940.

Craig, Rob. *It Came from 1957: a Critical Guide to the Year's Science Fiction, Fantasy and Horror Films*. McFarland, 2013.

Dahl, Roald. *Kiss Kiss*. Michael Joseph, 1959.

Daily Variety Television Reviews, 1946-1956 (vol. 1). Garland Publishing, Inc., 1989.

Dawidziak, Mark. *The Barter Theatre Story: Love Made Visible*. The Appalachian Consortium, 1982.

Ehrenstein, David. *Open Secret (Gay Hollywood 1928–1998)*. William Morrow and Company, Inc., 1998.

Garden, Mary and Biancolli, Louis. *Mary Garden's Story*. Simon and Schuster, 1951.

Goethe, Johann Wolfgang von. *The Metamorphosis of Plants*. The MIT Press, 2009.

Hagen, Uta. *Respect for Acting*. Macmillan, 1973.

Hofler, Robert. *The Man Who Invented Rock Hudson, the Pretty Boys and Dirty Deals of Henry Willson*. Carroll & Graf Publishers, 2005.

James, David E. and Hyman, Adam, eds. *Alternative Projections: Experimental Film in Los Angeles, 1945-1980*. John Libbey Publishing, 2015.

Johnson, William. *Focus on the Science Fiction Film*. Prentice Hall, 1972.

Kafka, Franz. *Verwandlung*. Kurt Wolff Verlag, 1915.

Kanin, Garson. *Born Yesterday*. The Viking Press, 1946.

Kearney, Leslie. *Tchaikovsky and His World*. Princeton University Press, 1998.

Kübler-Ross, Elisabeth. *On Death and Dying*. Macmillan, 1969.

Lamparski, Richard. *Whatever Became Of...?, Eighth Series*. Crown Publishers, 1982.

Maltin, Leonard. *2010 Movie Guide*. Signet, 2009.

Mann, William J. *Behind the Screen: How Gays and Lesbians Shaped Hollywood, 1910–1969*. Viking, 2001.

Matheson, Richard. *The Shrinking Man*. Gold Medal, 1956.

——. *The Shrinking Man*. Gauntlet Publications, 2001.

——. *The Path: a New Look at Reality*. Tor Books, 1999.

McKenna, Harold J., ed. *New York City Opera Sings: Stories and Productions of the New York City Opera 1944-79*. Richard Rosen Press, Inc., 1981.

McKinney, Robert L. *If You Like Us, Talk About Us: The Life and Times of Robert H. Porterfield*. Barter Media, 2006.

Morgan, Charles. *The Flashing Stream*. Macmillan & Co. Ltd, 1939.

Nelson, C.M. *Barren Harvest*. Crime Club/Doubleday, 1949.

Osteried, Peter. *Die Filme von Jack Arnold: Konig des Phantastischen Films*. Mpw Medien Publikations, 2012.

Ovid. *Metamorphoses*. Harvard University Press/William Heinemann Ltd, 1916.

Percival, Howard W. *Thinking and Destiny*. Word Publishing Inc., 1961.

Pirandello, Luigi. *Sei personaggi in cerca d'autore*. Bemporad, 1921.

—— ——. *Six Characters in Search of an Author*. Methuen Drama, 1979.

—— ——. *Uno, nessuno e centomila*. Bemporad, 1926.

—— ——. *One None and a Hundred Thousand*. E.P. Dutton & Co., 1933.

Poznansky, Alexander, ed. *Tchaikovsky through Others' Eyes*. Indiana University Press, 1999.

Powell, Matthew O.P. *God Off-Broadway: the Blackfriars Theatre of New York*. Scarecrow Press, 1998.

Rampersand, Arnold. *The Life of Langston Hughes, Volume II: 1941-1967, I Dream a World*. Oxford University Press, 2002.

Rathbone, Basil. *In and Out of Character*. Doubleday & Company, Inc., 1962.

Reemes, Dana M. *Directed by Jack Arnold*. McFarland & Company, Inc., Publishers, 1988.

Russell, Rosalind and Chase, Chris. *Life Is A Banquet*. Random House, 1977.

Schnelle, Frank, ed. *Hollywood Professional: Jack Arnold und seine Filme*. Verlag Robert Fischer + Uwe Wiedleroither, 1993.

Shakespeare, William. *The Two Gentlemen of Verona*. Oxford University Press, 2008.

Shapiro, Jerome F. *Atomic Bomb Cinema*. Routledge, 2002.

Shearer, Stephen Michael. *Beautiful: The Life of Hedy Lamarr*. St. Martin's Press, 2010.

Thurber, James. *The 13 Clocks*. Simon & Schuster, 1950.

Tzu, Lao. *Tao Te Ching*. Macmillan, 1989.

Variety Film Reviews 1907-1980. Garland Publishing, Inc., 1983.

Vaughn, Robert. *A Fortunate Life*. Thomas Dunne Books/St. Martin's Press, 2008.

Warren, Bill. *Keep Watching the Skies! American Science Fiction Movies of the Fiftes, vol. 1*. McFarland & Company, Inc., Publishers, 1982.

Weaver, Tom. *Science Fiction and Fantasy Film Flashbacks*. McFarland & Company, Inc., Publishers, 1998.

——————. *I Was a Monster Movie Maker: Conversations with 22 SF and Horror Filmmakers*. McFarland & Company, Inc., Publishers, 2001.

Williams, Tennessee. *A Streetcar Named Desire*. New Directions, 1947.

ARTICLES

Archerd, Armand. "'Good Old Days' Vanish for Juvenile Hopefuls." *Pottstown (PA) Mercury*, August 26, 1961.

"Around the Dial." *Hazleton (PA) Standard-Speaker*, June 1, 1963.

Ashby, Bernice. "Backstage." *Sydney Morning Herald*, January 12, 1963.

Askew, Rual. "Top Star Contender Ready for Whatever is Demanded." *Dallas Morning News*, March 5, 1957.

Belser, Emily. "Actor Finds Movie Life Has Headaches." *Kingsport (TN) News*, July 5, 1956.

Carroll, Harrison. "Behind the Scenes in Hollywood." *Tyrone (PA) Daily Herald*, July 20, 1961.

Hartl, John, "The Incredible Shrinking Man: to Inherit the Universe, Man Must Truly Know What It Is to Be Meek," *Cinefantastique*, volume 4, number 2, 1975.

Heimer, Mel. "My New York." *Kane (PA) Republican*, October 10, 1956.

Kelley, Bill. "Jack Is Back." *Cinefantastique*, volume 4, number 2, 1975.

McGee, Mark and Frank, Susan. "Interview: Classic Sci-Fi Film Director Jack Arnold." *SPFX*, n. 10, 2002.

"Miss Russell Wins Ham for Effort." *New York Times*, May 27, 1953.

"New 'Hawaiian Eye' Actor Had Many Other Roles." *Dover (OH) Daily Reporter*, December 17, 1960.

Newsom, Phil. "Foreign Press Commentary" (UPI). *Shamokin (PA) News-Dispatch*, June 22, 1960.

Scott, Vernon. "Hollywood." *New Philadelphia (OH) Daily Times*, April 8, 1961.

Starr, Eve. "Inside Television." *Pottstown (PA) Mercury*, August 12, 1961.

Thomas, Bob. "Inside Hollywood": "Grant Williams Anything But Nervous." *Newport (RI) News*, February 8, 1957.

"TV Scout Reports." *Abilene (TX) Reporter-News*, July 13, 1962.

"TV Star Rises From Stinker To Thinker Actor." *Provo (UT) Daily Herald*, February 2, 1959.

"Williams' Urge to Act Stronger than Sea Life." *Arizona Republic* (Phoenix, AZ), August 13, 1961.

Acknowledgments

RESEARCHING A BIOGRAPHY puts an author in the position of asking many people for help; this is natural enough. Asking for help, however, means disrupting people's routines, and putting an implicit choice before them: to go beyond the call of duty (whatever that duty might be) or to stay within the safe boundaries of their lives. Soon, it becomes clear who offers that help begrudgingly, and who offers it happily; who is generous, who stingy; who courteous and polite, who dismissive. Happiness, generosity, politeness and courteousness are neither obligations nor duties; they are personality traits that one has or does not have, for whatever reason. I was lucky to cross paths with many happy, generous, polite, and courteous persons in my search for help, and I thought their personality traits ought to be acknowledged.

For his selfless and enthusiastic support, and for his invaluable research suggestions, many, many thanks to the very gracious and urbane C. Robert Rotter of www.glamourgirlsofthesilverscreen.com. This book and its author owe him a lot, and might feel emboldened to call him a friend.

My affectionate thanks and love to my dear friends for their ongoing support and for their readiness in helping when asked: David Rodgers and Sarah Lilly of Los Angeles, Benjamin Hoyer and Thomas Martin of New York.

For their gracious sharing of memories of their teacher, thanks to Williams' former acting students Isabel Fisher, Ken Mulroney, and Melissa Ward.

For her willingness to reminisce and dig into her memories of Grant Williams from greener California days, and for her warmth, Nina Ingris has my gratitude.

Ditto to the gracious and generous June Moncur Waite, for sharing her remembrance of things past.

For responding to an improbable inquiry from thousands of miles away, my thanks to Shirley Knight.

My most heartfelt thanks go to Dollie Banner of Jerry Ohlinger's Movie Material Store in New York for her unswaying help in searching for material—and searching, and searching again.

For his blog, *Poseidon's Underworld*, and for his help in adding important research sources to this book, thanks to Jon Vater. Likewise, my thanks go to Alexis Hunter, Richard Koper, and Tom Weaver for their practical suggestions and for their help.

For their cheerful assistance in solving documentary conundrums, many thanks to: Russell Franks, M.L.I.S., Librarian for Special and Archival Collections, Phillips Memorial Library, Providence College; Robert Hofler; Kristine Krueger, Margaret Herrick Library, Academy of Motion Picture Arts and Sciences; Brandon Murray of the Dallas History and Archives Division, Dallas Public Library, Dallas, Texas; Michael North, Head, Reference and Reader Services, The Theater Playbills and Program Collection, Rare Book and Special Collection Division, The Library of Congress, Washington, D.C.; Scott Sanders, Archivist at Antioch College; Nancy Webster of the Highland Park Public Library; Claude Zachary of USC Special Collections.

Many thanks to Jeremy Wright, Managing Director, and to Karen N. Rowe, Administrative Associate of the Barter Theatre, Abingdon, Virginia, for generously searching their archives in my stead and for making some invaluable photographs available to me.

Thanks also to Jenni Matz, Senior Producer at the Archive of American Television, and to Author Larry James Gianakos.

Many thanks to the wonderful Rocco Romano and Lorenzo Slama of Legatoria Romano Cartabianca, for printing and binding little masterpieces instead of plain drafts of the many incarnations of the evolving manuscript.

About the Author

A BILINGUAL DUAL CITIZEN, Giancarlo Stampalia received his B.A. from Columbia University in New York, then studied screenwriting and playwriting at the University of Southern California in Los Angeles, devoting several years to playwriting and directing. For his play *Devil's Advocate*, he received a nomination as Best Playwright from the L.A. Weekly Annual Theater Awards in Los Angeles. In 1997 his book *Strehler dirige* ("Strehler Conducts"), about the work of seminal Italian theater Director Giorgio Strehler, was published by Marsilio Editori in Venice. A collaborator of film festivals over the years, Stampalia

Portrait of the author.
Photo: Juan Bastos, Los Angeles, 2015.

has taught creative writing and film history. He is currently working on a volume about American theater Director Robert Wilson, and on another about the film work of American Actor Richard Harrison. He lives in Trieste, Italy.

Index

Made in United States
North Haven, CT
13 May 2024

52472287R00226